WHEN THE KJV DEPARTS FROM THE "MAJORITY" TEXT

****

HOLDING TO EVERY WORD OF OUR STANDARD BIBLE

****

WITH MANUSCRIPT DIGEST

J. A. Moorman

ISBN 978-1-56848-098-5

All Scripture quotes are from the King James Bible except those verses compared and then the source is identified.

Address All Inquiries To:
The Dean Burgon Society
900 Park Avenue
Collingswood, New Jersey, 08108
U.S.A.

Phone: 856-854-4452
Orders: 1-800-John 10:9
FAX: 856-854-2464

E-mail:BFT@BibleForToday.org
Website: www.DeanBurgonSociety.org

BIBLE FOR TODAY #1617
Web: www.biblefortoday.org
E-mail: bft@biblefortoday.org

Formatted by **TOP**:
The **O**ld **P**aths Publications, Inc.
Directors: H. D. & Patricia Williams
142 Gold Flume Way
Cleveland, GA 30528
Web: www.theoldpathspublications.com
Email: TOP@theoldpathspublications.com
Jeremiah 6:16

1.0

DEDICATION

It is my pleasure to dedicate this volume to Dr. H.D. Williams, M.D., Ph.D. whose considerable writings have strongly defended the Text and Translation of our Authorized Bible, and whose publishing expertise have *multiplied the seed sown* (II Corinthians 9:10) in spreading abroad works dedicated to this cause. Without his skill and labors the publication of this book would not have been possible.

J. A. Moorman,
London, England, October 19, 2010

Heaven and earth shall pass away, but my words shall not pass away.

(Matthew 24:35)

TABLE OF CONTENTS

PREFACE

The debate over the King James Bible is as crucial as any we face today. A nation, church, individual is only as strong as its Bible and view of the Bible. If the Bible in hand is no longer seen as a final court of appeal, then *the foundations have been removed and what can the righteous do.* Psalms 11:3. "What does God's Word say," has now been replaced by an anemic, "How does this version render the passage." Replacement bibles are no longer extensively read, study-worn and memorized. They have not remotely achieved the stature of a "standard". A spiritual poverty now ensues.

It is a fact that believers holding to the AV and its underlying Text will generally have a conviction and confidence in their Bible that those using the modern versions simply do not have. Detractors may say it is "misguided", but the heartfelt conviction is there all the same. There is an inbred assurance that in the Standard Bible we possess the Words of God. For the other side it is far more tentative. They are still looking. They have still not after these millennia come up with a finalized Text of Scripture. That our confidence is not misguided is demonstrated by the many Biblical promises that God would preserve His Words throughout the passage of time. That: *Heaven and earth shall pass away, but my words shall not pass away.* Matthew 24:35. Christ here promises *verbal* preservation of His Words for all time!

The true historical outline of the key epochs in the Bible's transmission history is self-evident. And, it is evident that this transmission history will be in complete accord with His promises of the preservation of His Words. Given the nature of the subject before us it is crucial that this be clearly set forth.

KEY EPOCHS OF THE BIBLE'S PRESERVATION HISTORY

The promise from Matthew 24:35 along with a significant number of other passages state clearly that the written Words of God would be verbally preserved. That these Words would be available for every generation, and that despite corrupting influences these Words would be kept pure and could be readily recognized. This principle was set out at the beginning.

> *For this commandment which I command thee this day, it is not hidden from thee, neither is it far off. It is not in heaven, that thou shouldest say, Who shall go up for us to heaven, and bring it unto us, that we may hear it, and do it? Neither is it beyond the sea, that thou shouldest say, Who shall go over the sea for us, and bring it unto us, that we may hear it, and do it? But the word is very nigh unto thee, in thy mouth, and in thy heart, that thou mayest do it.* Deut. 30:11-14.

In line with this promise we will find these Words in the commonly received, traditionally accepted, generally available, and widely dispersed Text.

    We therefore **do expect** to find the Words that our Lord promised would not pass away in those Old Testament Scriptures long guarded over by the Hebrew scribes and culminating in the work of the later Masoretic scribes.

    We do expect to find these Words in the early missionary centers of manuscript proliferation such as Antioch. The Traditional Text has been rightly called the Antiochan Text.

    We do expect to find these Words in the "sectioned" Scriptures, known as lectionaries, and read daily throughout the year in early Greek churches. The standardized formatting of the lectionary manuscripts is now known to be very old, likely before 300AD, and probably earlier. This, because of its textual implications, is a fact grudgingly admitted by modern textual criticism, (See "The Greek Lectionaries of the NT", *The Text of the N.T. in Contemporary Research*, pp. 63,64). If the formatting is early there is every likelihood that the Traditional Text contained in existing lectionary manuscripts is also just as early. The two were never separated. Much like the work of the Masoretic scribes, the lectionary system placed a preservative fence around the inspired New Testament Words. An Aleph-B kind of text was never used in lectionary services.

    We do expect to find these never to pass away Words during the 8th Century changeover from uncial to minuscule script. Nearly every minuscule manuscript is of the same kind that underlies our King James Bible. Modern textual critics as Barbara Aland and Klaus Wachtel are at a loss to explain this. ("The Greek Minuscule Manuscripts of the NT", *The Text of the N.T. in Contemporary Research*, p. 44). The scribes who undertook this laborious and meticulous work were obviously convinced as to what constituted the True Text. Would not their vantage point give them a nearer and clearer view into the previous textual history than that of Aland and Wachtel – 1200 years later?

    We do expect to find these Words in the 16th Century, when printing presses across Europe began publishing large numbers of Bibles based on the newly printed Traditional-Received Text. During those days an Aleph-B kind of Bible was never brought to the press in Europe's publishing houses. In the providence of God the great Reformation Bibles based on the Traditional Text would be the first to be widely published. They were given the right to speak first!

    We do expect to find these Words underlying that Bible which by every standard became the Standard Bible, and that for the last 400 years. Apart from the Authorized Version there is no other Bible in English or in any other language that has even remotely achieved its status as a Standard.

    We do expect further, that these are the very words that will be preserved intact through the ages, and will be the basis of the judgments both of the saved (II Cor. 5:10) and of the lost (Rev. 20:10-12) at the end of the ages. See John 12:48.

    This is the only transmission history of the Text that accords with the promises of God to preserve verbally His Words. There is none other!

    Therefore **we do not expect** to find these Words in the modern Critical Text, for that text is a product of theological rationalism. It is an attempt to resurrect the corrupted text of Alexandria, a text that historically did not spread much beyond the sands of Egypt, nor for that matter from one of its long secluded resting places in the Vatican Library or a monastery at the foot of the traditional Mount Sinai.

We do not expect to find the Traditional Text in the Latin Vulgate, for that version was locked away in Catholic churches, kept from the people, and read by only a very few priests. God's Words were not preserved in their being hid but in their being dispersed abroad.

And now coming to our subject **we do not expect** that the time-honored Words of our Traditional Text will in any way be superseded by recent attempts to publish a new so-called majority text edition – editions which are shown to depart from the Traditional Text in some 1800 places. This would mean that after so long a time God's people have been wrong as to the identity of a significant number of God's Words, and that the promises of preservation have had no exactitude for previous generations. Further, if these recent attempts did in effect represent the "final form" of God's inspired and preserved Words, we would expect to see some acknowledgement on the part of believers in the publication of translations based on these editions. The printing presses have been silent, none have thus far been published.

Therefore when we consider these matters we have good grounds when we say: We believe the Greek, Hebrew and Aramaic Words that underlie the King James Bible are the very words inspired by the Holy Spirit and preserved verbally across the centuries. We believe that the transmission history briefly stated here accords perfectly with our Lord's promise in Matthew 24:35 that *Heaven and earth shall pass away, but my words shall not pass away.*

Regarding the subject of this book, *WHEN THE AUTHORIZED VERSION DEPARTS FROM THE "MAJORITY" TEXT*, it goes without saying that the Authorized Version is practically always the Majority Text. In contrast with the modem translations, the KJV has numerically overwhelming manuscript support. It is, of course, known that a number of passages, e.g., Acts 8: 36 ,37; 1 John 5: 7 do not appear to have majority support in the extant manuscripts. But what are we now to say when evidence is brought forward which purports to show that in nearly 1800 places the AV is based upon a Text containing minority reading? And, of these 1800 differences nearly one third directly affect the KJV translation. See page 14.

A great deal is available demonstrating how the KJV lines up against the sparsely supported readings of the Alexandrian Text, but not so much concerning this other side. Two more recent publications call for a closer look at the matter: the Hodges and Farstad *Greek New Testament According to the Majority Text*, and the Robinson and Pierpont *New Testament in the Original Greek: Byzantine Textform*. Some have suggested that with these publications a key area in our defense of the Standard Bible has been breached. The following pages give detailed evidence that this is definitely not the case.

Much of the following material was gathered in the years from 1986 to 1988, this revised edition takes into account the more recent work by Robinson and Pierpont. The author gratefully acknowledges his debt to those who have labored in the defense of the Authorized Version and Received Text. It is hoped that this study will give assistance in one area of that defense.

J. A. Moorman
London, England October 2010

But he answered and said, It is written, Man shall not live by bread alone, but by every word that proceedeth out of the mouth of God.

(Matthew 4:4)

INTRODUCTION

A NEW TURN IN THE OLD STRUGGLE

Generally the defense of the King James Version has been a one-on-one debate with the Critical Text (Nestle-Aland, UBS). Much has been written and many arguments for and against have been raised. The issue however remains the same—the vast majority of manuscripts on the KJV side versus a few old and disused ones for the Critical Text and modern versions.

In more recent times a different element has been introduced (though aspects of it have long been recognized), with the publication of: *The Greek New Testament According to the Majority Text* (1982), under the editorship of Zane C. Hodges and Arthur L. Farstad. This was followed in 1991 by the publication of *The New Testament in the Original Greek: Byzantine Textform* edited by Maurice A. Robinson and William G. Pierpont. A second and slightly revised Hodges-Farstad (*HF*) edition appeared in 1985. The current Robinson-Pierpont (*RP*) edition was published in 2005.

On the positive side, these two works drive quite a few further nails into the coffin of the Critical Text and demonstrate how foolish it is to brush aside the testimony of overwhelming numbers of manuscripts in the matter of ascertaining the Text of Scripture. The *HF* edition contains an elaborate apparatus which makes more accessible two of the most important sources of MS data: The critical apparatus of Hermann von Soden (1913), and *Concerning the Text of the Apocalypse* by H. C. Hoskier (1929). In fact both editions are based upon and derived *virtually entirely* from von Soden and Hoskier. Other material referred to in *RP* is "confirmatory" (*RP* 2005 Preface p. ix). It may come as a surprise after all this time that the editors believed (rightly) that there was nothing in print that could approach these two works in the numbers of MSS they cite. Both von Soden and Hoskier, however, are tedious to use in the extreme.

While the introduction to *RP* describes the somewhat different approach it used regarding the von Soden and Hoskier material, the resultant text produced does not differ much from *HF*. In a 2010 interview, Robinson said that there were "somewhere around 220 differences total" (sermonindex.net). However *Bible Researcher.com* has produced a list which excluding minor editorial differences gives 147 differences for Matthew to Jude and 186 for Revelation, for a total of 333 differences. Therefore there is a more significant difference in Revelation

In the Manuscript Digest of this work there is a list of 375 passages in which the translation is affected and in which von Soden and Hoskier indicate that the AV/TR readings are substantially deficient in manuscript support. Here *RP* follows *HF* in all but 18 instances. Of the 18, 5 are in Revelation and 5 in John 8:1-11 (where both *HF* and *RP* give special emphasis).

While some will likely view *RP* as a refinement over *HF*, there was no advance in the gathering of MS citations (except in John 8). As with its predecessor the *RP* text does not extend beyond what could be derived from von Soden and Hoskier. Further it lacks the substantial apparatus provided by *HF*, and thus with *HF* you have a clear understanding of which manuscripts gathered by von Soden and Hoskier were used. Therefore in this presentation *HF* will be given priority as a basis of comparison with the AV/TR.

A TEXTUAL HALFWAY HOUSE

According to my count the *HF* Edition indicates that the Greek Text of our Authorized Version is represented by <u>minority</u> MS support in some 1800 readings. Maurice Robinson in the *RP* preface says: "There are approximately 1500 differences between any Receptus edition and either the present text or that of Hodges-Farstad" (p. 3). Thus while our opponents with their Nestle-Aland Text say the AV Greek Text is wrong in over 8000 places (See *8000 Differences...* by author), we now have a situation where our friends say it is off the mark in upwards of 1800 places.

Zane Hodges has been a good ally. Several of the consulting *HF* editors, Harry Sturz, Jakob Van Bruggen, Alfred Martin, and Wilbur Pickering have contributed strongly and written major works in the defense of the Traditional Text. Maurice Robinson in the *RP* 1991 Preface gives a convincing "Rebuttal of Hortian Logic" (p. 6 internet), and argues for a "return to external evidence following the sound principles of John W. Burgon..." (p. 5 internet). Nevertheless, with these two productions we have been left with a tentative, *not-quite-there* text. This fact is clearly stated.

> Scholarly discipline permeates the editor's logic and conclusions; yet Hodges and Farstad make no claim that this text In all Its particulars is the exact form of the originals (*HF* jacket, second edition).

> The editors do not imagine that the text of this edition represents In all particulars the exact form of the originals...It should therefore be kept in mind that the present work...is both preliminary and provisional (*HF* Introduction p. x).

> The present editors desire to make it absolutely clear that they are not tied to such an agenda in any way. Neither the Textus Receptus nor any English translation is in view under the Byzantine-priority theory -- only the restoration of readings considered most closely to reflect the original form of the Byzantine text, and ultimately the autograph. The Byzantine Textform does not concur with any Receptus edition, and clearly not with any English version presently available, including the KJV or NKJV (*RP* 1991 Preface p. 15 internet).

According to *HF* and *RP* we still do not have after nearly two thousand years a New Testament Text whose *Words* we can hold in complete confidence. How does such an admission compare with our Saviour's promise: *Heaven and earth shall pass away but by words shall not pass away*?

KEY ERRORS REGARDING
THE NEW "MAJORITY" EDITIONS

1. The editors do not want to be seen relying "too much" upon God's verbal preservation of the Text.
2. Their work is derived from a source which cites only a <u>minority</u> of MS evidence.
3. They have followed the wrong stream of MSS in the Book of Revelation.

These points along with a number of wider issues will be dealt with in the following chapters.

CHAPTER 1

SHOULD THE TRADITIONAL TEXT BE DEFENDED WITH LITTLE APPEAL TO THE PROMISE OF PRESERVATION

Scrivener and Hoskier in an earlier generation and Hodges, Pickering and Robinson with others in our day have made a substantial contribution in defending the Traditional Text against the Hortian theories. They have provided us with a great store of factual material. Their work has been thorough; they have insisted that shortcuts and superficial analyses will not do.

Hoskier well says:

> ... it is with minutiae we have to deal with at the outset ... Hort was too sweeping, and too much in a hurry to say the final word ...Exhaustive methods are the only ones worth using (*Genesis of the Versions*,London: Quaritch, 1911, pp vii-x).

And Hoskier did just that! With the possible exception of a Tischendorf or von Soden (both on the critical side), it is hard to think of anyone who labored so tirelessly with the actual manuscript evidence. But in Hoskier, Scrivener, and the *HF*, *RP* editors, little or no reference is made to God's promises of preserving verbally the Words of Scripture. In fact, Hodges and Farstad make absolutely no mention of it in their edition. Thus, the foundation for textual research has been taken away.

Wilbur Pickering is listed as one of the consulting editor's. His book, *The Identity of the New Testament Text* has done a great deal to clarify and cause a rethink concerning Westcott and Hort. He is careful to state that he believes in preservation, yet in the presentation of his material he says:

> I have deliberately avoided introducing any arguments based upon inspiration and preservation in the preceding discussion in the hope that I may not be misrepresented by critics in the same way that Burgon has been (*INTT* p. 153).

If critics misrepresent and become uncomfortable with the Bible's clear declaration of preservational truth, what does it matter? Who are we trying to please, God or man. Must we participate in their neutrality and unbelief in order to gain a hearing from them?

When an inquirer into the text of Scripture (even a defender of the Traditional Text) takes this neutral approach in accessing the evidence, it will inevitably lead down this dead-end street of having only a tentative Bible. Notice the disturbing kind of statement Pickering is prepared to make:

> We do not at this moment have the precise wording of the original text (INTT p. 153).
> When all this evidence is in I believe the Textus Receptus will be found to differ from the original in something over a thousand places (pp 232,233).
>
> Most seriously misleading is the representation that I am calling for a return to the

> Textus Receptus…While men like Brown, Fuller and Hills do call for a return to the TR as such. Hodges and I do not. We are advocating what Kurt Aland has called the majority text ("Queen Anne…And All That: A Response." *Journal of the Evangelical Theological Society*. June 1978, p. 165).

Also listed as a consulting editor to the Majority Text Edition is Harry A. Sturz. His book *The Byzantine Text-Type and New Testament Textual Criticism* strikes a devastating blow at arguments which seek to minimize the fact that distinctive Byzantine readings are found in the early papyri. He lists 150 Byzantine readings which though not supported by the early Alexandrian and Western uncials are read by the bulk of later MSS and by the early papyri. He lists a further 170 Byzantine readings which also run counter to Aleph B and company but find support from the Western MSS. These also are supported in the early papyri. And lest it be said that this papyri support is "only minimal," Sturz demonstrates papyri support for a total of 839 readings which in varying degrees would be classed as Byzantine. As the papyri is extant for only 30% of the New Testament, available evidence allows us to reasonably project that subsequent papyri finds would give similar support to the Byzantine text In those areas not now extant.

Sturz in addition presents a number of other not so well known areas of evidence for the Byzantine text. We owe him a great debt for his research. However when he seeks to deny the theological/supernatural arguments for the preservation of the text, he becomes unmoored. You may be forgiven if you have difficulty understanding the following statement or think it to be contradictory:

> It should be pointed out that providential preservation is not a necessary consequence of inspiration. Preservation of the Word of God is promised in Scripture, and inspiration and preservation are related doctrines, but they are distinct from each other, and there is a danger of making one the necessary corollary of the other. The Scriptures do not do this God, having given the perfect revelation by verbal inspiration was under no special or logical obligation to see that man did not corrupt it (The Byzantine Text…Nelson, p 38, emphasis mine).

Zane Hodges in seeking to deny the charge that he might be leaning a little toward a theological/supernatural stance in textual matters, gives the following reply when questioned about his contribution to the excellent book *Which Bible*.

> Finally. Fee…seems to wish to continue to tag me with a theological slant that I have explicitly disavowed. The fact that I allowed an article of mine to be reprinted in a volume all of whose perspectives I did not share should not be used against me… ("Modern Textual Criticism and the Majority Text: A Surrejoinder", JETS, June 1978, p. 163).

Maurice Robinson in the *RP* edition is to be commended for sharpening the focus of the arguments used against the Critical Text. Valuable insights are given. And, he does make a statement or two on behalf of preservation, but it is conditioned and counterbalanced by what is termed a "non-theological" approach. As with a number of others today (see the authors, *My Words Shall Not Pass Away – Denials From Nine Fundamental Bible Colleges*) Robinson believes the original text is *out there*, but it has not yet been fully identified and restored. It is therefore the goal of *RP* "to establish as nearly as possible the precise form of the original text" (*RP* 1991 Preface p. 16 internet). And: "The task set before God's people is to identify and receive the best-attested form of the Greek biblical text as preserved among the extant evidence." This can be done by "careful and judicious examination of the evidence" (*RP* 2005 Preface p. xxi). Thus after 2000 years we are still going to have to wait for a for a fully exact and reliable New Testament Text! The following statements by Maurice Robinson, beginning with his view of Edward F. Hills, do not add to our comfort:

> I would not consider anyone whose primary agenda was the defense of KJV exclusivity or primacy to be in any manner a forerunner of the Byzantine-priority or majority text position, but rather to reflect a more recent and less-than-scholarly development. This is the situation with Hills, who — regardless of all his former training and apparently favorable comments regarding the Byzantine or majority text — is never willing absolutely to reject any KJV reading derived from a minority of Greek manuscripts (or even no Greek manuscripts whatever!). Through scholastic sophistry similar to that applied by most other KJVOs, Hills ultimately defends every aspect of the KJV and its underlying text, regardless of where the factual data might point. Like most other KJVOs, Hills also ignores the methodological dichotomy whereby he on the one hand claims Byzantine superiority while on the other hand he denies such in favor of minority or unsupported readings — this demonstrates a KJVO mentality quite clearly (2010 Interview, sermonindex.net).

> Since the Receptus form of text does not provide an accurate reproduction of the common Greek manuscript tradition, the present edition strives to rectify that situation by presenting the readings of the Byzantine Textform in a more precise manner (*RP* 2005 Preface, p. i note).

> Certainly the *Textus Receptus* had its problems, not the least of which was its failure to reflect the Byzantine Textform in an accurate manner. But the Byzantine Textform is *not* the TR, nor need it be associated with the TR or those defending such in any manner... This includes all the various factions which hope to find authority and certainty in a single "providentially preserved" Greek text or English translation (usually the KJV). It need hardly be mentioned that such an approach has nothing to do with actual text-critical theory or praxis (*RP* 2005 Appendix, p. 533, note 2).

> Byzantine-priority provides no domain or shelter for those unwilling to labor diligently, or for unscholarly individuals whose goal is merely a biased theological perspective or the advocacy of a particular translation. Rather, the theory manifests a compelling and logical perspective which can stand on its own merits. It attempts to explain the evidential data preserved to critical scholarship in the quest toward the goal of establishing the original text of the canonical Greek New Testament (*RP* 2005 Appendix, p. 584).

> For advocates of the TR/KJV position, the "theological argument" regarding the conflict between God and Satan is <u>primary</u>, centering upon the "providential preservation" of a specific and unique text, unlike that found in any single manuscript or texttype, including the Byzantine Textform. For advocates of the Byzantine-priority hypothesis, the underlying theological factors take a <u>secondary</u> role in the realm of textual criticism. (*RP* 1991 Preface, p. 15 internet, emphasis mine).

Not withstanding Robinson's approach and assessment of Edward Hills, it is a welcome contrast to see this following appraisal.

> He [Hills] integrated the theological perspective with the discipline of New Testament text criticism. This is a taboo that recent Majority Text advocates have attempted not to transgress, preferring to work from within a purely scientific framework (Preface, Theodore Letis, *The King James Version Defended* by Edward F. Hills p. vi).

Which of the two views, a "primary" or a "secondary" view of providential preservation, best accords with our Lord's promise in Matthew 24:35: *Heaven and earth shall pass away but my words shall not pass away?*

CHAPTER 2

A WELL-INTENTIONED REACTION TO THE SILENCING OF THE MANUSCRIPT MAJORITY

For over a hundred years there has been a systematic attempt to replace and ignore the Traditional Text/King James Version, and yet without giving the majority of manuscripts a chance to speak. With respect to the silencing of this majority Zane Hodges with the other *HF* and *RP* editors have been outspoken critics.

TEXTUAL CRITICISM'S ATTITUDE TOWARD 5,555 GREEK MANUSCRIPTS

It may come as a surprise that only a relative few of the 5555 MSS now catalogued have been collated. As of August 2009 the Munster Institute listed 124 Papyri, 280 Uncials, 2808 Minuscules, and 2343 Lectionaries for a total of 5555 MSS. High percentage collation has been limited to the papyri fragments, earlier uncials, and a relative few cursives which show some departure from the Traditional Text. The "constant witnesses" in the Nestle-Aland Text are an example of these. The great mass of MSS have been all but ignored. The reason is quite simple. The overwhelming majority of manuscripts support the TR/KJV, and seeking out any further support is the last thing in which textual criticism is interested. Westcott and Hort certainly were not interested in giving the majority the chance to speak. They wove their theory around only a few MSS, and of these they had but a second-hand knowledge.

Bart Ehrman pointed out:

> Westcott and Hort collated no MSS themselves but instead applied themselves to the study of collations and apparatuses made by other scholars (see, for example, Introduction, 144). As a result, their knowledge of the documents was second-hand and partial ("Methodological Developments in the Analysis and Classification of New Testament Documentary Evidence", *Novum Testamentum*, 29 -1987, p. 8 note).

Concerning the number of MSS available in Hort's day. Frederik Wisse says:

> Hort knew of the existence of fewer than 1000 cursives, and that only 150 of these were available to him in complete collation. (*The Profile Method for the Classification and Evaluation of Manuscript Evidence*, Grand Rapids: Eerdmans, 1982, p. 2).

In the years since Hort we have 2,808 cursives and 2,343 lectionaries. Again, apart from a cursory glance to see if there might be a reading even partially supportive of the Aleph-B kind of text, they have been merely catalogued and ignored. Attention, instead has centered on the comparatively few papyri fragments, and what to do when they and other favored witnesses disagree with Aleph and B, (the source of eclecticism!). With regard to the large file of MSS on microfilm at the Institute in Munster, Kurt Aland had admitted:

> ...the main problem in N.T. textual criticism lies in the fact that little more than their

actual existence is known of most of the manuscripts...("The Significance of the Papyri..." pp. 330, 311, Quoted in *INTT*)

Aland's interest in the vast repository of MS evidence which he oversaw had its own particular agenda. Wisse explains:

> Yet Aland's interest in the minuscules is not for their own sake. He is no longer satisfied with Hort's judgment that the discovery of important cursive evidence is most improbable. He wants to find the few hypothetical nuggets which Hort did not think were worth the effort. Aland wants to be able to say that he has searched the minuscules exhaustively for anything of value. This search of course, presupposed that the minuscules as such are of little value...Minuscles have to pass a test before they are considered worthy of inclusion in a textual apparatus. All MSS which are generally Byzantine will fail (*Profile Method*, p. 4).

Therefore, when we read about many more cursives being cited in the later editions of the *Nestle-Aland Greek NT*; we are not to believe that a significant shift away from the Alexandrian text has taken place. The following should be read with a fair amount of salt as it betrays what Wisse says above:

> Beside the papyri and uncials this edition presents for the first time the full evidence of a great number of minuscules—not simply of such familiar minuscules as 33, 69, 1739, f I, f I3, etc, but of a whole series hitherto quite unknown. In a study of the text of all the minuscules, these have proved themselves of equal if not superior value than many of the uncials...The nineteenth century was the age of the uncials; the mid-twentieth century was the age of the papyri...But now we are entering the age of the minuscules...the continuing collation of minuscules at the Institute for New Testament Textual Research (in preparation for an *editio maior critical*) has led to further discoveries. These results will be duly presented in future editions...

> Only those Greek manuscripts can be mentioned here whose significance merits·their citation for each variant, i.e , the "constant witnesses," in contrast to the majority of the Greek manuscripts... (*Nestle-Aland 26th Edition*, pp 47*, 48*).

What this present "age of the minuscules" really meant to the editors of the Critical Text was the hope that they might find a little more support for their Aleph/B/Alexandrian kind of text. In fact, they did not find much support during their "age of the uncials." And despite initial promise the "age of the papyri" has become something of an embarrassment. So as far as finding anything that would even remotely strengthen their case for the Aleph-B Text from the MSS, the "age of the minuscules" was a kind of last hope.

ALEPH AND B STILL REIGN SUPREME
IN CRITICAL CIRCLES

Despite contrary appearances and talk of being eclectic, Aleph, B and their few allies still dictate the modern Critical Text, and the feeling prevails that no purpose would be served in giving the majority of MSS a greater voice. Though, for different reasons, J.K. Elliot in a review criticized this dependence on the few uncials:

> Metzger's *Commentary* is a valuable and stimulating starting place for discussing

variants. Its failing merely - and inevitably- reflect the failings of the United Bible Society Greek New Testament text as a whole. These are primarily its excessive respect for the readings of the so-called great uncials (especially Aleph B)...(*New Testament Textual Criticism, Its Significance for Exegesis, Essays in Honour of Bruce M. Metzger*, "An Eclectic Textual Commentary on the Greek Text of Mark's Gospel". Oxford: Clarendon Press, 181, p. 48).

Sturz adds:

UBS has a fondness for the shortest readings and also a preference for B which sometimes outstrips Westcott and Hort (Harry A. Sturz, *The Byzantine Text-Type and New Testament Textual Criticism*, Grand Rapids: Nelson, 1984. p 190).

With the unification and identical text that began with the Nestle–26 and UBS-3 editions. The Critical Text fell as much as ever under the magic wand of Codex Vaticanus.

THE REASON WHY THE MAJORITY CANNOT BE IGNORED

Wisse singles out the central reason why textual criticism cannot afford to pass over the great mass of manuscripts:

In a situation where MS evidence runs into more than 5000 separate items and a time span of more than fourteen centuries, it should be questioned whether all this evidence is relevant for the establishment of the original text. It may well be that the oldest copies in existence are adequate representatives of the MS tradition so that the rest can be ignored. After all, why start more than thirteen centuries after the autograph MS were written, and wade back through literally thousands of MSS in an immensely complicated process...To find the foundation of a building one does not first climb the roof; one starts somewhere below the ground floor.

This argument...forms the background for all those who consider it justified to ignore all, or almost all, minuscules...

There Is bascially only one argument which can circumvent the task of studying all the late minuscules...This argument is that among the early uncials there are MSS which stand in <u>a relatively uncorrupted tradition</u>, and which show all other text-types of the period to be secondary and corrupted. Only if this argument can be proved, and if it is clear from some sampling that late minuscules fall predominantly in the tradition of one of the corrupted texts, can we safely omit a full study of these MSS (*Profile Method*, p. 1,2, emphasis mine).

When Aleph and B, the two main pillars of the critical text, display 3,000 clear differences in the Gospels (Hoskier's count in *Codex B and Its Allies*); then what candidate do they propose for "a relatively uncorrupted tradition"? They have none! Yet they continue to work at the miserable business of keeping the vast majority of MSS out of public sight, and thus denying all the witnesses a chance to speak. The editors of *HF* and *RP* reacted against this exclusion and turned to the work of Hermann von Soden for help. Wisse sums it up:

Except in von Soden's inaccurate and unused pages, the minuscules have never been allowed to speak (*Profile Method*, p. 5).

For I testify unto every man that heareth the words of the prophecy of this book, If any man shall add unto these things, God shall add unto him the plagues that are written in this book: And if any man shall take away from the words of the book of this prophecy, God shall take away his part out of the book of life, and out of the holy city, and from the things which are written in this book.

(Revelation 22:18-19)

Chapter 3

HERMANN VON SODEN IN A NEW SUIT OF CLOTHES

The *HF* and *RP* editions are not based upon new collations of the manuscripts, but are derived almost entirely from *Die Schriften des neuen Testaments* (1913) by Hermann von Soden for Matthew to Jude, and H.C. Hoskier's *Concerning the Text of the Apocalypse* (1929) for Revelation. Thus, the *HF* and *RP* editions are von Soden and Hoskier newly outfitted.

VON SODEN'S WORK WAS A MASSIVE EFFORT

Coming first to von Soden, there is no question that the editors went to a printed source which provides far more MS information than any other. The Berlin professor, born in Cincinnati, educated at the University of Tübingen, cannot be ignored! A number of his key theories are clearly wrong. The presentation is complex. Hoskier said that it was "honeycombed with errors". But whereas Hort theorized without directly collating the MSS, von Soden examined more items than anyone before or since.

Yet von Soden was a rationalist. He showed very little regard toward the Received Text which had brought such inestimable blessing to Europe and the world, and sought instead to rewrite the Text of the New Testament on the basis of his collations and rather novel theory of textual history. The *HF* and *RP* editors have now utilized his data toward the same end. We will show that this is a mistake and that despite the massive scope of von Soden's work, it provides only a very small part of the total MS picture and cannot begin to be used in the way the *HF* and *RP* editors envisaged. Regarding von Soden's approach to the project, J. Harold Greenlee summarizes:

> Shortly before the turn of the century a wealthy German woman provided generous financial assistance to Hermann von Soden to produce a text of the N.T. on a scale never before equalled, Von Soden, a professor in Berlin, was to hire a considerable number of trained research assistants to examine all known MSS of the N.T. in the libraries of Europe and the Near East. (*Introduction to New Testament Textual Criticism*, Eerdmans, p 83).

Anyone who has gone through von Soden's apparatus cannot but marvel at the huge amount of MS data he gathered. While Tischendorf gathered extensive citations from the uncials, fathers and versions, von Soden sought to traverse the vast expanse of the cursive evidence. His work, however, did not as expected replace Tischendorf's 8th Edition as the standard tool in textual criticism, and it has often been termed "a magnificent failure."

Wisse says:

> Few scholarly undertakings have suffered a more curious fate than that of Hermann Freiherr von Soden. On the one hand, criticism could hardly have been more unanimous, more vociferous, and more devastating. Nonetheless, almost all of von Soden's critics have made extensive use of his work...An immediate and apprehensive reaction...was inevitable. The work claimed to be an exhaustive and definitive study of

the MS tradition of the Greek NT...Thus it seemed that all previous textual work had become obsolete; and that the main task of lower criticism of the NT had finally been accomplished...Nor was this first volume immune to a charge of scholarly arrogance. So sure was von Soden of the finality of his work that he adopted a totally new notation system (*Profile Method*, p. 9).

In addition to the fact of God's promises that He would preserve the Word's He inspired, there are conclusive reasons why von Soden cannot be used to reconstruct the Traditional and Received Text.

VON SODEN'S APPARATUS IS "HONEYCOMBED WITH ERRORS"

It would be impossible for a work of this magnitude to escape a reasonable amount of error, but with von Soden, it is said to have gone beyond acceptable limits. H.C. Hoskier was in a position to make an evaluation of the accuracy of the work. He writes:

I had looked for great things from Dr. von Soden's final volume of the Text. The earlier volumes were very heavy reading, but I expected that his Text and Critical notes would fill a gap in our studies.

Alas, he has but complicated our problems, and instead of writing a eulogy on his work, I regret to have to condemn it strongly...

As to the presentment of the combined critical material, after making every allowance for the division of work among forty people it can only be said that the apparatus is positively *honeycombed* with errors, and many documents which should have been recollated have not been touched, others only partially, and others again have been incorrectly handled (*JTS*, 15-1914, p. 307 emphasis mine).

Hoskier, over the next twenty pages, went on to document this assertion. Likely haste was involved, for von Soden admitted on his opening page that he lived in fear of dying before the work was finished:

In the end it seemed preferable to leave whatever incorrect numbers or letters or small oversights as had crept in, rather than delay the printing by further fine checking (translation from the German).

In fact von Soden did die shortly afterwards in an accident boarding a subway train in Berlin. Hoskier remarks on this tragedy:

As these last pages come to me for revision, I received the news of Hermann von Soden's sudden and untoward end. I regret that there has been so much to criticise as to his work. I wish I could have seen any way to modify it (*Codex B and its Allies*, Quartch, p. 461).

More recently though, this criticism has been countered. James Royse in 1979 wrote:

Von Soden's critical edition of the Greek N.T. has remained a principle source of information on the readings of many minuscules...however, there have been frequent charges of undue complexity and unacceptable inaccuracy...Most recently, W.J. Elliot has presented evidence to suggest that von Soden's inaccuracy is even more pervasive than was previously thought...In fact, however, Elliott gives a very misleading picture...apparantly because he has misinterpreted von Soden's system of notation.

Royce then, after giving a detailed examination of Elliott's criticism, says:

> In conclusion, then, von Soden's apparatus while neither thoroughly perspicuous nor completely reliable, does give us a good deal of information not available in Tischendorf. As long as this is so, and as long as no more recent critical edition of the New Testament exists, von Soden's apparatus must be utilized. This is admittedly a case of making do with what we have, but the accuracy of what we have is considerably better than Elliott would have us believe ("Von Soden's Accuracy," James R.Royce, *JTS*, 30-1979, pp. 166, 167, 171).

This brings us to Hodges and Farstad's rather positive initial statement concerning their reliance on von Soden. But as we will see they also express a substantial concern which goes beyond the following qualified view of Robinson and Pierpont (*HF*, xxii, xxiii).

> For the evidence of the Majority Text, the present edition rests heavily upon the information furnished by Hermann von Soden...Though this has been extensively checked with the Eighth Edition of Constantine Tischendorf, with the apparatus of S.C.E. Legg for Matthew and Mark, and with the apparatus of UBS-3 and Nestle-Aland-26, only rarely can von Soden's data be corrected with confidence (*HF* Introduction, p. xv).

And then *RP*:

> The primary source for establishing the readings of the Byzantine Textform remains the massive apparatus of Hermann Freiherr von Soden...Additional confirmatory material appears in various sources, including the UBS[4], NA[27], the IGNTP volumes, the Editio Critica Maior, and specific manuscript collations published within the Studies and Documents series and elsewhere.

> The *Text und Textwert* volumes are particularly useful in this regard: this series presents complete collation data regarding selected variant units throughout the New Testament. Within each variant unit, *Text und Textwert* cites *all* available Greek manuscripts in relation to their support of specific readings. These data provide primary confirmation regarding the status of Byzantine readings that previously had been established from earlier published sources. In particular, these full collation results tend to confirm the Byzantine group evidence presented in von Soden's early twentieth-century apparatus. In a similar manner, the Claremont Profile Method also tends to confirm von Soden's general reliability in regard to the identification of groups. Although von Soden cannot be relied upon when dealing with specific readings of individual manuscripts, his overall general reliability in regard to the larger groupings of texttypes and sub-types remains stable in view of the evidence provided by these outside sources (*RP* Preface, pp. ix,x emphasis mine)

"Von Soden can be trusted for his groups of MSS but not his individual MSS"! How then are we to view the 414 MSS he cites individually? Frederik Wisse in his *Profile Method* on Luke certainly brings us back to square one and back to Hoskier's verdict: The work is "honeycombed with error"!

> In order to make an independent judgment of the matter, a test was run to measure the extent of von Soden's inaccuracy. Luke 1 was chosen, since it is one of the sample chapters of the Profile Method, and, more importantly, hundreds of twice-checked

collations were available with microfilms through the office of the IGNTP in Claremont.

A careful count revealed that von Soden claims to use 120 MSS in the apparatus to Luke 1. It should be borne in mind that von Soden does not always use a MS throughout. A significant number of MSS were only partially collated. Why these MSS were not used in toto is not clear, but time and opportunity must have been the determining factors...

Through the good offices of the IGNTP, 99 of the 120 MSS could be checked...

Wisse goes on to explain how these 99 MSS were checked against 54 passages, 53 of which von Soden deals with. He then gives the shocking summary:

Once the extent of error is seen, the word "inaccuracy" becomes a euphemism. Of the 99 checked MSS, 76 were missing one or more times when they should have been cited, or were listed when they should not have been. This breaks down into 59 MSS which were missing in von Soden's apparatus from 1 to 4 times, and 39 which were added incorrectly from 1 to 6 times.

...von Soden's inaccuracies cannot be tolerated for any purpose. His apparatus is <u>useless for a reconstruction of the text</u> of the MSS he used (*Profile Method*, pp. 16, 17 emphasis mine).

Yet this is the primary source *HP* and *RP* used in their reconstruction of the New Testament Text.

VON SODEN WAS STRONGLY ALEXANDRIAN

Here Hermann von Soden's work is something of an enigma. He views the Byzantine Text (K) as being underived from and possibly as old as both the Alexandrian (H) and his more diverse Jerusalem (I) Text. This is certainly a departure from standard Westcott and Hort dogma. We would like to think that he arrived at this conclusion by his dealing with the large numbers of MSS rather than merely theorizing. However, his estimate of the K (Byzantine) Text is certainly not equal to the other two. And though von Soden's text is closer to the TR than other critical editions, yet his views and product are still firmly within the Alexandrian camp.

Hoskier says:

Von Soden's text is so thoroughly Alexandrian that it falls into line with Hort, irrespective of MS evidence. Among other things, it favours the imperfect over the aorist, just as the Alexandrians did, and favours the historic present on countless occasions... (*Codex B And its Allies* , p. 461).

What needs to be emphasized at this point is that anyone who seeks to gather Byzantine MS evidence from the standard sources - Alford, Tischendorf, Souter, Merk, Vogels, Nestle, Aland, or <u>von Soden</u> - is really getting only a few scraps from the table. The energies of these men have been expended elsewhere. Their labors toward the great mass of Byzantine MSS is limited to those places where there is departure from the TR. A clear example can be seen in the fact that von Soden individually cites all of the MSS which fall into his I and H groups, but with the exception of 55 directly K MSS lumps large numbers of Byzantine MSS under a few sigla.

Therefore *HF* and *RP* have based their editions upon an area of von Soden's work where he gave the least attention. And this brings us to the fatal flaw in their attempted reconstruction of the Text.

VON SODEN MADE ONLY A CURSORY SAMPLING
FROM AMONG THE VAST NUMBERS OF MANUSCRIPTS

Though faced with the impossibility of a task in which he clearly would have liked to have done much more, time, and importantly his interest in the "I" and "H" MSS prevented his team from making anything approaching a detailed survey of the Byzantine tradition. Von Soden did far more than anyone else. But, he did not see a majority of the MSS. He did not collate a majority of the MSS which he did see. And, among those which he did collate, only a relative few received a high percentage collation. Therefore, it is fair to ask: How can *HP* and *RP* reconstruct the God-honored Textus Receptus or for that matter the New Testament Text generally on the claim of majority MS support when neither they or von Soden or anyone else has even begun to collate the majority of MSS?

Metzger comments on the general situation:

> Obviously the most satisfying method of locating a newly discovered manuscript within the manuscript tradition of the New Testament is to compare it with each and all previously known manuscripts. This procedure, however, entails such an enormous amount of labor...that scholars are content to make analyses on a <u>selective basis</u> (*The Text of the NT*, p. 179 emphasis mine).

Regarding the *HF* edition at this point, Andrew Brown says:

> One can rarely be sure whether von Soden consulted all his manuscripts at the passage in question, or just <u>a representative sample</u>. And even where he does give figures, the resulting total does not constitute a majority of all the manuscripts which are now available. For these reasons the Hodges-Farstad edition should not be regarded as a definitive majority text until the necessary further collation work has been carried out (Trinitarian Bible Society Quarterly Record, January 1983, pp. 14-16 emphasis mine).

In fact, the *HF* editors themselves express serious reservation over this aspect of von Soden's material.

> As all who are familiar with von Soden's materials will know, his presentation of the data leaves much to be desired. Particularly problematical to the editors of this edition was the extent to which his examination of the K [Koine, Byzantine] appeared to lack consistency. As the specific statements show, at times <u>only a few·representatives</u> of Kx in the Gospels or of K in the Acts and Epistles were examined by him. How often this was true where he gives no exact figures we are left only to guess. His other K subgroups suffer from the same shortcomings. The generalized data of the other sources (such as Tischendorf or Legg) were of little value in correcting this deficiency. <u>In the final analysis, if the present edition was to be produced at all, the statements of von Soden had to be accepted</u>...What is urgently needed is a new apparatus covering the entire manuscript tradition. It should include complete collations of a very high percentage of the surviving majority text manuscripts (*HF*, xxii, xxiii emphasis mine).

The editors give an example of von Soden's fractional use of the materials on page xxii. He is shown to have consulted only 13 Kx MSS on Luke 22:30 (out of 300 accessible to him). Further examples are shown below. In the light of these admissions, we wonder why the *HF* and *RP* projects based upon von Soden were undertaken! It is also to be noted again that *RP* in its Preface does not wrestle over these matters to the extent that *HF* does.

When dealing with the errors in von Soden's work, Frederik Wisse gives a striking example of the fractional nature of his presentation (*Profile Method*, p 16). In Luke 1 von Soden cited 120 MSS; whereas Wisse profiled upwards of 1385! And, there is no reason to think that the situation is much different elsewhere. But now more specifically-

HOW MANY GREEK MANUSCRIPTS DID VON SODEN USE?

The following are the papyri, uncial and minuscule MSS which von Soden cited directly in his apparatus. To what extent they were all cited *consistently* is an open question. This list is based upon that prepared by Benedikt Kraft which converts the von Soden notations to the standard Gregory numbers. Each of these MSS belongs to one of von Soden's three broad groupings: I (Jerusalem), H (Alexandrian) and K (Byzantine). They total 414 MSS. Von Soden also gave numbers to an additional 27 uncials, but it is not clear to what extent he cited them.

P1 P2 P4 P5 p8 P13 P15 P16 PI8 P19 P20 P35 P36 = <u>13 Papyri MSS</u> (124 now extant)

01 02 03 04 05 06 07 08 09 010 011 012 013 014 015 017 019 020 021 022 023 024 025 026 027 028 029 030 031 032 033 035 036 037 038 039 040 041 042 043 044 045 046 047 049 050 051 052 053 054 058 059 065 067 068 070 071 074 078 080 083 084 085 087 091 099 0108 0109 0112 0116 0120 0121 0122 0124 0125 0127 0130 0139 0141 0162 0169 0170 0172 0173 = <u>84 Uncial MSS</u> (280 now extant)

1 2 4 5 6 7 13 16 21 22 27 28 33 35 36 38 42 51 57 60 69 71 79 81 88 91 97 104 115 118 124 138 139 157 160 172 174 175 177 179 181 185 201 203 206 209 213 216 218 221 223 226 229 230 241 242 245 248 249 251 255 256 257 262 263 265 267 270 273 279 280 291 296 307 314 317 319 323 325 326 330 337 346 348 3497 372 378 383 385 397 399 406 421 423 424 429 430 431 432 436 440 443 453 459 460 461 462 467 468 472 473 476 477 478 479 480 482 483 485 489 491 495 498 506 517 522 536 543 544 547 565 566 579 582 598 610 614 617 623 635 639 642 655 659 660 661 664 692 700 713 716 743 788 794 808 821 823 826 827 828 850 869 872 876 892 913 915 917 919 920 922 927 935 941 945 954 983 990 994 998 1010 1012 1038 1047 1071 1082 1093 1108 1149 1170 1175 1187 1188 1192 1207 1210 1216 1219 1220 1223 1229 1241 12112 1245 1279 1293 1295 1311 1319 1321 1346 1354 13551 1365 1375 1391 1396 1402 1405 1424 1515 1518 1522 1542 1555 1573 1574 1579 1582 1588 1604 1606 1610 1611 1654 1615 1689 1738 1739 1758 1765 1778 1819 1820 1827 1828 1829 1831 1835 1836 1837 1838 1845 1852 1859 1862 1867 1872 1873 1874 1876 1891 1894 1898 1908 1912 1934 1994 2004 2005 2014 2015 2016 2017 2020 2023 2026 2027 2028 2029 2031 2033 2036 2040 2043 2054 2055 2056 2057 2059 2060 2061 2064 2065 2066 2067 2068 2069 2080 20812086 2093 2115 2127 2138 2143 2145 2147 2180 2191 2193 2294 2329 2351= <u>317 Minuscule MSS</u> (2808 now extant. Total papyri, uncial and minuscule now extant not counting the 2343 lectionaries = 3212)

The great majority from among these 414 fall into his I category, which is basically the Byzantine Text with varying amounts of departure. A relative few are from his H (Alexandrian) Text. And, as shown below, from among those he cited directly only about 55 fall into his K (Byzantine) MS group. This shows where von Soden's interests lay!

The following shows the rather complex sub-groupings von Soden gave to his K MSS. He gave similar sub-classifications to the the I MSS. Excepting the three "lumped together" groups, shown here are the numbers of directly cited MSS in each.

K1	In the Gospels, he sites:	8 MSS
Ki	In the Gospels, he cites:	4 MSS
Kx	In the Gospels, he does not cite individually, but Hodges and Farstad say the group has more than 300 MSS	300 MSS
Kr	In the Gospels, he does not cite individually, but it is said to be much smaller than Kx:	? MSS
Kc	In the Gospels, he does not cite individually, it does not seem to be a significant number:	? MSS
A	In the Gospels, he cites:	4 MSS
K:Iota	In the Gospels, he cites:	3 MSS
K	In Acts to Jude, he cites:	9 MSS
Kc	In Acts to Jude, he cites:	9 MSS
Kr	In Acts to Jude, he cites:	4 MSS
Kc	In Revelation, he cites:	4 MSS
Ko	In Revelation, he cites:	9 MSS
K	In Revelation, he cites:	1 MSS

The K groupings whose numbers are known (excepting Kx) and whose MSS were directly cited, total 55 from among the 414. When von Soden cites for a given reading one of the three "lumped together" groups - Kx, Kr or Kc, we do not know how many MSS he actually looked at. While he does give some indication for Kx, the fact that he does not say anything for Kr or Kc indicates that it was probably only a cursory sampling. His statements on page xii of *Die Schriften des neuen Testaments* clearly show his approach and attitude toward the Byzantine MSS. It was anything but thorough and consistent.

> ...only collated in small numbers word for word at the beginning until the K-Text was established.

> ...collated Kr Texts as far as was necessary to establish the text in detail. In Kx Texts only those passages were examined on which the K-Text faltered.

> ...But because no individual weight is due these otherwise uncollated K-codices, It seemed that the quoting of the ratio of the Kx evidence would suffice (translated from the German).

Regarding this latter statement, von Soden infrequently cites the ratio of Kx MSS for and against a reading, and when he does it often betrays how few he actually consulted. The following example of these ratios in Mark 8, 9, 10 shows a surprising disparity of Kx MSS consulted:

8:7	83 for 81 against
8:26	96 for 69 against
8:38	5 for 8 against
9:1	3 for 10 against
9 :2	4 for 9 against
9:4	8 for 5 against
9:38	103 for 63 against
9:45	7 for 5 against
10:14	4 for 8 against
10:25	3 for 10 against
10:29	54 for 111 against
10:29	7 for 6 against

Thus for some readings, he consulted as many as 165 Kx MSS and for others only 13. He says that he only consulted the Kx MSS when the other K groups "faltered" (didn't agree). But with the possible exception of Kr in the Gospels, von Soden only bothered to give a few representative MSS to these other K groups. And thus it seems clear that these sub-groups with few MSS, when they were in agreement, in the determination of the text were allowed to overrule the witness of the much larger Kx group.

THE DIFFERENT APPROACHES OF *HF* AND *RP* TO VON SODEN

The impression is given in *HF* and *RP* that many hundreds of MSS have been brought forward in support of their reconstructed texts. But when the above is carefully considered this is far from the truth. The core of von Soden's work are the 414 MSS he cited and classified. Beyond these his treatment of the MSS can only be described as a cursory sampling. As the von Soden I Text "for the most part adheres to the majority form, although with frequent defections" (*HF* Introduction, p. xv), both the I and the K Texts were used by *HF* in preparing their *Majority Text*. The *RP* editors on the other hand did not use the I Text but limited themselves to the K Text and its sub-groupings in order to produce their *Byzantine Textform* or "Byzantine Consensus Text" (*RP* Preface, pp. ix, x).

Therefore in Matthew to Jude, *HF* appealed to a great many more of the 414 directly cited MSS than did *RP*. By my count, excluding 15 MSS for Revelation and excluding the "cursory sampled" groups, the *RP* Text is based on only 40 directly cited MSS for Matthew to Jude.

HF and especially *RP* have therefore based their texts on only a very small percentage of the 5555 MSS now extant. The one exception is in John 7:53 – 8:11 where they utilized von Soden's citations of over 900 MSS. According to Wisse, von Soden had hoped that this would provide a basis for group classification. It apparently did not! (See *Profile Method*, p. 12).

The *HF* and *RP* editions are based on only a small percentage of the Greek MS evidence. They have not considered the 2343 lectionaries. They have not taken account of the vast field of Patristic and Versional evidence. They express only a very limited view of verbal preservation. They cannot claim a valid basis for the "restoration of the text", which for us means the God-honored Words which underlie the Authorized Version (See for example *RP* Appendix, p. 544). Clearly in von Soden these two Greek editions chose a very faulty foundation.

Ye shall not add unto the word which I command you, neither shall ye diminish ought from it, that ye may keep the commandments of the LORD your God which I command you.

(Deuteronomy 4:2)

CHAPTER 4

THE BOOK OF REVELATION
IN THE *HF* AND *RP* EDITIONS

When we come to the Book of Revelation, *HF* and *RP* turn from von Soden to the far more secure ground of H. C.Hoskier. Yet there will not be much joy in this for those of us who hold to the Authorized Version, for in the case of the *HF* edition fully one-third (1/3) of the 1800 alterations which the editors make are from the Apocalypse, and based on Hoskier's data! The situation appears to be approximately the same for *RP*.

Herman C. Hoskier is generally a friend of the Traditional Text of the NT. His famous work *Codex B and Its Allies* is a devastating indictment against the so-called "pillars" of the Alexandrian Text. He is among that triumvirate of scholars, with Burgon and Scrivener, who stood against the stampede toward the Revised Text. Hoskier's scholarship and firsthand knowledge of the MSS command respect, and often from those who are opponents in textual matters.

J. Neville Birdsall is an example:

> But pride of place belongs to two more recent students who have devoted themselves solely to the problems of text. First to be named is Herman C. Hoskier, who made many valuable contributions to the textual cirticism of the New Testament as a whole, and in regard to the Revelation <u>gave thirty years to the task of collating all the available manuscripts of the book</u>. The result of this task are to be found in the two massive volumes of his, *Concerning the Text of the Apocalypse*. Hoskier as a theoretician of textual criticism was exceedingly eccentric nor was he gifted with a very felicitous style of English; but as a collator he was, as Kirsopp Lake testified, preternaturally accurate, so that all his works are valuable as repositories of raw material...for the Greek text of the Apocalypse his work stands as a *kteme eis aei* [an eternal possession] ("The Text of the Revelation of Saint John", *The Evangelical Quarterly*, 33-1961, pp. 228,229 emphasis mine).

At the outset, Bible believers will find reassuring Hoskier's basic conclusion concerning the 200 plus MSS he collated for Revelation:

> I may state that if Erasmus had striven to found a text on the largest number of existing MSS in the world of one type, he could not have succeeded better, since his family-MSS occupy the front rank in point of actual numbers, the family numbering over 20 MSS, beside its allies (*The John Rylands Bulletin* 19-1922/23. p. 118).

So, what went wrong? Why this wholesale departure by *HF* and *RP* from the Received Text in the Book of Revelation? Unlike von Soden, we cannot argue that Hoskier looked at only a minority of the MSS or that his work was characterized by low percentage collation, or that it was "honeycombed with error". In fact, his work was very accurate and dealt with most of the extant MSS containing Revelation. So again, how can we account for his material being used to introduce so many departures from the Received Text? The answer is basically two-fold:

1. Both *HF* and *RP* chose to base their text in Revelation on a large group of MSS which generally align with the 10ᵗʰ century uncial MS 046. *RP* calls this group "Q"; we will call it 046. Hoskier did not indicate a preference for 046 but merely cited the data. The KJV/TR adheres to an equally large group of MSS associated with (and often containing) an influential commentary on Revelation by Andreas, Bishop of Caesarea in Cappadocia. This commentary is said by *RP* to have been written in the 4ᵗʰ century (*RP* Preface, p. xii).

2. The second major error is that the *HF* editors did not allot to the Andreas group all the MSS due to it. Thus, the 046 group is made in their edition to look larger than the Andreas. The *RP* editors do not explain their procedures to the extent of *HF*, and though their resultant text differs somewhat, they are clear in stating that they followed the 046 group.

These two basic procedures led to the many changes which the *HF* editors readily admit:

> Additionally, the number of disagreements with the Oxford Textus Receptus was much greater than in the other books of the New Testament (*HF* Introduction, p xl).

They also say:

> Here also, as in the John passage, the results are presented as *provisional* and *tentative*…it remains for the community of New Testament scholars to weigh these data in the light of the projected stemma (p. xxxiii emphasis mine).

Before examining the two major MSS groupings in Revelation (Andreas and 046) we should note at the outset:

THE UNIQUE POSITION OF REVELATION
IN THE MANUSCRIPT HISTORY

It is not surprising that this book which so mightily tells of Christ's Second Coming and Satan's defeat, should itself be the chief object of Satan's attack. The "official" church, both East and West, but especially East, was slow to accept the book as canonical. The rebukes to the seven churches in Asia may have come too close to the bone. "Wordsworth conjectures that the rebukes of Laodicea in Revelation influenced the council of Laodicea [4ᵗʰ century] to omit Revelation from its list of books to be read publicly" (*JFB Commentary*, Vol. VI, p. lxii). There was also a strong bias against the book's millennial doctrine. As there also is today!

Further, Greek MSS containing Revelation are not nearly as plentiful as in the rest of the NT. Many of the extant MSS (Hoskier says 40) are bound up with writings other than the NT. Revelation was not used in the lectionary services of the Eastern Church, and therefore, the lectionary MSS do not contain it.

In passing, it is interesting to note that while extant MSS of the Syriac Peshitta do not have Revelation, yet earlier editions must have contained it. For Ephrem Syrus (died 373), who was considered the greatest father in the Syrian church, quotes Revelation repeatedly <u>in Syriac</u>. He did not know Greek! (See *The Greek New Testament*, Henry Alford, vol. IV, p. 202)

But whatever the position may have been in the official church, *the common people heard him gladly* (Mark 12:37). And God has preserved this book which concludes our Bible through the priesthood of believers.

THE TWO MAIN MANUSCRIPT GROUPINGS IN REVELATION

Unlike the rest of the NT in which the KJV/TR type of MSS totally dominate the field numerically, the same is not the case with Revelation. Among the 256 (just above 300 now) MSS which Hoskier collated, it is two rather than one group that are seen to dominate. Zane Hodges presented an excellent study on this textual phenomena:

> The cursive evidence does not reveal a single type of text decisively dominating the field. Instead of this, there is a most striking bifurcation of the cursive witnesses as revealed by the surviving manuscripts. On the one hand is found the uncial 046 standing at the head of a large band of cursive manuscripts, the hard core of which is about eighty strong. On the other hand stands another large group, approximately equal in size, whose text is connected with that used by Andreas of Caesarea [in Cappadocia, Asia Minor]...Most of the remaining cursives, with the exception of a few which are related to the uncials A and C, are found to be texts which have experienced mixture of these two basic types.
>
> But this cleavage In the cursive testimony is rendered even more striking because it is found to be remarkably sharp. To prove this, if one works his way carefully through Hoskier's second volume, he will find that on page after page of the apparatus these two cursive groups stand apart from each other and render confllcting testimony where there are significant variants. What is even more, the uncial manuscripts on which modern editors have placed such great reliance are discovered to vacillate surprisingly from side to side.("The Ecclesiastical Text of Revelation," *Bibllotheca Sacra*, April 1961, p 115).

Again, s noted, the Andrean MSS will often contain Andreas' commentary along with the text.

CHARACTERISTICS OF THE ANDREAS AND 046 MSS

1. As to which would receive more support from the uncials, Hodges says:

> On the whole the Andreas group receives stronger uncial support throughout the book than does the 046 coterie, but Aleph and A and C and P47 disagree frequently among themselves ...Although belonging to the same basic Egyptian family, the elder uncials along with P47 exhibit exceptional fluidity...But while P47 and Aleph seem more inclined to go with 046, and A and C tend to favor Andreas, the groupings by no means consistently follow these lines ("Ecclesiastical Text", p. 115, 120).

This vacillation of the old uncials between Andreas and 046 indicates that their characteristic readings are in fact older than the early uncials. Hodges explains:

> One inference from all this is obvious. There is nothing here to suggest that the fundamental cleavage between Andreas and 046 was of late origin. Indeed, the uncertainty which the leading ancient manuscripts exhibit hints strongly that the two major cursive streams can only meet back, perhaps far back, of the fourth century. Aleph, generally assigned to that era, shows the most pronounced signs of wavering between the two cursive groups...

> The confusion among the uncials is profound, and there is not wanting in this a hint that the editors of the uncials themselves or of their ancestral exemplars exercised their critical faculties extensively in adjudicating the rival claims of the Andreas and 046 branches of the tradition, and that no panacea for doing so was known to any of them. Hence they strike out in differing directions repeatedly...

> No text prevailed in the Byzantine Church. Instead, two forms of text were used and copied—often side by side in the same monastery—down through the Middle Ages (pp. 120, 121).

Here we have a good example of how a large group of late MSS can give a far clearer picture of the original autographs than the early uncials.

2. Regarding the comparative age of the two streams, Hoskier presents a somewhat different view than the above and shows the Andrean to be much older:

> ...the B [046] revision, which was made in the 7th century and has so largely influenced one-half or one-third of the cursive MSS (*Text Apocalypse*, vol. I, p. xxvii).

> As to the 1 family [Adreas, Erasmian]... The large group 119-123-144-148-158 is also independent, and through its Syriac strain going back to a very ancient substratum (p xxxiii).

> ...the leading problem is the B (046) recension. Strange that, as in the other books, the great Vatican codex B occupies the most prominent position among the materia critica, so here another MS also designated B should seem to hold the key to the position of the fortress we are trying to penetrate (p xxxv)!

> 119-123 further emphasize the great age of the Erasmian or 1 group (p. 12).

HF agrees, the Andrean text is very old:

> There Is no reason why the parental exemplar of the Andreas text-type could not go back well into the second century (*HF* Introduction, p. xxxvi).

3. Regarding the all-important question of which of the two groups aligns more closely with the printed Received Text underlying the Authorized Version, Hodges says:

> ...the Textus Receptus much more closely approximates Andreas than 046 - in fact, hardly resembles the latter group at all ("Ecclesiastical Text," p. 121 emphasis mine).

To this question Hoskier likewise leaves us in no doubt:

> We trace the origin of the B (046) group not further back than 8th or possibly 7th century. Now many many cursives are identified with this family group, whereas in the main our Textus Receptus is not, and has at any rate avoided the bulk of this revision (*Text Apocalypse*, p. xxxvii).

> ...This is what we mean when we say it Is dangerous to tamper with the oldest readings of the TR (p. xii).

> This may be the proper place to emphasize why the Textus Receptus of the Apocalypse is intrinsically good. Apoc. #1, on which It was founded, is an old text. See how it comes

out in Hippolytus…(p. xivii).

It is a clear and established fact that the TR and #47 are infinitely closer to Hippolytus' text of A.D. 225, than were either Aleph in 375, C and A in 550, P in 700, B (046) in 800 (p. xivii).

4. Regarding the place each text gives to the Deity of Christ and other Trinitarian doctrines: A number of passages show the testimony is stronger in the Andrean MSS. The *HF* apparatus indicates that the 046 MSS unite to exclude the following readings, whereas the Andreas MSS give at least partial and often full support for their inclusion.

1:8	the beginning and the ending
1:11	I am Alpha and Omega, the first and the last
19:1	Lord (partial)
20:9	from God
21:3	and be their God (partial)
21:4	God (partial)

5. Regarding the grammatical form, there are indications that the Andrean text is superior:

…reflect…a stylistic improvement (*HF* Introduction, p. xxxvi),

Now, of course, this issue of grammatical smoothness has been used as argument against the Received Text and Byzantine MSS generally. It is said that "They reflect editorial revision designed to improve the flow and syntax." Textual criticism has long implied that the rougher the grammar the more likely it is to be the original reading. But why must the Holy Spirit in inspiring the Words of Scripture be accused of using rough grammar? Did not the Divine Author know how to use "proper Greek"!

Therefore, in light of the above, why did *HF* and *RP* choose the 046 rather than the Andreas MSS as the basis for their text of Revelation?

Their choice seems to have been influenced to a large degree by the work of Josef Schmid who in turn built "heavily upon the data furnished by Hoskier" (*HF* Introduction p. xxxii. See also *RP* Preface pp. xii, xiii). Schmid labored for many years in seeking to construct a history of the text of Revelation. His conclusions were published in 1955. It is a large work with valuable material, but is put under a shadow by the strange conclusion that the true text of Revelation is to be found in the uncials A and C, and the early commentary by Oecumenius. He seeks further support for his text from five minuscules and the Coptic versions. He goes so far as to give the name "Neutral" to these witnesses. Thus, along with other textual critics, he disregards the majority for a handful of Alexandrian MSS. Zane Hodges gives an able refutation of Schmid's theory in "The Critical Text and the Alexandrian Family of Revelation," *Bibliotheca Sacra*, April 1962.

Nevertheless, Hodges and Farstad (and *RP*) were influenced by Schmid's opinion that the Andreas text was a recension:

There is no reason why the parental exemplar of the Andreas text-type could not go back well into the second century.

But, as Schmid has also concluded, the Andreas text-form is a recension in which many of its readings are gratuitous revisions of the original text. These revisions often reflect either a <u>stylistic improvement</u> or a <u>reverential embellishment</u> (*HF* Introduction, p. xxxvi. *RP* Preface, pp. xii, xiii emphasis mine).

If the Andreas text goes back "well into the second century," then that means it is not very far from the Apostle John himself. And if this text has a long history of transmission and was used as the base for our Reformation Bibles, and if the alternative text (O46) by their admission is "not identical with the original text," and has "at least two obvious scribal errors" (*HF* Introduction, p. xxxiv), and as we know did not become the base of the printed Bibles; then the <u>stylistic improvements</u> and <u>reverential embellishments</u> in the Andreas text must be very obvious and numerous for it now to be discarded. The *HF* editors, however, give only two examples of this kind of "defect" in the Andreas text.

1. Their example of "reverential embellishment":

In Rev. 1:11, the Andreas MSS read (as does the AV): *I am Alpha and Omega, the first and the last*. The Alexandrian witnesses P47. Aleph, A, C, unite with the 046 MSS and other cursives to omit the words.

About 57 of the MSS Hoskier collated have the passage. There is also strong internal evidence for its inclusion. After the Superscription (1:1-3), and Salutation (1:4-8), John, beginning at 1:9 describes his first meeting with the Glorified Christ on the island of Patmos. He hears the voice in 1:10, receives the command in 1:11, and turns to see the speaker in 1:12. In verse 11 it would be strange if the speaker did not first reveal his identity before giving to John such an all-embracing commission.

2. Their example of "stylistic improvement":

In 16:3-17, the 046 MSS read: *the second angel*, and then omit "angel" in the third to seventh vials. The Andreas MSS (and KJV) include the word in each vial (except for the first vial which 046 also leaves out).

If the sequence was going to be abbreviated would it not be more likely that "angel" would be inserted with the first vial and then left out in each of the succeeding ones? Placing it in only the second is awkward and gives the impression that something is amiss in the text.

The *HF* apparatus indicates strong MS support for the inclusion of "angel". In their apparatus, a and b represent the 046 type of MSS, d and e the Andreas, and c somewhere in between.

<u>"angel" included</u>	<u>"angel" omitted</u>
16:4 bcde	a, Egyptian uncials
16:8 bcde , Aleph	a, other Egyptian uncials a, Egyptian uncials
16:10 bcde	a, Egyptian uncials
16: 12 bcde (pt)	a e(pt), Egyptian uncials
16:17 bcde	a, A

The above illustrates the Alexandrian tendency to shorten the text.   It is also worth noting that in the trumpet sequence (chs. 8 and 9), there is no omitting of "angels" from the text. Certainly from these two examples, the editors case for "gratuitous revision" in the Andreas text is not convincing. Again we must ask—Why does Textual Criticism often attribute to the Holy Spirit inspired autographical Text readings which are grammatically rougher and less reverential? Of course in many instances they do not believe in verbal inspiration.

HOW MANY ANDREAS MANUSCRIPTS?

At this point, there is confusion in the different presentations. In his "Ecclesiastical Text of Revelation" Hodges says Andreas and 046 are "approximately equal in size". He quotes Schmid who verifies that they both have eighty MSS (p. 115). *RP* also speaks of them being "approximately equal" (*RP* Preface, p. xii). However the list in the *HF* Edition has 046 outnumbering Andreas by as much as three to one. In addition, there is Hoskier's statement that the twenty-plus Erasmian MSS are the largest single group.

Hodges and Farstad give the following breakdown:

Total number of minuscules in Hosker's list	256
MSS not collated by him	-41
MSS which they believed to be copies of existing ones	-11
Total independent MSS collated by Hoskier	204

The HF editors divide the MSS into five groups. These form a transition or shading from 046 MSS in Group a to Andreas in Group e. It is noteworthy that their total is over one hundred short of Hoskier's initial count.

Group a:	The 046 MSS, including 046	74
Group b:	Contains a shortened form of the Andreas commentary, but often aligns with 046. Hoskier calls the group "Coptic."	10
Group c:	Similar to the text found in the Complutenslan Polyglot, it is a mixture of 046 and Andreas	29
Group d:	Associated with, and generally supports the Andreas text. Hoskier said that it has an Egyptian background and calls it "Egyptian"	13
Group e:	The Andreas MSS, among which are contained all but one of Hoskiers twenty "Erasmian" MSS	24
	Total:	**150**

Allowing a and b, and d and e to group together, the 046 MSS in *HF* outnumber Andreas 84 to 37. By this reckoning the editors have their "majority" text in the Book of Revelation:

> … the editors have not detected any convincing reason to reject the joint testimony of a and b when they concur (*HF* Introduction, p. xxxiv).

But, were Hodges and Farstad right to remove so many MSS from Hoskier's list, and how many of these belong to the Andreas group? They have given the impression that the Andrean

MSS are outnumbered by over two to one. The evidence presented below demonstrates that this is not the case.

The researches of Josef Schmid provide important information at this point. In his *Studien Zur Geschichte Des Griechischen Apokalypse-Textes* he describes 83 MSS which contain the Andreas commentary. These he divides into 12 groups (vol. 1, pp. 1-78). They do not include 13 further MSS which contain a shortened version of the Andreas commentary, (Hoskier's "Coptic"). Apart from this latter it is to be emphasized that there is a basic cohesiveness in the text that became associated with Andreas. In other words, these MSS are not so grouped merely because they contain the commentary.

83 ANDREAS MANUSCRIPTS

The list is in the order of the Gregory numbers followed by Hoskier's numbers. An asterisk indicates that the MS is listed by Hodges and Farstad in either their Md or Me groups. Then follows Schmid's group designation, and finally the group designation of Hoskier. You will notice that Hoskier termed a great many of these MSS "Erasmian" and others "Egyptian". This latter is not to be confused with the Alexandrian type of text. Though it does demonstrate something of an Egyptian background, it is only slightly removed from the kind of text Erasmus used, and can be grouped with it. If anything, the Alexandrian type of text shows a greater affinity with the 046 MSS in Revelation. One demonstration of this is Hodges and Farstad group Mb (Hoskier's "Coptic") with Ma.

025-P, Schmid lists with, but does not place in, one of the Andrean groups.
    Hoskier does not give its group.
051 (Hoskier's E), Schmid-f, Erasmian MSS in this group.
052 (Hoskier's F), Schmid-l, Hoskier-Erasmian.
*1(1), HF-Me. Schmid-a, Hoskier-Erasmian.
35 (17), Schmid-c, Erasmian MSS in this group.
82(2), HF-Ma, Schmid lists with, but does not place in one of the Andrean groups.
    He indicates that the text belongs to 046. Hoskier does not give its group.
88(99), Schmid-i , Erasmian MSS in this group, Hoskier-Egyptian.
94(18), Schmid lists with, but does not place in one of the Andrean groups.
    Hoskier-an independent MS.
*181(12), HF-Me, Schmid-b , Hoskier-eclectic, but a brother of the Erasmian group.
205(88), Schmid-g, Hoskier-Erasmian , missing.
205 Abschr (101), a copy of the above.
209(46), Schmid-d, Hoskier-Erasmian.
254(251), Schmid-c, Erasmian MSS in this group.
*598(204), HF-Me, Schmid-h, Hoskier-Erasmian.
632(22), HF-Ma, Schmid-g, Erasmian MSS in this group. Hoskier- somewhat
    independent, "yet gives a very good account of the best traditional text."
743(123), Schmid-d, Hoskier says "743 and 2067 further emphasize the great age of the
    Erasmian group."
*1384(191), HF-Md, Schmid-i, Hoskier -Egyptian.
1678(240), Schmid-l, Erasmian MSS in this group.

1685(198), Schmid-i, Egyptian MSS in this group, missing.
*1732(220), HF-Md, Schmid-i, Hoskier-Egyptian.
1773 (-), Schmid does not group.
1778 (203), Schmid-l, Erasmian MSS in this group.
*1876(135), HF-Md, ·Schmid-i, Hoskier-Egyptian.
2004(142), HF-Ma, Schmid does not group. Hoskier does not list among the groups.
*2014(21), HF-Md, Schmid-i, Hoskier-Egyptian.
*2015(28), HF-Md. Schmid-i, Hoskier Egyptian.
2019(36), Schmid does not group, Hoskier calls it "a grand church standard".
2020(38), Schmid-l, Erasmian MSS in this group.
2023(49), Schmid-f, Erasmian MSS in this group.
*2026(59), HF-Me, Schmid-e , Hoskier-Erasmian.
*2028(62), HF-Me, Schmid-c, Hoskier-Erasmian.
*2029(63), HF-Me, Schmid-c, Hoskier-Erasmian.
*2031(67), HF-Me, Schmid-f, Hoskier-Erasmian.
*2033(72), HF-Me, Schmid-c, Hoskier-Erasmian.
*2034(73), HF-Md, Schmid-i, Hoskier-Egyptian.
*2036(79), HF-Md, Schmid-i, Hoskier-Egyptian.
2036 Abschr(79a), copy of above, Hoskier did not collate.
*2037(80), HF-Md, Schmid-m, Hoskier-Egyptian.
*2038(81). HF-Me, Schmid-h , Hoskier-Erasmian.
2040(95), Schmid lists with, but does not place in one of the Andrean groups, Hoskier
    places in a sub-group of Coptic family (Mb).
2042(100), Schmid-i, Hoskier-Egyptian.
*2043(103), HF-Md, Schmid-i, Hoskier Egyptian.
*2044(136), HF-Me, Schmid-c, Hoskier-Erasmian.
2045(137), Schmid-g, Hoskier-Erasmian.
*2046(138), HF-Md, Schmid-m, Hoskier-Egyptian.
*2047(139), HF-Md, Schmid-i, Hoskier-Egyptian.
2051 (144), Schmid-d, Hoskier-Erasmian.
*2052(145), HF-Me, Schmid-c, Hoskier does not list among the groups.
*2054(147), HF-Me, Schmid-c , Hoskier-Erasmian.
2055(148), Schmid-d, Hoskier-Erasmian.
*2056(120), HF-Me, Schmid-f , Hoskier-Erasmian.
*2057(121), HF-Me, Schmid-e, Hoskier-Erasmian.
2058(122), HF-Ma, Schmid lists with, but does not place in one of the Andrean groups.
*2059(152), HF-Me, Schmid-b , Hoskier-Erasmian.
*2060(114), HF-Me, Schmid-h, Hoskier - some divergence toward the Complutensian.
2063(116), Schmid-f, Erasmian MSS in this group. Hoskier neglects.
2064(158), Schmid-d, Hoskier-Erasmian.
*2065(159), HF-Me, Schmid-n , Hoskier-Erasmian.
2066(118), Schmid-i, Egyptian MSS in this group, Hoskier did not collate.
2067(119), Schmid-d, Hoskier-Erasmian (see 743).
*2068(162), HF-Me, Schmid-c , Hoskier-Erasmian.
*2069(163), HF-Me, Schmid-c , Hoskier-Erasmian.

2071(167), Schmid-g, Erasmian MSS in this group. Hoskier does not list among the groups, mentions it as being "our latest cursive."

2073(169), Schmid-f , Erasmian MSS in this group.

*2074(174), HF-Md, Schmid-i, Hoskier-Egyptian.

2080(170), Schmid-l, Erasmian MSS in this group.

*2081(179), HF-Me, Schmid-b , Hoskier-Erasmian.

*2082(112), HF-Md, Schmid-i, Hoskier-Egyptian.

*2083(184), HF-Me, Schmid-c , Hoskier-Erasmian.

2091(189), Schmid-e , Hoskier-Erasmian.

*2086 (208), HF-Me, Schmid-c. Hoskier-Erasmian.

2254(216), Schmid-f , Erasmian MSS in this group.

2259(213), Schmid-b , Erasmian MSS in this group. Hoskier did not collate.

*2286(241), HF-Me, Schmid-h, Hoskier indicates Syriac tendencies.

*2302(193), HF-Me, Schmid-h , Hoskier indicates Syriac tendencies.

2361(-), Schmid-c, Erasmian MSS In this group.

2428(-), Schmid-a, Erasmian MSS In this group.

2429(-), Schmid-n, 2065 from this group is Erasmian.

2432(-), Schmid-n, 2065 from this group is Erasmian.

2433(-), Schmid-l, Erasmian MSS in this group.

2435(-), Schmid-d, Erasmian MSS in this group.

Fragment Bodl. Baroc. gr. 212, Schmid-f, Erasmian MSS in this group.

Fragment Paris B.N. gr. 475. Schmid lists with, but does not place in one of the Andrean groups.

A survey of these 83 MSS· demonstrates that the great majority as regards their text clearly belong to the Andrean group. The question must then be asked, Why did not Hodges and Farstad allow their witness to be fully counted? Schmid seems to give the answer:

> For the reconstruction of the Andreas-Text...only 39 MSS remain as valuable (II, p. 26).

In his work, Schmid has printed out in full the entire Andrean text of the Book of Revelation. He felt that a selection of 39 of its MSS was sufficient to determine the text. It is, therefore, hardly fair for the *HF* editors to list the <u>full</u> evidence for the 046 text and then merely present Schmid's <u>selection of 39 MSS</u> for the Andrean. Especially when on the next page, after listing and dividing the 046 MSS into 19 groups, Schmid speaks of over 30 which "can be ignored." Why did not the editors also deduct these from their Ma list?

HOW COHESIVE ARE THE 046 MANUSCRIPTS?

One example of why this question should be raised is that a sizable number of the 74 MSS which Hodges and Farstad list under Ma were classified by Hoskier as being Erasmian and Egyptian.

Hoskier says that six are Erasmian.

385 (29)	808(149)
429(30)	893 (186)
522 (98)	2349 (129)

And fully seventeen are placed by Hoskier in his Egyptian group. Remember, this group is not Alexandrian but is supportive the Andrean MSS.

93(19)	935(153)
149(25)	1597(207)
201(94)	1728(211)
203(107)	1734 (222)
366(84)	1849(128)
386 (70)	1948(78)
452 (42)	2021(41)
467(53)	2025 (58)
506(26)	

Nearly one-third of the MSS in the *HF* "majority" group would normally be expected to be classified with Andreas. Notice that none of these 23 MSS contain the Andrean commentary and are not listed among the 83 MSS given above. It may be expected therefore that a number of additional MSS not containing the commentary, are in fact Andrean as concerning their text.

It is fair to say, that whatever their other conclusions might be, the researches of Schmid and Hoskier demonstrate the superiority of the Andreas text over the 046. Schmid certainly gives tacit acknowledgement of the important nature of the Andreas text by laboring to reproduce it in full; something he does not do for 046 or the other smaller groups. Hoskier's comments given above leave us in no doubt as to where his preferences lie.

In the light of the evidence, Hodges' and Farstad's (and also *RP*) use of the 046 MSS to alter the text of Revelation from the Textus Receptus in over 600 places, was no less an error of judgment than their use of von Soden in altering the rest of the NT!

We could not end this chapter on a better note than by repeating Hoskier's statement given at the beginning:

> I may state that If Erasmus had striven to found a text on the largest number of existing
> MSS in the world of one type, he could not have succeeded better...

Here then is a powerful example of God's guiding providence in preserving the text of Revelation.

O praise the LORD, all ye nations: praise him, all ye people. For his merciful kindness is great toward us: and the truth of the LORD endureth for ever. Praise ye the LORD.

(Psalms 117:1-2)

CHAPTER 5

SUPPORT FOR "MINORITY" PASSAGES IN THE AUTHORIZED VERSION

THE MANUSCRIPT DIGEST

We have demonstrated the basic fallacies of Hodges and Farstad (and similar for *RP*) in using von Soden's material to introduce 1200 changes into the text of Matthew to Jude, and using the 046 MSS to alter the text of Revelation in 600 places. These two factors account for nearly all of the differences between their Text and that which underlies the KJV. Yet, after taking this into account, there does appear to be a number of readings in the King James Version which on the basis of <u>current information</u> seem to have a minority of MS support. In the following pages, we will show that there is in fact substantial support for these passages.

SEVERAL PRINCIPLES TO KEEP IN MIND

1. In the previous pages we have shown that the defense of the King James Bible has been the very last thing on the mind of Textual Criticism. Almost all energy has been directed toward "reconstructing" the text on the basis of a few old uncials, and ferreting out what little support can be gathered for these MSS. The evidence gathered here in behalf of the passages in question is perhaps as extensive as any now available. Yet, in comparison to what could be gathered by a first-hand search of <u>all the MSS</u> currently extant, it is likely to be only a fraction of the true picture.

2. Our extant MSS reflect but do not determine the Text of Scripture. The Text was determined by God in the beginning (Psa. 119:89 Jude 3). After the advent of printing (AD 1450), the necessity of God preserving the MS witness to the Text was diminished. Therefore, in some instances the majority of MSS extant today may not reflect at every point what the true, commonly accepted, and majority reading was 500 years ago.

3. The MSS Hoskier gathered on Revelation should be viewed in this light. Though he collated a majority of the available MSS, yet his 200 plus can only be considered a small fraction of the total MS tradition of the book. They cannot be used to reconstruct the Text. Also, if we went strictly by the majority of extant Greek MSS we would not be able to include the Book of Revelation at all, for only one in fifty MSS contain it. There was a bias in the Greek speaking East against the book, and it was not used in the lectionary services.

4. This leads to another point which is often overlooked. Certainly in Revelation, and to a lesser extent in the rest of the New Testament, we must occasionally look to the Latin West for corroboration on a disputed Greek reading. The Latin Christians who opposed Rome had a far more vital faith than that which usually characterized the Greek East. We look to

them for our spiritual heritage, and they were an important channel through which God preserved His Word.

5. Christ promised that the Holy Spirit. would guide believers of each generation "into all truth" (John 16:13). With regard to the Text of Scripture, "all truth" was found in one primary source with some corroboration from another. The primary source during the manuscript period was the Greek speaking East with occasional refinement and verification from the Latin and Syriac areas.

6. When a version has been *The Standard* as long as the Authorized Version, and when that version has demonstrated its power in the conversion of sinners, building up of believers, sending forth of preachers and missionaries on a scale not achieved by all other versions and foreign language editions combined; the hand of God is at work. Such a version and its underlying Text must not be tampered with. And in those comparatively few places where it <u>seems</u> to depart from the majority reading, it would be far more honoring toward God's promises of preservation to believe that it is the so called "majority" that has strayed rather than the Words underlying the Authorized Version.

7. It is therefore a reasonable position based on the Bible's many statements of preservation to say that that our Standard Bible of 400 years <u>identifies perfectly</u> in its underlying Text the true, inspired, preserved and *once delivered* (Jude 3) Hebrew, Greek and Aramaic Words of Scripture. Therefore our position is in complete contrast to that of *HF* which says: "The editors do not imagine that the text of this edition represents in all particulars the exact form of the originals...It should therefore be kept in mind that the present work...is both preliminary and provisional (*HF* Introduction, p. x). Likewise it contrasts with *RP*: "The divinely preserved autograph text exists and functions within the framework of *all* existing Greek source documents...(*RP* Preface, p. xxii emphasis theirs).   In effect *RP* means that the True Text is "out there" but it has not yet been fully identified.

A SUMMARY OF THE *HF* DEPARTURES FROM THE TEXT OF THE AUTHORIZED VERSION

The apparatus of *HF* allows for a count to be made of the differences between their Text and the Scrivener Text which purports to underlie the AV. The *RP* editors do not provide an apparatus and a direct count of their differences with the AV was not made. However, what we have seen from their procedures lets us know that their differences are about the same as those in *HF*. In short, of the nearly 1800 differences in the *HF* Text, 559 directly affect the KJV translation.

Deviations from the KJV Text (i.e. the Scrivener Text). This does not include many of the proper names; and on one occasion two divergent readings were combined:	1794
Among these 1794 there are a number of readings which deviate from the edition of the TR which *HF* used, but in fact unite with the KJV Text. See Appendix 1:	-56

Changes in the *HF* Text which <u>do not affect</u> the AV English wording:	-1179
Total HF changes which <u>do affect</u> the AV English wording:	559
KJV readings (among the 559) which according to the *HF* apparatus either approach, equal or exceed the HF reading in the preliminary manuscript evidence. See Appendix 3:	-184
Translatable KJV readings which according to initial evidence appear deficient in manuscript support:	375
"Minority" readings in Matthew to Jude based on the collations of von Soden:	221
"Minority" readings in Revelation based on the collations of Hoskier:	154

FORMAT OF THE MANUSCRIPT DIGEST

Listed below are what modern criticism would call the 375 "most vulnerable" readings in the KJV New Testament. These are the passages with the "least" manuscript support. They would average out to less than two per page. At first sight this seems to pose a problem for the Bible believer. But keep in mind that it is nowhere nearly so great a problem as NIV and NASV adherents whose Text is based on only a small fraction of the MSS. For our case the known support for so-called "deficient" AV readings is usually quite substantial.

Evidence in the Manuscript Digest is listed only for the KJV reading. It is to be assumed that the commonly cited manuscripts in modern editions will generally support either the *HF*, *RP* or CR (Critical Text, Nestle-Aland) reading.

ORDER IN WHICH EVIDENCE IS PRESENTED

First the Authorized Version reading (AV) is given, followed by the HF, RP andCR reading. This second reading is given in the KJV vernacular, so that the difference can be easily seen. The Greek text of the AV reading is assumed to be Scrivener's *The Greek Text Underlying the English Authorized Version of 1611*. See Appendix 1.

1. The first line of evidence for the AV reading, gives the four great pre-KJV English versions (Tyndale-1525, Great-1539, Geneva-1560, Bishops-1568). This is followed by three standard editions of the Received Text (Stephanus-1550, Beza-1598, Elziever-1624).

2. The second lines of evidence present the Greek witnesses: the Papyri (P66, P75 etc), the Uncials (Aleph B Theta 046...), the Minuscules (1, 209, 1689...). This is often followed by "indications" of von Soden. We say "indications" because the MSS listed are from von Soden's group designations and cannot always be relied upon. The Greek MSS are given their Gregory number. Papyri support is generally not known for these readings and lectionary evidence is given infrequently.

3. The third lines give the versional evidence: Old Latin (a g2 m etc.), Vulgate (Clementine, gat...), Syriac (Peshitta, Harclean...), Coptic (Sahadic, Bohairc), Gothic, Armenian, Georgian, Ethiopic, Arabian, Persian. Individual MSS are cited for the Old Latin. Editions are cited for the Syriac and Coptic. Both MSS and editions are cited for the Vulgate. In the

case of the secondary versions, i.e., the Ethiopic, it is usually to be assumed that an edition is being referred to. When a primary version is listed alone it indicates that a consensus of its MSS and editions support the reading.

4. The fourth lines give evidence of the Church Fathers. These entries generally includes the city or area associated with their ministry and the probable date of death. Unless the word "Latin" is given, it is to be assumed that the Father's Scripture quotation was in Greek.

SYMBOLS AND ABBREVIATIONS

AV, KJV	The Authorized Version
HF, RP	The Hodges-Farstad, Robinson-Pierpont Editions
CR	The Critical Text, i.e., Nestle-Aland, United Bible Societies Editions, which have an identical text
Asterisk *	The original wording of a MS which had been subsequently altered
cor, 2nd cor	Scribal alterations to the manuscript's original reading
( )	The manuscript supports the reading but with minor variation. Parentheses around von Soden's citations indicates that there may be a higher than usual degree of uncertainty in the citation.
[CR]	The editors of the Critical Editions express doubt over the reading they have chosen
P1, P46, etc.	Papyri MSS, written in uncial (large lettered) script. First to third century
Aleph, A, Theta, 046,etc	Uncial MSS, third to tenth century
1, 399, 1546, etc	Minuscule or cursive (small lettered) manuscripts, tenth to sixteenth century
Family 1	Five MSS which form the basis of the so-called Caesarean Text: 1, 118, 131, 209, 1582
Family 13	Thirteen MSS also associated with the "Caesarean" Text: 13, 69, 124, 174, 230, 346, 543, 788, 826, 828, 983, 1689, 1709
I iota, I pi, etc.	von Soden's manuscript groupings. His "I" (Jerusalem) MSS are basically Byzantine with some divergence
Vulgate: gat fuld, etc	Early vulgate manuscripts

SOURCES USED FOR THE DIGEST

The following were consulted for the entire New Testament. and are given in the approximate order of the amount of material they provided for the digest. See the Bibliography.

1. Von Soden
2. Tischendorfs - 8th Edition
3. Nestle-Aland-26th Edition
4. Alford

5. United Bible Societies-3rd Edition
6. Metzger's Textual Commentary

The following provided evidence for a portion of the New Testament.

1. Alands Synopsis: The four Gospels
2. Legg: Matthew and Mark
3. International Greek New Testament Project: Luke 1-14
4. Hoskier: Revelation
5. Charles: Revelation

For the LORD is good; his mercy is everlasting; and his truth endureth to all generations.

(Psalms 100:5)

THE MANUSCRIPT DIGEST

MATTHEW 3:8
AV   Bring forth therefore fruits meet for repentance
HF RP CR   ...fruit...
Tyndale Great Geneva Bishops Steph Beza Elz.
L U 28 33 267 472 726 828 998 1010 1194 1675 many others.
Old Latin: a g2 m; Syriac: Peshitta Sinaitic Curetonian Palestinian; Armenian.
Tatian, Syria, 172 Teritullian, N. Africa, Latin, 200 Lucifer, Cagliari, Latin, 370
Basil, Cappadocia, 379 Ambrose, Milan, Latin, 397   Chrysostom, Constantinople, 407
Augustine, Hippo, Latin, 430 Cyril, Alexandria, 444 "Speculum", Pseudo-Augustine, Latin, V
"Opus Imperfectum", XI Theophylact, Bulgaria, 1077   Euthymius, Zigabenus, 1116.

MATTHEW 3:11
AV CR he shall baptize you with the Holy Ghost, and *with* fire!
HF RP   omits "and *with* fire"
Tyndale Great Geneva Bishops Steph. Beza Elz.
Aleph BCD (supplied) K L M U W Gamma Delta Theta Pi 399 472 476 485 565 655 660 700
945 998 1093 1094 1355 1365 1604 1606 1675.
von Soden indicates: Most Egyptian mss., I eta (1 22 118 209 1192 1210 1582), I iota (13 69 124
174 230 346 543 788 826 828 1689), I beta (16 348 477 1216 1279 1588), I pi (N Sigma Phi), I
kappa (A 229 248 280 473 482 489 1219 1346 1354), I sigma (157 245 291 713 1012).
Old Latin; Vulgate; Syriac: Peshitta Curetonian Harclean; Coptic: Sahadic Bohairic; Other
Versions.
Justin Martyr, 165   Tatian, Syria, 172   Irenaeus, Lyons, Latin, 178
Origen, Alexandria, Caesarea, 254   Cyprian, Carthage, Latin, 258   Eusebius,
Caesarea, 339   Hilary, Poictiers, Latin, 367   Cyril, Alexandria, 444.

MATTHEW 4:10
AV CR Get thee hence, Satan
HF RP adds "behind me"
Tyndale Great Geneva Bishops Steph. Beza Elz.
Aleph B C D (apparently) K P S V W Delta Theta Sigma 0233   family 1 and 13,
13 22 27 40 124 251 265 273 372 399 472 489 543* 565 700 892*
1079 1219 1223 1355 1546 1582   many others.
von Soden indicates: Most Egyptian mss., I eta (1 118 209 1192 1210), I Iota (13 69 174 230 788
826), I pi (N Phi), I r (262 566 1187 1555 1573).
Old Latin: f k; Vulgate: early mss Clementine; Syriac: Peshitta Harclean Palestinian; Coptic:
an early Sahadic ms Bohairic (pt) Middle Egyptian; Georgian.
Ignatius, Antioch, 110 Tatian, Syria, 172   Irenaeus, Lyons, 178
Tertullian, N.Afrlca, Latin, 220 Origen, Alexandria, Caesarea, 254 Peter,
Alexandria, 311 Juvencus, Latin, 330 Hilary, Poictiers, Latin, 367, Jerome, Latin, 420
        Pseudo-Ignatius, V.

MATTHEW 4:18
AV   And Jesus, walking by the sea
HF RP CR   omit "Jesus"
Tyndale Great Geneva Bishops   Steph. Beza Elz.
E (L) Delta Omega 472 517 many others.
Von Soden does not cite.
Old Latin: a c ff l h m; Vulgate;   Armenian.
"Speculum", Pseudo-Augustine, Latin, V

MATTHEW 5:27
AV   Ye have heard that, it was said by them of old time
HF RP CR   omits "by them of old time"
Tyndale Great Geneva Bishops   Steph. Beza Elz.
L M Delta Theta 0233   family 1 and 13   4 21 33 124 245 251 273 399
440 489 543 600 659 713 892 1010 1012 1093 1229 1293 many other s.
Von Soden indicates: I iota (13 69 174 230 346 788 826 828 983 1689), I beta (16 348 477 1216 1279 1579 1588), I r (262 566 1187).
Old Latin: aur c ff1 g1 g2 h l m r2; Vulgate; Syriac: Curatonian Harclean (with asterisks) Palestinian; Georgian.
Irenaeus, Lyons, Latin, 178   Origen (pt.) Alexandria, Caesarea, 254
Cyprian, Carthage, Latin, 258   Eusebius, Caesarea, 339 Hilary, Poictiers, Latin, 367
Chrysostom, Constantinople" 407.

MATTHEW 5:47
AV CR   And if ye salute your brethren only
HF RP   ...friends...
Tyndale Great Geneva Bishops   Steph. Beza Elz.
Aleph B D Z family 1 and 13   22 372 472 543 660 892 1582 many others.
Von Soden indicates: Most Egyptian mss., I eta (1 22 118 209 1192 1210 1582), I iota (13 69 124 174 230 346 543 788 826 828 983 1689).
Old Latin: except k f (h gap); Vulgate; Syriac: Peshitta Curetonian Palestinian; Coptic: Sahadic Bohairic; Ethiopic; Arabic; Persian.
Tatian, Syria, 172   Cyprian, Carthage, Latin, 258.

MATTHEW 6:18
AV   thy Father, which seeth in secret, shall reward thee openly
HF RP CR   omits "shall reward thee openly"
Tyndale Great Geneva Bishops   Steph. Beza Elz.
E Delta 16 21 27 28 71 118 124 157 209 346 372 440 472 485 543 655 788 1009 1012 1071 1093 1195 1246 1230 1241 1253 1546 1579 2174 many others.
Von Soden indicates: I beta (348 477 1279).
Lectionaries: 547 950 1663.
Old Latin: a b c g1 h k; Syriac: an early Palestianian ms; Armenian; Georgian; Ethiopic.
Ephraem, Syria, 373.

MATTHEW 7:14
AV   Because strait is the gate
HF RP CR (what? who? how?) strait is the gate
Tyndale Great Geneva Bishops   Steph. Beza Elz.
Aleph* B N-c X-c l-c 118-c 157 372 477* 700c 1010 1071 1365 1546 (apparently) others.
Von Soden indicates: I eta (1 22 118 209 1192 1210 1582).
Lectionaries: 10 32 76 1043 1627 1642.
Old Latin: m; Vulgate including an early ms; Coptic: Sahadic Bohairlc; Armenian; Georgian.
Origen, Alexandria, Caesarea, 254 Gregory Nazianzen, Constantinople, 389
Gaudentius, Brescia, Latin, 406 Theodore, Mopsuestia, 428
"Speculum" Pseudo- Augustine, Latin, V.
The interrogative of HF RP CR is barely translatable. Alford says it was a clerical error.

MATTHEW 8:5
AV   And when Jesus was entered into Capernaum
HF RP CR   ...he...
Tyndale Great Geneva Bishops   Staph. Beza Elz.
C* 2nd.cor. L 71 1170 1374 many others according to Tischendorf.
Old Latin: (c); Vulgate including 2 early mss. Syriac: Peshitta Harclean.
Tatian, Syria, 172.

MATTHEW 8:25
AV   And his disciples came to *him*
HF RP   ...the disciples...
CR   ...they...
Tyndale Great Geneva Bi shops Steph. Beza Elz.
C* W X Theta Sigma Phi   family 1   213 472 517 544 566 945 990 1012 1195 1424 1582 1604
1646 many others.
Von Soden indicates: I eta (1 22 118 209 1192 1210 1582), I phi (7 267 349 659 954 1391 1402
1606 1675 2191), I pi (N 080), I r (262 1187 1555 1573).
Lectionary majority.
Old Latin: b gl (q); Vulgate: Clementine; Syriac: Peshitta Sinaitic
Harclean Palestinian; Coptic: Middle-Egyptian; Gothic Georgian Ethiopic.
Tatian, Syria, 172.

MATTHEW 9:36
AV   because they fainted
HF RP CR   ...they were distressed
(Tyndale Great Geneva Bhishops , probably support the KJV)   Steph. Beza Elz.
L V 7 349 517 659 954 1194 1424 many others.
Von Soden indicates: I phi (7 267 349 517 659 954 1188 1391 1402 1424 1675 2191).
Old Latin: d; Syriac: (Peshitta) (Sinaitic); Georgian.

MATTHEW 10:8
AV   cleanse the lepers, raise the dead

HF RP   cleanse the lepers
CR   raise the dead, cleanse the lepers
Tyndale Great Geneva Bishops   Steph. Beza Elz.
16 348 372 1093 1579 others.
Syriac: Pashitta.
Cyril, Alexandria, 444.
Though in a different sequence (as CR), "raise the dead" is found in many of the mss, including:
Aleph* B C* D N family 1 and 13 33 565 892 1010.
Old Latin Vulgate Syriac-Sinaitic Coptic-Sohairic Ethiopic, etc

MATTHEW 12:8
AV   For the Son of man is Lord even of the sabbath day
HF RP CR   omits "even"
Tyndale Great (Geneva)   Steph. Beza Elz.
1 33 157 348 372 476 565 659 713 726 1093 1391 1396 many others.
Von Soden indicates: I eta (1582), I iota (69 124 174 788), I phi (349 517 954 1188 1424 1675).
Old Latin: f; Vulgate: including an early ms. Syriac: Harclean.

MATTHEW 12:32
AV CR neither in this world
HF RP neither in this present world
Tyndale Great Geneva Bishops   Stepha Beza Elz.
Aleph B C D N W Sigma Phi 1 21 22 33 157 270 372 399 443 517 713 726 1582 1604 2145 many others.
Von Soden indicates: Most Egyptian mss, I iota (13 69 124 174 230 346 543 788 826 828 983 1689), I phi (M 27 71 160 349 692 945 954 990 1010 1194 1207 1223 1293 1675), I kappa (726 1200 1375).
Tatian, Syria, 172   Origen, Alexandria, Caesarea, 254.
Another well-attested Greek variant reads as the AV.

MATTHEW 12:35
AV   A good man out of the good treasure of the heart
HF RP CR   omits "of the heart"
Tyndale Great Geneva Bishops   Stepha Beza Elz.
L   family 1   33 118 157 209 (372) 399C 517 689 713 1093 1365 1689.
Von Soden indicates: I eta (1582).
Old Latin: (f) ff2 m; Vulgate; Syriac: Sinaitic Curetonian Palestinian
Tatian, Syria, 172 Clement, Alexandria, 215 Odgen, Alexandria, Caaserea, 254
Chrysostom, Constantinople, 407.
Many other witnesses support the inclusion of "heart" but add "his".

MATTHEW 14:19
AV   on the grass, and took the five loaves
HF RP CR   omits "and"
Tyndale Great Geneva Bishops   Stepha Beza Elz.

Aleph C* Ic (X?) 067   245 472 485 1010 1012 1093 1293 1295 others.
Old Latin: ffl h; Coptic; Armenian.
The translation difference here, if any, is very slight.

MATTHEW 18:19
AV   Again I say unto you
HF RP [CR]   Again, verily, I say unto you
Tyndale Great   Stepha Beza Elz.
Aleph D L M N O W Gamma Delta Sigma   1 245 892 1012 1279 1295 1346 1354 1355 1582 1604
2145 many others.
Von Soden indicates: Most Egyptian mss., I eta (1582).
Old Latin: aur d ff2 l r2; Vulgate; Syriac: Peshitta HarcLean Palestinian; Coptic: Bohairic;
Armenian; Georgian.
Tatian, Syria, 172 Origen , Alexandria, Caesarea, 254
A Greek variant with ample support reads with the AV.

MATTHEW 18:29
AV   I will pay thee all
HF RP CR   omits "all"
Tyndale Great Geneva Bishops   Steph. Beza Elz.
Aleph-c C-2nd cor. (K) L W Gamma Theta Pi   family 13   1 16 22 28 33 69 124 157 245 291 443
543 544 565 (660) 1012 1093 1207 1223 1241 1293 1295 1355 1391 1402 1574 1579 1582 1604
(1689) 2145 many others.
Von Soden indicates: I iota (13 174 230 346 788 826 828 983), I phi (349 517 954 1424 1675),
I kappa (A? 229 248 265 270 280 482 489 726 1200 1219 1346 1375).
Old Latin: aur c f ff1 g2 l q; Vulgate; Syriac: Peshitta Harlean-mg Palestinian; Coptic: Sahadic
Bohairic; Ethiopic.
Chrysosotom, Constantinople, 407.

MATTHEW 20:21
AV   the one on thy right hand, and the other on the left
HF RP CR   ...on thy left
Tyndale Great Geneva Bishops   Steph. Beza Elz.
D W Theta   family 1   22 33 118 174 209 489 565 892 1375 1582 many others.
Old Latin: aur b c d e ff1,2 m r1,2; Vulgate; Coptic: Middle Egyptian; Armenian.
Origen, Alexandria, Caesarea, 254.

MATTHEW 20:22
AV   of the cup that I shall drink of, and to be baptized
HF RP   ...or to be baptized
CR   omits "and to be baptized"
Tyndale Great Geneva Bishops   Steph. Beza Elz.
5 71 440 443 473 482 655 659 700 892 1170 1207 1216 1355 1402 1574 1588 others.
Syriac: Peshitta.
Chrysostom, Constantinople, 407.

In contrast to the CR text there is overwhelming support for inclusion of the words concerning baptism. The HF RP is close to the KJV.

MATTHEW 20:26

AV RP   Whosoever will be! great among you, let him be your minister
HF CR   ...shall...
Tyndale Great Geneva Bishops   Steph. Beza Elz.
Aleph - 2nd cor H L M S X 047   4 22 27 28 157 268 273 291 440 482 485 544 565 659 660 700 892 1010 1200 1355 1375 1391 1396 1574 1606 1609 1689 many others.
Von Soden indicates: I Phi (160 945 990 1207 1223 1293), I kappa (A? 265 489 1219 1346), I r (262 566 1187 1555 1573).
Old Latin: aur f ff1 g1,2 l; Vulgate; Coptic: Bohairic Middle Egyptian; Armenian; Georgian; Ethiopic.
Tatian, Syria, 172   Origen , Alexandria, Caesarea, 254
Chrysostom, Constantinople, 407   Jerome, Latin, 420 John, Damascus, 749

MATTHEW 21:14

AV CR   And the blind and the lame came to him
HF RP   ...lame and the blind...
Tyndale Great Geneva Bishops   Steph. Beza Elz.
Aleph B D L W Theta   family 13   1 4 33 69 157 543 700 713 892 954 990 1207 1223 1582 many others.
Von Soden indicates: Most Egyptian mss, I iota (13 124 174 230 :346 788 926 029 993 1689), I phi (160 945 1010 1293).
Old Latin: aur b c d f ff1,2 g1 h l g r2; Vulgate; Syriac: Peshitta (Palestinian); Coptic: Bohairic; Armenian; Georgian; Ethiopic.
Origen, Alexandria, Caesarea, 254.

MATTHEW 22:7

AV   But when the King heard *thereof*, he was wroth
HF RP   And When that King heard
CR   But the King was wroth
Tyndale Great Geneva Bishops   Steph. Beza Elz.
(Theta) (family 13)   34 69 124 543.
Did not use Von Soden.
Old Latin: aur ff1 g2 h (l) r2; Vulgate; Syriac: (Peshitta) Palesrtinian; Coptic: (Bohairic) (Middle Egyptian).
Irenaeus, Lyons, Latin, 178   Eusebius, Caesarea, 339   Lucifer, Cagliari, Latin, 370.
In contrast to CR, there is strong support for inclusion of the word 'heard'
A well attested Greek variant; reads as the KJV (indicated here by the bracketed witnesses).   The HF RP is close to the KJV.

MATTHEW 23:25

AV CR   but within they are full of extortion and excess
HF RP   ...unrighteousness...

Tyndale Great Geneva Bishops   Steph. Beza Elz.
Aleph B D L Delta Theta Pi Phi   family 1 and 13   22 33 69 124 238 270 (473) 517 543 565 892 1010 1293 1354 1402 1424 1574 1682 2145 many others.
Von Soden indicates: Most Egyptian mss, I eta (1 118 209 1192 1210), I iota (13 174 230 346 543 788 926 1675), I phi (349 954 1188 1675), I beta (16 349 477 1216 1279 1579 1588), I kappa (A ? 265 489 1219 1346).
Old Latin: a c (d) ff2 h (other Old Latin readings are close to the AV);
Syriac: Harclean; Armenian.
Basil, Cappadocia, 379.

MATTHEW 23:36
AV CR   Verily I say unto you, All these things shall come
HF RP   ...that all these things...
Tyndale Great Geneva Bishops   Steph. Beza Elz.
Aleph B D L W Theta Sigma Phi   family 1   22 28 124 174 517 700 788 992* 1592 many other:s.
Von Soden indicates: Most Egyptian mss, I eta (1 118 209 1192 12110), I iota (174), I pi (N O).
Old Latin (except f g1) Vulgate Georgian Ethiopic.
Irenaeus, Lyons, Latin, 178   Lucifer, Cagliari, Latin, 370   other Fathers.

MATTHEW 24:17
AV   not down to take any thing out of his house
HF RP CR   ...to take the things...
Tyndale Great Geneva Bishops   Stepha Beza Elz.
D (E*) W Theta   family 1   28 33 245 544 565 700 945 1293 1295 1402 1424 1582 many others.
Von Soden indicates: I eta (1 22 118 209 1192 1210), I phi (349 517 954 1188), I beta (16 340 477 1216 1279 1579 1588).
Old Latin; Vulgate; Syriac: Peshitta Palestinian; Armenia; Georgian; Ethiopic.
Tatian, Syria, 172   Irenaeus, Lyons, Latin, 178 Hippolytus, Portus, 220
Origen , Alexandcia, Caesarea, 254   Cyprian, Carthage, Latin, 258
Epiphanius, Cyprus, 403   Isidore, Pelusium, 435   Caesarius, Aries, Latin, 542.

MATTHEW 25:44
AV   Then shall they also answer him
HF RP CR   ...they themselves...
Tyndale Great Geneva   Steph. Beza Elz.
Aleph* (apparently) 700.
Old Latin: f h m r2; Vulgate: Clementine em gat ing mm.
A Greek variant with ample support reads with the KJV.

MATTHEW 26:38
AV CR   Then saith he unto them
HF RP   ...saith...Jesus
                   Steph. Beza Elz.
P37 (other papyri) Aleph A B C* D I L W Theta Sigma 067   family 1   21 29 33 69 124 270 291 443 659 700 726 892 998 999 1200 1360 1374 1375 1574 1582 2145 many others.

Von Soden indicates: Most Egyptian mss, I eta (1 22 118 209 1192 1210), I iota (174 788 983 1689), I pi (N Phi).
Old Latin: b c ff1,2 g1,2 l q; Vulgate; Syriac: Peshitta Sinaitic Palestinian; Coptic: Sahadic Bohairic; Armenian; Georgian; Ethiopic.
Chrysostom, Constantinople, 407

MATTHEW 26:52
AV CR   for all they that. take the sword shall perish with the sword
HF RP   ...shall die...
Tyndale Great Geneva Bishops   Steph. Beza Elz.
P37 Aleph A B C D E G L W Theta Pi Sigma Phi   family 1   23 33 71 124 157 229 482 495 517 700 892 954 998 999 1010 1012 1295 1424 1582 1675 many others.
Von Soden indicates: Most Egyptian mss, I eta (1 22 118 209 1192 1210), I phi (349 1188), I pi (N), I kappa (248 265 270 280 473 489 726 1200 1219 1346 1354 1375).
Old Latin; Vulgate; Syriac: Sinaitic Palestinian; Coptic: Sahadic Bohairic; Armenian; Georgian.
Origen, Alexandcia, Caesarea, 254   Hilary, Poictiers, Latin, 367
Basil, Cappadocia, 379   Chrysostom, Constantinople, 407.

MATTHEW 26:70
AV CR   But he denied before *them* all
HF RP   ...before them all
"them" is not italicized in the four English versions, but as the evidence of the editions show this may be translational and not textual. Steph. Beza Elz.
Aleph B C-2nd cor D E G L Z Theta Signa 090   family 13 (except 124)   4 33 69 71 157 229 213 348 482 700* 892 990 998 999 1010 1012 1200 1216 1293 1295 1355 1360 1473 many others.
Von Soden indicates: Most Egyptian mss, I iota (13 174 230 346 543 788 826 828 983 1689), I pi (N).
Old Latin; Vulgate; Syriac: Peshitta (apparently) and others; Coptic: Sahadic Bohairic; Other versions.
Origen, Alexandria, Caesarea, Latin, 254.

MATTHEW 27:35
AV   casting lots: that it might be fulfilled which was spoken by the prophet, They parted my garments among them, and upon my vesture did they cast lots
HF RP CR   casting lots (rest of verse omitted)
Tyndale Great Geneva   Steph. Beza Elz.
Delta Theta Phi   family 1 and 13   4 22 262 273 348 349 517 566 954 1187 1279 1379 1424 1555 1573 1579 1675 others.
Von Soden indicates: I iota (13 69 124 174 230 346 788 826 903 1689).
Old Latin: a aur b c d g2 h q r1 r2; Vulgate: Clementine.
Eusebius, Caesarea, 339   Pseudo-Athanasius, VI.

MATTHEW 27:41
AV CR   with the scribes and elders
HF RP   adds "and Pharisees"

Tyndale Great Bishops   Steph Beza Elz.
(Aleph) A B L Theta   family 1 and 13 (except 346)   33 69 124 238 543 700 713 892 1295 1582 1604 many others.
Von Soden indicates: Most Egyptian mss, I eta (1 22 118 209 1192 1210), I iota (13 174 230 788 826 828).
Old Latin: including aur c ff1 g1,2 1; Vulgate Coptic: early Sahadic mss Bohairic Middle Egyptian; Armenian; Georgian; Ethiopic.
Eusebius, Caesarea, 339 Augustine, Hippo, Latin, 430.

MATTHEW 28:19
AV CR Go ye therefore, and teach all nations
HF RP omits "therefore"
Tyndale Great Geneva Bishops   Steph. Beza Elz.
B W Delta Theta Pi Sigma Phi 074   family 1, 13 (by itself)   28 33 174 265 280 346 348 565 892 1010 1012 1187 1219 1241 1293 1346 1355 1582 1604 2145 many others.
Von Soden indicates: Most Egyptian mss, I eta (1 22 118 209 1192 1210), I pi (N).
Old Latin c e f ff1,2 g1 l q; Vulgate; Syriac: Peshitta Harclean Palestinian; Coptic: Sahadic Bohairic-pt Middle Egyptian; Armenian; Ethiopic.
Cyprian, Carthage, Latin, 258   Hilary, Poictiers, Latin, 367   Zeno, Verona, Latin, 372.

MARK 1:16
AV   he saw Simon and Andrew his brother
HF RP he saw Simon and Andrew, his brother to Simon (difficult to translate)
CR   he saw Simon and Andrew, the brother of Simon.
Tyndale Great Geneva   Bishops Steph. Beza Elz.
D G W Gamma Theta   28 33 245 372 495 579 713 1355 1360 1424 1555 1606 many others.
Von Soden indicates: I beta (16 348 477 1216 1279 1579 1588).
Old Latin: (except a r1); Vulgate; Syriac: Peshitta Sinaitic; Coptic: Bohairic-pt. Ethiopic.
Tatian, Syria, 172.

MARK 2:9
AV   *Thy* sins be forgiven thee
HF RP CR Thy sins are forgiven
Tyndale Great Geneva   Bishops Steph. Beza Elz.
A C D S Gamma Delta Theta Phi 090 0130   22 131 265 330 372 485 726 945 998 1047 1071 1093 1194·1223 1375 1396 1555 1606 2145 others.
Von Soden indicates: I iota (983 1689), I beta (16 348 1279 1579).
Old Latin: including c e l r1 d; Vulgate; Syriac: Palestinian.
Tatian, Syria, 172   Eusebius, Caeaacea, 339.
There may not be a translational issue in this passage. The variation in the text may fall under the category of "orthography".

MARK 3:32
AV   thy mother and thy brethren
HF RP [CR]   adds "and thy sisters"

Tyndale Great Geneva   Steph. Beza Elz.
Aleph B C G K L W Delta Theta Pi 124), Sigma Phi   family 1 and 13 (except 124)   372 472 485 495 543 565 827 892 1009 1012 1047 1071 1079 1082 1195 1241 1360 1365 1375 1402 1424 1515 1546 1555 1573 1588 1082 1195* 1241 1604 2148 2174 many others.
Von Soden indicates: Most Egyptian mss., I eta (1 22 118 209 872 1192 1210 1582 2193), I iota (13 69 230 346 788 826 983 1689), I phi (349 517 1675), I omega (213 443 1574 2145), I pi (N), I kappa (265 489 1219 1346).
Lectionary majority.
Old Latin: aur e l r1; Vulgate, including early mss; Syriac: Peshitta Sinaitic Harclean;
Coptic: Sahadic Bohairic; Armenian; Georgian; Ethiopic.
Tatian, Syria, 172 Hegemonius (?), 350   Faustus, Milevis, Latin, IV/V.
"It is extremely unlikely that Jesus' sisters would have joined in publicly seeking to check him in his ministry" (Metzger, Textual Commentary).

MARK 4:4
AV   and the fowls of the air came and devoured it up
HF RP CR   omits "of the air"
Tyndale Great Geneva   Bishops Steph. Beza Elz.
D G M   89 115 179 248 249 256 273 472 477 486 495 569 713 892 1375 others.
Lectionaries 50 51 others.
Old Latin: including a ff1 g2 i q r1;
Vulgate: Clementine gat.

MARK 4:9
AV   And he said unto them, He that hath ears
HF RP CR   omits "unto them"
Tyndale Great Geneva Bishops   Steph. Beza Elz.
M - 2nd cor mg S? W   7 118 238 239 242 243 249 252 267 372 477 486 487 489 659 713 others.
Lectionary 251.
Coptic: Sahadic an early Bohairic ms.

MARK 6:2
AV   which is given unto him, that even such
HF RP CR   ...him, and such
Geneva   Steph. Beza Elz.
372 470 474 485 486 954 1038 1396 many others.
Syriac: Palestinian.
A well attested Greek variant reads with the AV.

MARK 6:15
AV   That it is a prophet, or as one of the prophets
HF RP CR   omits "or"
Tyndale Geneva Bishops   Steph. Beza Elz.
Delta Phi   1 28 251 2145 others.

Von Soden indicates: I eta (lB 209 1192 1210).
Syriac: Harclean Palestinian; Armenian.
The context and the last clause of the verse requires the connective "or".

MARK 6:33
AV   And the people saw them departing
HF RP CR   omits "the people"
Tyndale Great Geneva Bishops   Steph. Beza Elz.
W   family 13   69 124 others.
Von Soden indicates: I iota (13 69 230 346 543 768 826 993 1689).
Syriac: (Peshitta); Coptic: Sahadic.
Tatian, Syria, 172.
The clause and those which follow require the inclusion of "the people". There can be no seeing without people, (see the NASV). The parallel passages in Matthew and Luke have the words.

MARK 6:44
AV   And they that did eat of the loaves were about
HF RP [CR]   omits "were about"
Tyndale Great Geneva Bishops   Steph. Beza Elz.
(Aleph) (Theta)   family 1   4 28 274 372 (565) (700) 892 others.
Von Soden indicates: I eta (1 118 209 1192 1210 1582 2193).
Armenian.
A well attested Greek variant (a few of the witnesses noted here by brackets) reads as the KJV.

MARK 9:7
AV   and a voice came out of the cloud, saying
HF RP CR   omits "saying"
Tyndale Great Geneva Bishops   Steph. Beza Elz.
A D L W (Delta) Theta Phi Psi   family 1 and 13   7 28 33 69 71 115 124 157 179 245 267 372 482 543 565 692 700 713 1071 1093 1223 1241 1396 1573 1606 1675 many others.
Von Soden indicates: I eta (1 118 209 1192 1210 1582 2193), I iota (13 124 230 346 788 826 983 1689), I phi (M 27 1194), I beta (16 348 477 1216 1279 1579 1588).
Old Latin (except k); Vulgate; Syriac: Peshitta Harclean-with asterisks; Coptic: Sahadic; Ethiopic; Armenian.
Tatian, Syria, 172   Origen, Alexandria, Caesarea, 254.

MARK 10:28
AV   Then Peter began to say unto him
HF RP CR omits "Then"
Tyndale Great Geneva Bishops   Staph. Beza Elz.
D   118 209 245 248 251 372 472 544 1030 1093 1278 1515 1542 1573 1604 1654 2145 many others.
Von Soden indicates: I phi (7 115 179 267 659 827 1082 1391 1402 1606 2191).
Old Latin (except f r2)   Vulgate Syriac: Peshitta Harclean; Ethiopic.
A well attested Greek variant reads with the KJV, as does a second variant.

MARK 11:32
AV   But if we shall say, Of men
HF RP CR But shall we say, Of men?
Tyndale Great Geneva Bishops   Steph. Beza Elz.
D W O   family 13   28 69 118 209 372 472 473 543 (565) 700 1047 1207 1515 1542 1654 2145 many others.
Von Soden indicates: I iota (13 124 230 346 788 826 983 1689).
Old Latin (except k); Vulgate; Syriac: Peshltta (according to Alford) Sinaitic Harclean; Armenian; Georgian; Ethiopic.
Tatian, Syria, 172.
Three additional Greek variants would read as the KJV.

MARK 12:23
AV   In the resurrection therefore
HF RP CR   omits "therefore"
Tyndale Great Geneva Bishops   Steph Beza Elz.
A C D G K M W Z Theta Pi Sigma   28 33 124 242 495 543 565 579 892 1009 1047 1071 1079 1216 1230 1360 1241 1542 1546 1646 2174 many others.
Von Soden indicates: I eta (1 22 118 209 872 1192 1210 1582 2193).
Lectionary majority.
Old Latin; Vulgate; Syriac: Peshitta Curetonian Harclean; (Armenian); Ethiopic.
Tatian, Syria, 172.
A well attested Greek variant reads with the AV; Some of von Soden's citations may overlap into this variant.

MARK 12:32
AV   for there is one God; and there is none other but he
HF RP CR   for he is one; and...
Tyndale Great Geneva Bishops   Steph. Beza Elz.
D E F G H (W) Theta 092 family 13, 1 4 28 61 71 245 267 273 300 472 495 543 700 945 954 1071 1093 1194 1223 many others.
Von Soden indicates: (the evidence includes witnesses which have an article before "God"), I alpha (067 79 279 372 406 565 1542 1654), I iota (13 69 124 230 346 788 826 983 1689), I beta (16 348 477 1216 1279 1579 1588) •
Old Latin (except l r2; Vulgate, including Clementine; Syriac: Sinaitic: Curetonian Palestinian; Coptic: Sahadic Bohairlc; Armenian; Georgian.
Eusebius, Caesarea, 339 Marcellus , cited by Eusebius   Hilary, Poictiers, Latin, 367.

MARK 13:32
AV   But of that day and *that* hour
HF RP CR   ...day or hour
Tyndale Great Geneva Bishops   Stepha Beza Elz.
Aleph D F S* W Theta   family 1 and 13   7 26 29 69 115 124 157 237 245 251 267 349 472 477 495 543 565 700 1047 1082 1229 1279 1574 1588 many others.
Von Soden indicates: I alpha (79 279 406 544 1542 1654), I eta (1 118 209 1192 1210 1582 2193),

I iota (13 230 346, 788 826 983 1689).
Old Latin: a aur g2 i k g r1,2; Vulgate;   Syriac:Peshitta, Sinaitic; Coptic: Sahadic Bohairic-pt.
Armenian; Georgian; Ethiopic.
Tatian, Syria, 172   Irenaeus, Lyons, Latin, 178 Hilary Poictiers, Latin, 367
Basil, Cappodocla, 379   Epiphanius, Cyprus, 403 Augustine, Hippo, Latin, 430.

MARK 14:30
AV   Verily I say unto thee, That this day
HF RP CR   ...That, thou, this day
Tyndale Great Geneva Bishops   Stepha Beza Elz.
Aleph C D Delta Phi   family 13   7 22 115 245 330 472 495 544 659 827 992 954 1355 1391 1515
1675 1689* others.
Von Soden indicates: I beta (16 349 477 1216 1279 1579 1588).
Old Latin (except c k); Coptic: Sahadic;   Georgian.
Tatian, Syria, 172.

MARK 14:45
AV CR   he goeth straightway to him, and saith
HF RP   ...and saith to him
Geneva   Steph. Beza Elz
Aleph A B C K L M U W X Delta Pi* Psi   family 1 and 13 (except 124)   7 115 179 251 713 892
1039 1071 1093 1542 1573 1606 many others.
Von Soden indicates: Most Egyptian mss, I eta (1 118 209 1192 1210 1502 2193), I iota (13 69
230 346 543 788 826 983 1689), I phi (517 1424 1675), I omega (443 1574 2145), I kappa (229
265 280 482 489 121913461354).
Old Latin: f1;   Vulgate; Syriac: Harclean; Coptic: Sahadic Bohairic; Georgian; Ethioplc.

MARK 15:18
AV RP CR   Hail, King of the Jews
HF   Hail, the King of the Jews
Tyndale Great Geneva Bishops   Steph. Beza Elz.
Aleph B D M P S V X Theta Lambda Psi 047 0250   family 1   22 28 213 230 251 262 291 349
565 661 700 1012 1207 1542 1606 many others.
Von Soden indicates: I eta (1 118 209 872 1192.1210 1582 2193).

MARK 16:8
AV   And they went out quickly, and fled from the sepulchre
HF RP CR   Omits "quickly"
Tyndale Great Geneva Bishops   Steph. Beza Elz.
E   238 239 440 475-2nd cor   477 486 488 489 1071 others.

LUKE 3:19
AV   Herodias his brother Philip's wife
HF CR   omits "Philip' s"
Tyndale Great Geneva Bishops   Steph. Beza Elz.

A C K W X Pi Psi 22 33 213 291 544 565 579 713 945 1012 1071 1207 1223 1424 1604 2145 others.
Von Soden indicates: I eta (1 1582 2193), I phi (349 517 954 1424 1675), I kappa (229 248 265 270 280 473 482 489 726 1200 1219 1346).
About 48 of the IGNTP cursives (see Introduction to Digest).
Syriac: Peshitta Harclean; Coptic: early Sahadic mss Bohairic; Ethiopic.
Tatian, Syria, 172.

LUKE 3:33
AV RP   Aminadab...Aram...Esrom
HF   Aminadab...Joram...Esrom
CR   Aminadab...Adim...Ram (or Arni)...Hezron
Tyndale (Great) Geneva (Bishops) Steph. Beza (Elz).
A D E G H U Pi 33 565 (1071) 1079 1230 1253 (1424) many others.
Did not use Von Soden or IGNTP.
Lectionary 184.
Old Latin: a aur c d f ff2 (g1) l q r1; Vulgate; Syriac: Peshitta; Gothic; Georgian.

LUKE 4:8
AV RP   for it is written
HF CR omits "for"
Tyndale Great Geneva Bishops   Steph. Beza Elz.
U Delta Lambda 0116   7 69 262 267 372 472 476 659 713 1012 1093 1194 1396 1555 1604 1654 many others.
Von Soden indicates: I iota (13 69 124 230 346 543 826 983 1689), I phi (349 517 954 1424 1675), I beta (16 477 1216 1279 1579 1588).
I omega (213 1071 1574).
About 47 of the IGNTP cursives.
Old Latin: b q; Coptic: Sahadic.
Tatian, Syria, 172.

LUKE 5:36
AV   the piece that was *taken* out of the new agreeth not
HF RP omits "the piece"
CR   puts "agreeth not" in the future tense
(Tyndale) (Great) Geneva Bishops Steph. Beza Elz.

1. Inclusion of "piece"
Aleph B C (D) L W X Lambda 1 7 33 69 157 213 251 267 659 660 1012 1039 1071 1229 1360 1606 2145 many others.
Von Soden indicates: Most Egyptian mss, I eta (1 22 1192 1210 1592 2193), I iota (13 69 124 230 346 543 789 826 983 1689), I phi (349 1188 1424 1675), I beta (16 349 477 1216 1279 1579 1581), I r (262 1197 1555 1573).
About 60 of the IGNTP cursives.
Old Latin; Vulgate; Syriac: Peshitta, Harclean; Coptic; Armenian.

2. "agreeth not" in the present tense
E F H K M (R) S U V Gamma Delta Lambda Pi many others.
Von Soden indicates the great mass of Byzantine cursives.
About 115 of the IGNTP cursives.
Old Latin; Vulgate; Syriac: Peshitta Harclean; Coptic; Gothic; Armenian; Ethiopic.

LUKE 6:7
AV CR   And the scribes and Pharisees watched him
HF RP   omits "him"
Tyndale Great Geneva Bishops   Steph. Beza Elz.
P4 Aleph B D L W X family 13   22 33 157 213 477 713 892 1071 1241 1424 1555 1604 many others.
Von Soden indicates: Most Egyptian mss, I iota (13 69 124 230 346 543 788 926 983 1689), I phi (349 517 954 1424 1675).
About 28 of the IGNTP cursives.
Syriac: Peshitta Harclean Palestinian; Coptic; Armenian; Ethiopic.
Ambrose ?, Milan, Latin, 397   Cyril, Alexandria, 444.

LUKE 6:9
AV CR   to save life, or to destroy *it*
HF RP   ...or to kill *it*
Tyndale Great Geneva Bishops   Steph. Beza Elz.
P4 Aleph B D L W X Psi   family 1 and 13   69 157 251 291 660 892 1038 1071 1093 1241 1604 others.
Von Soden indicates: Most Egyptian mss, I eta (1 22 118 209 1192 1210 1582 2193), I iota (13 124 230 346 543 788 826 983 1689).
About 40 of the IGNTP cursives.
Old Latin; Vulgate; Syriac: Peshitta Harclean-mg Palestinian; Coptic; Gothic; Armenian.
Marcion 130, quoted by Tertullian 220.

LUKE 6:10
AV   And looking round about upon them all, he said to the man
HF RP CR   ...he said to him
Tyndale Great Geneva Bishops   Steph. Beza Elz.
Aleph D L W X family 1 and 13   33 69 124 157 213 998 1071 1093 1346* 1604 others.
Von Soden indicates: I eta (1 22 118 209 1192 1210 1582 2193), I iota (13 230 346 543 788 826 983 1689), I beta (16 348 477 1216 1279 1579 1588).
About 29 of the IGNTP cursives.
Old Latin; Vulgate; Syriac: Harclean-mg (Palestinian); Coptic; Armenian; Ethiopic.
Tatian, Syria, 172.

LUKE 6:26
AV   Woe unto you, when all men shall speak well of you

HF RP CR omits "unto you"
Tyndale Great Geneva Bishops   Steph. Beza Elz.
D W* Delta 69 472 1038 1424 others.
Von Soden indicates: I phi (349 517 954 1675).
About 12 of the IGNTP cursives.
Old Latin: b r1,2; Syriac: Peshitta Sinaitic; Coptic: Sahadic Bohairic; Armenian; Ethiopic.
Irenaeus, Lyons, Latin, 178   Macarius, Egypt, 391   Chrysostom, Constantinople, 407.

LUKE 6:28
AV   Bless them that curse you, and pray
HF RP CR   ... curse you, pray
Tyndale Great Geneva Bishops   Steph. Beza Elz.
W   251 472 716 1229.
About 18 of the IGNTP curasives.
Old Latin: ff2; Vulgate: Clementine; Syriac: Peshitta; Ethiopic.
Marcion, 130 Justin Martyr, 165   Clement, Alexandria, 215   Tertullian, N. Africa, Latin, 220
Adamantius (?), 300.

LUKE 7:12
AV CR   and much people of the city was with her
HF RP   omits "was"
Tyndale Great Geneva Bishops Beza Elz.
P75 Aleph B C L X Theta Xi 33 69 124 700 1071 others.
Von Sod
en indicates: Most Egyptian mss., I iota (13 124 230 346 543 788 826) •
About 19 of the IGNTP cursives.

LUKE 7:31
AV   And the Lord said, Whereunto shall I liken the men
HF RP CR   omits "And the Lord said"
Tyndale Great Geneva Bishops   Steph. Beza Elz.
M-mg. others.
Von Soden does not cite.
About 2 of the IGNTP cursives.
Old Latin: f g2; Vulgate: Clementine; Persian.

LUKE 8:8
AV   And other fell on good ground
HF RP CR   ...into...
Tyndale Great Geneva Bishops   Steph. Beza Elz.
D W 047   4 124 157 251 372 495 660 700 945 954 1047 1241 1354 1355 1396 1424 1582 2145
2193 others.
About 26 of the IGNTP cursives.
Old Latin a c d.
Justin Martyr 165.

At the time of sowing, the seed falls "upon" rather than "into" the ground.

LUKE 8:34
AV   they fled and went and told *it*
HF RP CR   omits "and went"
Geneva Bishops   Steph. Beza Elz.
440 472.
About 5 of the IGNTP cursives.
Ethiopic.
The parallel passage in Matthew reads with the KJV.

LUKE 8:51
AV   Peter, and James, and John
HF RP CR   Peter, and John, and James
Geneva Bishops   Steph. Beza Elz.
Aleph A L S X Lambda   33 157 213 262 372 700 892 1071 1093 1187 1194 1241 1424 1606 many others.
Von Soden indicates: Most Egyptian mss, I phi (349 517 954 1675), I beta (16 348 477 1216 1279 1579 1588).
About 29 of the IGNTP cursives.
Old Latin: (ff2 g1,2); Vulgate: Clementine; Syriac: Peshitta Sinaitic Curetonian;
Coptic: Sahadic-pt. Bohairic; Gothic; Armenian; Ethiopic.
Why should the regular order be changed?

LUKE 9:1
AV   Then he called his twelve disciples
HF RP CR   ...the twelve
(Geneva) Steph. Beza Elz.
C-3rd cor. E F H U   48 157 251 440 472 476 655 998 1010 1216-mg. 1344 1604 1689 many others.
Von Soden indicates: I phi (7 267 659 1606 2191).
About 21 of the IGNTP cursives ,
Lectionary majority.
Old Latin: including b ff2 g1 l q r.
Tatian, Syria, 172.

LUKE 9:23
AV CR and take up his cross daily, and follow me
HF RP   omits "daily"
Tyndale Great Geneva Bishops   Steph. Beza Elz.
P75 Aleph* A B K L M R W X Theta Xi Pi Psi family 1 and 13 33 69 72 124 131 700 892 others.
Von Soden does not cite.
About 49 IGNTP curstves.
Old Latin: aur f g1,2; Vulgate: including am fuld em forj; Syriac: Peshitta Curetonian
Harclean-with asterisk; Coptic: Sahadic Bohairic; Gothic; Armenian; Ethiopic.

Jerome 420, cites early mss   Chrysostom, Constantinople, 407.

LUKE 10:12
AV   But I say unto you
HF RP CR omits "But"
Tyndale Geneva   Steph. Beza Elz.
Aleph D M S V W Theta Xi   213 245 251 472 565 660 713 892 945 1038 1047 1194 1355 1424 1574 many others.
Von Soden indicates: I eta (22 118 209 1192 1210) 1675), I phi (349 517 954 1675), I beta (16 348 477 1216 1279 1579 1588), Kl (Omega 461 655).
About 44 of the IGNTP cursives.
Old Latin: a f q; Vulgate: early mss; Syriac; Palestinian; Coptic:Bohairic.
Tatian, Syria, 172.

LUKE 10:20
AV   but rather rejoice, because your names
HF RP CR   omits "rather"
Geneva Bishops   Steph. Beza Elz.
X Psi 1574 others.
About 5 of the IGNTP cursives.
Cyril, Alexandria, 444 (2 citations).

LUKE 11:6
AV CR   For a friend of mine in his journey is come to me
HF RP   omits "of mine"
Tyndale Great Geneva Bishops   Steph. Beza Elz.
P75 Aleph A B C L U X Theta   7 22 157 267 472 713 716 1071 1229 2144 many others.
Von Soden indicates: Most Egyptian mss, I ets (1 1582 2193), I iota (13 69 124 230 346 543 788 826), I phi (349 517 1424 1675), I beta (16 348 477 1216 1279 1579 1588), I kappa (Pi 229 248 265 270 280 473 482 489 726 1200 1219 1375).
About 62 of the IGNTP cursives.
Old Latin (except c); Vulgate; Syriac: Curetonian Harclean; CopticBohairic;
Armenian; Ethiopic.

LUKE 11:11
AV   or if *he asks* a fish
HF RP omits "if"
CR   omits "or if"
Tyndale Great Geneva Bishops   Steph. Beza Elz.
Cursive support.
Did not use Von Soden.
About 15 of the IGNTP cursives.
A Greek variant reads with the KJV. The fact that "if" is included in the first and third questions of verses 11, 12 indicates that it should also be in the second.

LUKE 13:20

AV CR   And again he said
HF RP   omits "And"
Tyndale Great Geneva Bishops   Steph. Beza Elz.
P45 P75 Aleph B G L Theta 070   157 372 990 1012 1194 many others.
Von Soden indicates: Most Egyptian mss, I eta (1 22 118 209 1192 1210 1582 2193), I iota (13 69 124 230 346 543 788 826 983 1689).
Old Latin; Vulgate; Syriac: Harclean Palestinian; Coptic: Bohalric; (Armenian); (Ethiopic).

LUKE 13:29

AV CR   and from the north
HF RP   omits "from"
Tyndale Great Geneva Bishops   Steph. Beza Elz.
B L R Psi   family 13 69 372 892 1012 1582 many others.
Old Latin: including a a2 d f i l q; Syriac: (Peshitta) (Curetonian) Palestinian.
Tatian, Syria, 172.

LUKE 13:35

AV   and verily I say unto you
HF RP CR   omits "verily"
Geneva Bishops   Steph. Beza Elz.
Many cursives (according to Tischendorf).
Von Soden does not cite.

LUKE 14:5

AV   Which of you shall have an ass or an ox
HF RP CR   have a son or an ox
Tyndale Great Geneva Bishops   Steph. Beza Elz.
Aleph K L X Theta Pi Psi   family 1 and 13   33 157 213 291 440 892 990 1071 1079 1093 1207 1223 1230 1241 1253 1355 1396 1546 1604 1646 many others.
Von Soden indicates: Most Egyptian mss, I eta (1 22 118 209 1192 1210 1582 2193), I iota (13 69 124 230 346 543 708 826 983 1689), I kappa (229 248 265 270 280 473 482 489 726 1200 1219 1346 1375).
Lectionary 547.
Old Latin: a aur b c ff2 i l r1; Vulgate; Syriac: (Sinaitic) Palestinian;
Coptic: Bohairic Fayyumic.

LUKE 17:4

AV   turn again to thee, saying
HF RP   omits "to thee"
Tyndale Great Geneva Bishops   Steph. Beza Elz.
Cursive support.
Von Soden indicates: I eta (1 22 118 209 1192 1210 1582 2193).
The well attested Greek variant followed by CR reads as the KJV (see NASV).
The personal force of the repentance is lessened without "to thee".

LUKE 17:9
AV   commanded him? I trow not
HF RP   commanded? I trow not
CR   commanded?
Tyndale Great Geneva   Bishops Steph. Beza Elz.
D X   family 13   69 others.
Von Soden indicates: I iota (13 124 230 346 543 788 826 983 1689).
Old Latin; Vulgate; Syriac: Peshitta; Coptic: Bohairic Ethiopic.
Tatian, Syria, 172 Cyprian, Carthage, Latin, 258.

LUKE 17:24
AV   so shall also the son of man be in his day
HF RP CR omits "also"
Bishops Steph. Beza Elz.
D   71 157 472 many others.
Von Soden indicates: I pi (N).
Old Latin: b c e i s; Armenian; Ethiopic.

LUKE 17:34
AV CR   the one shall be taken
HF RP   omits "the"
Tyndale Great Geneva Bishops   Steph. Beza Elz.
P75 Aleph B Theta 063   family 1 and 13   69 124 157 251 485 716 892 1071 1229 others.
Von Soden indicates: Most Egyptian mss, I eta (1 22 118 209 1192 1210 1582 2193), I iota (13 230 346 543 788 826 983 1689).
Coptic: Bohairic.
Eusebius, Caesarea, 339.
The translation difference here is marginal.

LUKE 17:35
AV CR   the one shall be taken
HF RP   omits "the"
Tyndale Great Geneva Bishops   Elz.
P75 Aleph-1st cor B D R W Theta Omega   family 1 and 13   69 251 291 579 660 1241 many others.
Von Soden indicates: I eta (1 22 118 209 1192 1210 1582 2193), I iota (13 69 124 230 346 543 788 826 983 1689).
Coptic: edition of Schwartze.
There may not be a translatable difference.

LUKE 17:36
AV   Two *men* shall be in the field; the one shall be taken, and the other left.
HF RP CR   omits entire verse
Great (in italics) Bishops Beza Elz.
D 030 039   4 229-c 262 265-c 476 489-c 700 716 988 1012 1071 1187 1194 1230 1241 1355 1396

1573 1555 (2148) 2174 many others.
Von Soden indicates: I iota (13 124 230 346 543 826 973 1689), I phi b (7 267 659 1606 2191), I Beta (16 348 477 1216 1279 1579 1588).
Lectionary: 185 1579.
Old Latin: a aur b (c) e f ff2 i l q (r1); Vulgate; Syriac: Peshitta Sinaitic Curetonian Harclean; Armenian; Georgian.
Tatian, Syria, 172 Eusebius, Caesarea, 339 Ambrose, Milan, Latin, 397
Augustine, Hippo, Latin, 430.
Erasmus and the first three editions of Stephanus omit the passage. Stephanus in his fourth edition includes it.

LUKE 20:1

AV CR   the chief priests and the scribes came upon *him*
HF RP   the priests and...
Tyndale Great Geneva Bishops   Steph. Beza Elz
Aleph B C D L M N O R W Theta Psi   family 1 and (13)   4 7 33 157 213 291 659 713 716 892 1047 1093 1200 1241 1424 1604 many others.
Von Soden indicates: Most Egyptian mss, I eta (1 22 118 209 1192 1210 1582 2193), I iota (13 69 124 230 346 545 788 826 983 1689), I phi (27 692 1194).
Old Latin (except a); Vulgate; Syriac; Coptic; Armenian; Ethiopic.
A Greek variant with different word order supports the reading "chief priests".

LUKE 20:9

AV [CR]   A certain man planted a vineyard
HF RP   omits "certain"
Tyndale Great (Geneva) Bishops   Stepha Beza Elz.
A W O   family 13   69 124 157 251 443 447 544 660 713 1071 1093 1195 1241 1344 1365 1604 2148.
Von Soden indicates: I iota (13 230 346 543 788 826 983 1689), I phi (7 267 659 1606 2191).
Lectionary majority.
Old Latin: g1 r1; Syriac: Peshitta Sinaitic Curetionian Harclean; Armenian; Georgian.
Tatian, Syria, 172   Theodoret, Cyrus, 466.

LUKE 20:19

AV [CR]   and they feared the people: for they perceived
HF RP   omits "the people"
Tyndale Great (Geneva) Bishops   Stepha Beza Elz.
Aleph A B C D E H K L H R U W Delta Pi   4 21 28 251 440 472 660 716 1047 1071 1093 1207 1229 1355.
Von Soden indicates: I eta (1 22 118 209 1192 1210 1582 2193), I iota (13 69 124 230 346 543 788 826 983 1689), I phi (27 692 1194), I sigma (157 245 291 1012), I kappa (229 248· 265 270 280 473 482 489 726 1200 1219 1346 1375).
Old Latin; Vulgate; Syriac; Coptic; Gothic.

LUKE 20:31
AV   the seven also: and they left no children
HF RP CR   omits "and"
Tyndale Great Geneva Bishops   Elz.
G K H P-c W Gamma Theta Pi   family 13 1 251 660 716 1047 1071 1093 1187 1207 1223 1229 1241 1279 1335 many others.
Von Soden indicates:. I eta (22 118 209 1192 1210 1582 2193), I iota (13 124 230 346 543 788 826 1689), I phi (27 71 692 1194), I sigma (291 713 1012), I kappa (229 248 265 270 280 473 482 489 726 1200 1219 1346 1375).
Old Latin: including a c f 1; Vulgate; Syriac: Peshitta Harclean; Gothic; Armenian.
Tatian, Syria, 172.

LUKE 21:16
AV CR   brethren, and kinsfolk, and friends
HF RP   kinsfolk, and friends, and brethren
Tyndale Great Geneva Bishops   Stepha Beza Elz.
Aleph (A) B D M R U W 713 1012 1047 1071 1223 1229 1355 manyothers.
Von Soden indicates: Most Egyptian mss, I eta (1 22 118 209 1192 1210 1582 2193), I iota (13 69 124 230 346 543 788 826 983), I kappa (K Pi 229 248 265 473 482 489 1219 1346).
Syriac: Peshitta Curetonian Palestinian.
Origen, Alexandria, Caesarea, 254.

LUKE 23:25
AV   And he released unto them
HF RP CR   omit "unto them"
Tyndale Great Geneva Bishops   Steph. Beza Elz.
K M Pi   family 1 and 13   7 251 291 440 659 660 1071 1187 1207 1216 1223 1279 1355 1604 many others.
Von Soden indicates: I eta (1 22 118 209 1192 1210 1582 2193), I iota (13 69 124 230 346 543 826 983 1689), I phi (27 692 1194), I kappa (229 248 265 270 280 473 482 489 726 1200 1219 1346 1375).
Old Latin (except a); Vulgate; Syriac:Peshitta Curetonian Harclean-with obelus;
Armenian; Ethiopic.
Tatian, Syria, 172.

LUKE 23:55
AV   And the women also, which came with him
HF RP CR   omits "also"
Geneva   Steph. Beza Elz.
Cursives.
Von Soden seems indicate support from: D, 3 others.
Old Latin: c r; Coptic: Sahadic.

JOHN 1:28
AV   These things were done in Bethabara beyond Jordan

HF RP CR   ...Bethany...

Tyndale Great Geneva Bishops   Steph. Beza Elz.

(Aleph-c) C-2nd cor (K) U Gamma Pi-c Psi* (apparently) family 1 and 13   22 33 69* 262 346 477 826 892-mg 983 1093 1207? 1230 1354 1365-c 1546 1646-c (1646*) 1675* (apparently) many others.

Von Soden indicates: I eta (1 22 1192 1210 1582 2193), I kappa (265 489 1219 1346) I r (262 566 1187 1555 1573), Von Soden also indicates that the mass of mss designated as "Koine r" support the KJV.

Lectionaries 70-c 1231.

Syriac: Sinaitic Curetonian (Palestinian mss); Coptic: Sahadic; Armenian; Georgian; Slavonic.

Origen, Alexandria, Caesarea,254   Eusebius, Caesarea, 339   Epiphanius, Cyprus, 403 Chrysostan, Constantinople, 407   Jerome, Latin, 420   Suidas, 980 Euthymius, Zigabenus, 1116.

Origen mentions that though many mss had the reading "Bethany", in his travels he could not locate such a place·near Jordan (Metzger, Textual Commentary).

JOHN 1:41

AV   Which is, being interpreted, the Christ

HF CR   omits "the"

Geneva Bishops Steph. Beza Elz.

71 1194 others.

Coptic: Bohairlc; Armenian.

Cyril, Alexandria, 444.

Of the 19 times the title "Christ" stands by itself in the Gospel of John, only twice (4:25 9: 22) is the Greek article not used. Here it is most appropriate.

JOHN 1:43

The day following Jesus would go forth into Galilee

HF RP CR   ...he...

Tyndale Great Geneva Bishops   Steph. Beza Elz.

E F G H U Gamma 4 20 71 213 251 348 440 476 477 655 713 726 1093 1194 1229 1241 1574 many others.

Von Soden indicates: I phi (7 185 267 659 1606 2191).

Syriac: Peshitta; Persian.

Tatian, Syria, 172.

As verse 43 begins a new paragraph in the development of the narrative, the inclusion of Jesus' name is much more appropriate than the use of a pronoun.

JOHN 2:22

AV   his disciples remembered that he had said this unto them

HF RP CR   omits "unto them"

Geneva   Steph. Beza Elz

K T 245 348 477 544 1207 1223 others.

Von Soden indicates: I kappa (229 248 270 280 473 482 489 726 1200 1219 1346 1375) •

JOHN 3:25
AV   between *some* of John's disciples and the Jews
HF RP CR   ...and a Jew
Tyndale Great Geneva Bishops   Steph. Beza. Elz.
P66 Aleph* G Theta Lambda-c Pi-c   family 1 and 13   69 71 124 482 565 1071 1187 1194 1253
1355 1365 others.
Von Soden indicates: I eta (1 22 118 209 1210 1582 2193), I iota (13 230 346 543 788 826 983
1689),) K iota (850 1819 1820), C (050 0141 138 139 397 821 869 994).
Lectionary 105.
Old Latin: (a) sur b c (d) e (f) ff2 (j) l (q) (r1); Vulgate; Syriac: Curetonian Palestinian, early
mss.; Coptic: early Sahadic mss.
Bohairic; Gothic; Georgian; Ethiopic.
Origen , Alexandria, Caesarea, 254   Cyril, Alexandria, 444.
The phrase 'a Jew' would be unique in John (Metzger, Textual Commentary).

JOHN 3:28
AV CR   Ye yourselves bear me witness, that I said
HF RP   omits "me"
Geneva   Steph. Beza Elz.
P66 A B D G K L S U W - supplied Delta Theta Lambda Pi Psi 063 (apparently) 083 086
(apparently)   family 13   7 21 33 124 209 270 280 291 348 482 495 565 659 700 713 892 1010
1071 1079 1223 1230 1241 1242 1354 1365 1546 1547 1579 1646 many others.
Von Soden indicates: Most Egyptian mss, I eta (1 22 118 1210 1582 2193), I omega (213 1321
1574 2145), I pi (N), I kappa (1346), I r (1187 1555), C (050 0141 138 139 397 821 869 994), N
(249 317 423 430 743).
Lectionary majority.
Old Latin: a b c d (e) f ff2 i q; Vulgate; Syriac: (Peshitta Sinaitic Curetonian Harclean
Palestinian ??); Coptic: early Sahadic mss Bohairic Fayyumic; Armenian; Georgian?
Cyprian, Carthage, Latin, 258 Eusebius, Caesarea, 339 Chrysostom,Constantinople, 407
Cyril, Alexandria, 444   Other fathers.

JOHN 4:3
AV CR   He left Judea, and departed again into Galilee
HF RP   omits "again"
Tyndale Great Geneva Bishops   Steph. Beza Elz.
P66 P75 B-2nd cor C D L M W-supplied Theta 053 083 086 0141   family 1 and 13   3 124 185
213 245 251 291 346 565 713 892 1010 1093 1170 1242 1293 others.
Von Soden indicates: Most Egyptian mss, I eta (1 22 118 209 1210 1582 2193), I iota (13 69 230
543 788 826 983 1689), K iota (850 1819 1820), C (050 0141 138 139 397 821 869 994).
Old Latin: including a b c e f ff2 l; Vulgate; Syriac: Peshitta Sinaitic Curetonlan Palestinian;
Coptic: Sahadic Bohairic; Armenian; Ethiopic.
Epiphanius, Cyprus, 403.

JOHN 6:24
AV   they also took shipping

HC RP CR omits "also"
Tyndale Great Geneva Bishops   Steph. Beza Elz.
U Gamma   33 213 348 485 565 1071 1216 1223 1279 others.
Von Soden indicates: I eta (1 22 118 209 1210 1582 2193), N (249 317 423 430 743).
Tatian, Syria, 172

JOHN 6:45
AV CR Every man therefore that hath heard, and hath learnt
HF RP   ... that hears...
Tyndale Great Geneva Bishops   Steph. Beza Elz.
P66 P75 Aleph A B C K L T Theta Pi   185 213 291 544 565 713 1071 1093 1170 1188 1223 1242 1355 many others.
Von Soden indicates: Most Egyptian mss, I eta (1 22 118 209 1210 1582 2193) , I iota (13 69 124 230 346 543 788 826 983 1689) , I beta (16 348 477 1216 1279 1579 1588), I kappa (229 248 270 482 489 726 1200 1219 1346 1375), K iota (850 1819 1820), C (050 0141 138 139 397 821 869 994).
Old Latin: c f ff2 r; Vulgate.
Origen, Alexandria, Caesarea, 254   Cyril, Alexandria, 444.

JOHN 7:16
AV   Jesus answered them, and said
HF RP CR Jesus therefore answered...
Tyndale Great Geneva Bishops   Steph. Beza Elz.
D L X Psi   21 33 71 213 485 544 565 579 713 788 others.
Von Soden indicates: I eta (1 22 118 209 1210 1582 2193), K iota (850 1819 1820), C (050 0141 138 139 397 821 869 994).
Old Latin: including a e ff2 l; Vulgate; Syriac: Peshi tta Curetonian; Coptic: Sahadic Bohairic; Armenian.
Tatian, Syria, 172   Cyril, Alexandria, 444.

JOHN 7:29
AV   But I know him: for I am from him
HF RP CR omits "But"
Great Geneva Bishops   Steph. Beza Elz.
P66 Aleph D N X   33 71 213 251 291 565 660 945 1071 1194 1223 1241 2145 many others.
Von Soden indicates: I eta (1 22 118 209 1210 1582 2193), I beta (16 348 477 1216 1279 1579 1588), I kappa (A? 229 248 270 280 482 489 726 1200 1219 1346 1375).
Old Latin: including b c f ff2 r; Syriac: Peshitta Curetonian Harclean Palestinian;
Coptic: Bohairic; Gothic; Ethiopic.
Tatian, Syria, 172   Hilary, Poictiers, Latin, 367   Cyril, Alexandria, 444.

JOHN 7:33
AV   Then said Jesus unto them
HF RP CR   omits "unto them"
Tyndale Great Geneva Bishops   Steph. Beza Elz.

T 053   565 892 (1241) others.
Von Soden indicates: I eta (1 22 118 209 1210 1582 2193), I beta (16 348 477 1216 1279 1579 1588).
Old Latin: (c) g; Vulgate: Clementine; Syriac: Sinaitic; Coptic: Sahadic; Ethiopic.
Tatian, Syria, 172 Cyril, Alexandria, 444.

JOHN 8:4

AV   this woman was taken
HF [RP has "woman"] we found this *woman*
Tyndale Great Geneva Bishops   Steph. Beza Elz.
K Pi   1010.
Supported by the von Soden M5 grouping which has 280 cursives.
The CR reads with KJV and is supported by: D, 1, Old Latin and Vulgate witnesses, von Soden's M1 grouping·(possibly 25 cursives). Further variant support is found in von Soden's M2, 3, 4 groupings (probably over 80 cursives).

JOHN 8:5

AV RP   Now Moses in the law commanded us
HF   Now in our law Moses commanded
Tyndale Great Geneva Bishops   Steph. Beza Elz.
Supported by von Soden's M5 grouping (about 280 cursives) and part of M1 (probably 20 cursives).
The CR and a variant reads with the KJV and is supported by: K U Pi Lambda family 13, 1 700 892, Old Latin and Vulgate witnesses, von Soden's M3-pt, M4 groupings (probably 40 cursives).

JOHN 8:9

AV RP   And they which heard it, being convicted by *their own* conscience
HF CR   omits: "being convicted by *their own* conscience"
Geneva Bishops   Steph. Beza Elz.
E G H K S 118 209.
Supported by von Soden's M5 (280 cursives), M6-pt. (about 125 cursives), M7 (260 cursives).
Coptic: Bohairic.

JOHN 8:9

AV   and the woman standing in the midst
HF RP CR   and the woman being in the midst
Tyndale Great Geneva Bishops   Steph. Beza Elz.
1 892.
Supported by von Soden's M1 grouping (about 20 cursives).
Old Latin-pt; Vulgate; Syriac: Palestinian; Ethiopic.
See the awkward NASV translation of this passage.

JOHN 8:10
AV RP   Jesus...and saw none but the woman
HF   Jesus saw her and said
CR   Jesus said
Tyndale Great. Geneva Bishops   Steph. Beza Elz.
E G F (apparently) H K.
Supported by von Soden's M5 grouping (280 cursives), M7 (260 cursives).

JOHN 8:10
AV   he said unto her, Woman
HF   omits "unto her"
RP   omits "woman"
Tyndale Great Geneva Bishops   Steph. BezaElz.
E F G H K M S Gamma others.
Old Latin: e ff2 g l-mg; Vulgate; Syriac: Palestinian; Armenian; Ethiopic.
The CR reads with the KJV, supported by : Gamma, 1 28 892 1010, Old Latin and Vulgate
witnesses; Coptic: Bohairic-pt; von Soden's M1 pt (probably about 20 cursives), M2 (40
cursives), M3-pt. (about 10 cursives), M4 (about 10 cursives).

JOHN 8:10
AV RP   where are those thine accusers
HF   where are thine accusers
CR   where are they
Tyndale Great Geneva Bishops   Steph. Beza Elz.
E F G K   118 209.
Supported by von Soden's M5 grouping (280 cursives), M6-pt, (probably about 125 cursives),
M7 (260 cursives).
Coptic: Bohairic Ethiopic.

JOHN 8:11
AV RP   sin no more
HF CR   from now on sin no more
Tyndale Great Geneva Bishops   Steph. Beza Elz.
E F G H K Gamma 28.
Supported by von Soden's M4-pt (probably about 10 cursives), M5 (280
cursives).
Old Latin: aur e

JOHN 8:54
AV   of whom ye say, that he is your God
HF CR   ...our God
Tyndale Great Geneva Bishops   Steph. Beza Elz
P66* Aleph B* D F X Psi   4 13 245 270 346 399 660 700 892 1009 1010 1017 1079 1093 1188
1216 1223 1242 1354 1424 1546 1555 1582 2148 many others.
Von Soden indicates: I phi (7 185 267 659 1606 2191), I beta (16 348 477 1216 1279 1579 1588),

I omega (213 1321 1574 2145), N (249 317 423 430 743).
Lectionary support is strong.
Old Latin: a b c d e ff2 l q; Vulgate: Clementine;   Syriac: Palestinian;
Coptic: an early Bohairic ms.
Tatian, Syria, 172   Tertullian, N. Afica, Latin, 220, Chrysostom, Constantinople, 407
Cyril, Alexandria, 444.

JOHN 9:20
AV   His parents answered them
HF RP But his parents answered them
CR   His parents answered then
Tyndale Great Geneva Bishops   Steph. Beza Elz.
D Theta family 1 565 1010.
Old Latin-pt; Vulgate.
The reading "them" rather than "then" is indicated by von Soden as being in the
vast majority of cursive mss, also A Gamma Delta Lambda Pi.
As the word translated "but" is often left untranslated, the HF RP could read as the KJV.
Von Soden indicates that the word is omitted in a large number of mss.

JOHN 9:28
AV   Then they reviled him
HF RP They reviled him
CR   And they reviled him
Tyndale Great Geneva Bishops   Steph. Beza Elz.
Family 13   69 others.
Von Soden indicates: I iota (13 69 124 230 346 543 788 826 983 1689).
Lectionary 184.
Old Latin: c ff2; Vulgate: Clementine; Gothic.
A well attested Greek variant could translate as the KJV. The CR is close.

JOHN 9:36
AV   He answered and said, Who is he, Lord
HF RP CR   ...and who...
Tyndale Great Geneva Bishops   Steph. Beza Elz.
(Aleph*) L Theta   245 1079 1241 1321 1546 others.
Von Soden indicates: I kappa (A? 229 248 270 280 489 726 1200 1219 1346 1375).
Old Latin: aur b c e f ff2 l (q); Vulgate; Syriac: (Peshitta); Coptic: Sahadic (an early Bohairic
ms.); Georgian.
Tatian, Syria, 172   Origen, Alexandria, Caesarea, 254.

JOHN 10:8
AV   All that ever came before me are thieves and robbers
HF RP   omits "before me"
Tyndale Great Geneva Bishops   Steph. Beza Elz.
Theta   family 1   124 565 1365 others.

Von Soden indicates: I eta (1 22 118 209 1210 1582 2193), K iota (850 1819 1820).
Vulgata: foss; Armenian; Georgian.
Valentinians, II Clement, Alexandria, 215   Origen, Alexandria, Caesarea, 254
Arnbrsosiaster, Latin, 384 "Quaestions", Latin, among the works of Augustine, 430
Nonnus, Panopolis, 431   Cyril, Alexandria, 444.
The well attested CR reads with the KJV.

JOHN 14:30
AV   for the prince of this world cometh
HF RP CR   omits "this"
Tyndale Great Geneva Bishops   Steph. Beza Elz.
1 138 346 565 579 1093 1582 many others.
Von Soden indicates: I iota (13 543 788 826 983 1689), K iota (850 1819 1820).
Old Latin; Vulgate; Syriac: Palestinian; Coptic: Sahadic Bohairic.
Hippolytus, Portus, 235   Origen, Alexandria, Caersarea, 254
Hilary, Poictiers, Latin, 367   Athanasius, Alexandria, 373   Basil, Cappadocia, 379
Macarius, Egypt, 391   Chrysostom, Constantinople, 407 Cyril, Alexandria, 444
Theodoret, Cyrus, 466.
It is *this* world that Satan rules.

JOHN 16:3
AV   And these things they will do unto you, because
HF RP CR   omits "unto you"
Tyndale Great Geneva Bishops   Steph. Beza Elz.
(Aleph) D L Psi 0141 family 1 and 13 (33) 69 213 482 544 565 660 713 1071 1093 1187 1194
1195 1207 1223 1321 1365 1375 2145 many others.
Von Soden indicates: Most Egyptian mss, I eta (1 22 118 209 1210 1582), I iota (13 230 346 543
788 826 983 1689) , C (050 0141 138 139 397 821 869 994), N (249 317 423 430 743).
Lectionary majority.
Old Latin: a c d f ff2 g; Vulgate: Clementine; Syriac: Harclean-with asterisk Palestinian;
Coptic: Sahadic Bohairic Achimic-2; Armenian; Ethiopic; Georgian

JOHN 16:15
AV   that, he shall take of mine, and shall shew *it* unto you
HF RP CR   ...he takes...
Tyndale Great Geneva   Steph. Beza Elz.
Aleph-c (A) K V Pi 4 13 69 124 213 291 543 544 954 many others.
Von Soden indicates: I beta (348 477 1279), I kappa (229 248 270 280 473 482 489 726 1200
1219 1346 1375).
Old Latin: b c f ff2 g m q; Vulgate; Coptic: Sahadic Bohairic; Ethiopic.
Hilary, Poictiers, Latin, 354   Cyril, Jerusalem, 386.

JOHN 16:33
AV   In the world ye shall have tribulation
HF CR   ...ye have...

Tyndale Great Geneva   Beza Elz.
D 0141 family 1 and 13   69 472 477 892-supplied 998 1216 1579 many others.
Von Soden indicates: I iota (13 124 230 346 543 788 826 983 1689), K iota (850 1819 1820), N (249 317 423 430 743).
Old Latin; Vulgate: including am fuld em taur; (Gothic); Armenian;Ethiopic.
Origen, Alexandria, Caersarea, 254   Cyprian, Carthage, Latin, 259
Dionysius, Alexandria, 265 Eusebius, Caesarea, 329 Hilary, Poictiers, Latin, 367
Athanasius, AlexandrIa, 373 Basil, Cappodocia, 379 Chrysostom, Constantinople, 407
Cyril, Alexandria, 444.

JOHN 17:2

AV RP CR   that he should give eternal life
HF   ...shall give...
Tyndale Great Geneva   Steph. Beza Elz.
Aleph-2nd cor A C G K (L) M S (W) X Omega 053 0141 0250   33 348 399 472 495 1071 1279 many others.
Von Soden indicates: K iota (850 1819 1820).
Cyril, Alexandria, 444.
The translation difference is marginal and may fall into the area of orthography.

JOHN 17:20

AV CR which shall believe on me through their word
HF RP which believe...
Tyndale Great Geneva Bishops   Steph. Beza Elz.
D-2nd cor apparently many others.
Von Soden only cites briefly.
Old Latin: a c e f g q; Vulgate; Coptic: Sahadic Achimic-2 Proto-Bohairic; Ethiopic.
Origen, Alexandria,Caesarea, 254   Cyprian, Carthage, Latin, 258 Hilary, Poictiers, Latin, 367

JOHN 18:25

AV   He denied *it*, and said
HF RP CR Then he...
Tyndale Great Geneva Bishops   Steph. Beza Elz.   CR
Aleph A B C*D-supplied H L S U X Pi 138 291 440 565 660 713 1223 1355 1360 many others.
Von Soden indicates: Most Egyptian mss, I eta (1 22 118 209 1210 1582 2193), I iota (69 124 788), I omega (213 1071 1321 1574 2145), I pi (N), I kappa (482 489 726 1200 1219 1346 1375), 1820), K iota (850 1819 1820).
Old Latin b e ff2 g q; Vulgate; Syriac: Harclean; Coptic: Sahadic;Armenian.

JOHN 19:6

AV CR Crucify *him*, crucify *him*
HF RP Crucify *him*, crucify him
Tyndale? Great? Geneva   Steph. Beza Elz.
P66 A? B L W Psi family 1 245 others.
Von Soden indicates: I eta (1 118 209 1210 1582).

Old Latin: aur e; Vulgate: am tol em forj ing mt taur; Syriac: Palestinian-c.
Hilary, Poietiers, Latin, 367   Chrysostom, Constantinople, 407
Augustine,
Hippo, Latin, 430   Cyril, Alexandria, 444.

JOHN 19:38
AV CR   And after this...besought Pilate
HF RP   omits "And"
Geneva   Steph. Beza Elz.
Aleph A B D-supplied H LUX Pi-2nd cor   1 69 348 659 713 998 1071 1170 1242 2145 many others.
Von Soden indicates: Most Egyptian mss, I eta (118 209 1210 1582), I iota (13 124 230 346 543 788 826 983 1689), I pi (N), K iota (850 1819 1820), C (050 0141 138 ·139 397 821 869 994), N (249 317 423 430 743).
Old Latin (except ff2); Vulgate;   Syriac: Harclean Palestinian; Coptic: Bohairic-Codex Diez; (Ethiopic).
Cyril, Alexandria, 444.

JOHN 20:39
AV   Thomas, because thou hast seen me
HF RP CR omits "Thomas"
Tyndale Great Geneva Bishops   Steph. Beza Elz.
Cursives.
Von Soden does not cite.
Vulgate: Clementine foss rom mt others; Persian.
In such a direct reprimand, it would seem strange for Christ not to use Thomas' name at least once.

ACTS 3:20
AV   Jesus' Christ, which before was preached unto you
HF RP CR   ...appointed...
Tyndale Great Geneva Bishops   Steph. Beza Elz.
Cursives.
Von Soden does not cite.
Vulgate; Coptic: Bohairic.
Origen , Alexrandria, Caesarea, 254   Cosmas, Indicopleustes, 550.
The Jews rejection of the previously preached message (see 3:18) is a key point at issue here.

ACTS 5:3
AV   and to keep back *part* of the price
HF RP CR and to keep back to thee *part* of the price
Tyndale Great Geneva Bishops   Steph. Beza Elz.
P8 P74 Aleph A B E   323 614 945 1175 1739 many others.
Von Soden indicates: Most Egyptian mss, I a1 (88 181 431 915 917 1829 1874), I a2 (5 489 623 927 1827 1838 1873 2143), I b1 (429 522 1758 1831 1891), I b2 (440 2298), Ic (255 257 383 385

913 1108 1245 1518 1611 1765 2138 2147).
Old Latin-pt.
Chrysostom, Constantinople, 407.

ACTS 5:23
AV   and the keepers standing without before the doors
HF RP CR   omits "without"
Tyndale Great Geneva Bishops   Steph. Beza Elz.
Cursives.
Von Soden does not cite.
Chrysostom, Constantinople, 407.

ACTS 5:25
AV   and told the, saying
HF RP CR   omits "saying"
Geneva   Steph. Beza Elz.
36 others.
Von Soden indicates: I a1, Andreas mss. (307 453 610).
Old Latin-pt; Armenian; Ethiopic.
Lucifer, Cagliari, Latin, 370.

ACTS 6:13
AV [CR]   blasphemous words against this holy place
HF RP   ...the...
Tyndale Great Geneva Bishops   Steph. Beza Elz.
B C   5 33 36 69 323 460 467 489 623 642 808 927 945 1739 1827 1838 1845 2143 2147 2180 2298 2495 many others.
Von Soden indicates: Most Egyptian mss., I a1 (88 181 307 453 610 915 917 1829 1898), I b1 (242 429 522 1758 1831 1891).
Old Latin: h p t; Vulgate: tol; Syriac: Pehsitta Harclean; Coptic: Sahadlc Bohairic.
Gregory, Nyssa, 394   Chrysostom, Constantinople, 407   Proclus, Constantinople, 446.

ACTS 7:37
AV   A prophet shall the Lord your God raise up
HF RP   the Lord our God...
CR   God...
Tyndale Great Geneva Bishops   Steph. Beza Elz.
P   1 33 36 69 104 216 242 326 429 431 919 920 1319 1522 1827 1829 1831 1845 1873 2127 2143 many others.

ACTS 8:10
AV CR   To whom they all gave heed
HF RP   omits "all"
Bishops   Steph. Beza Elz.
Aleph A B C D E   36 81 88 322 323 460 915 1311 many others.

Von Soden indicates: Most Egyptian mss., I a1 (181 431 917 1829 1874 1998), I a1 Andreas mss. (36 307 453 610), I a2 (5 467 489 623 927 1827 1838 1873 2143), I b1 (206 242 429 522 536 1758 1831 1891), I c1 (1108 1245 1518 1611 2138), I c2 (257 385 614 913 1610).
Vulgate; Syriac: Peshitta Harclean; Coptic: Sahadic Bohairic; Ethiopic; Armenian.
Chyrsostom, Constantinople, 407.

ACTS 8:37
AV   And Philip said, If thou believest with all thine heart, thou mayest. And he answered and said, I believe that. Jesus Christ is the Son of God.
HF RP CR   omits entire verse
Tyndale Great Geneva Bishops   Steph. Beza Elz.
E   4 36 88 97 103 104 242 257 307 322 323 395 429 453 464 467 629 630 913 945 1522 1739 1765 1877 1891 others. Note: the above and following witnesses include those with minor variation.
Von Soden indicates: I b1 (522 1758) , I b2 (2298).
Lectionary 59.
Old Latin: ar c? e gig h l m ph r; Vulgate: Clementine am-2 tol demid; Syriac: Harclean-wi th asterisk; Coptic: Middle Egyptian; Armenian, Georgian.
Irenaeus, Lyons, Latin, 178   Tertullian, N. Africa, Latin, 220 Cyprian, Carthage, Latin, 258
Ambrosiaster, Latin, 384 Paclanus, Barcelona, Latin, 392 Ambrose, Milan, Latin, 397
Augustine, Hippo. Latin, 430 "Praedestinatus", Latin, 434   Bede, England, Latin, also cites Greek mss, 735   Theophylact, (cor), Bulgaria, 1077.

ACTS 9:5,6
AV   *it is* hard for thee to kick against the pricks. (6) And he trembling and astonished said, Lord what wilt thou have me to do? And the Lord said unto him
HF RP CR   omits entire passage
Tyndale Great Geneva Bishops   Steph. Beza Elz.
629-Latin; Old Latin: ar c h l p ph t; Vulgate: Clementine fuld demid; Armenian?; Georgian; Slavonic; (Ethiopic).
Hilary, Poictiers, Latin, 367   Lucifer, Cagliari, Latin, 370 Ephraem, Syria, 373
Ambrose, Milan, Latin, 397 Theophylact, Bulgaria, 1077.
Hills says that the passage is present at the end of Acts 9:4 in E, 431 and the Syriac Peshitta (KJVD p. 201).
ACTS 9:17
AV CR   the Lord, *even* Jesus...hath sent me
HF RP   omits "*even* Jesus"
(Geneva) Bishops   Steph. Beza Elz.
P45 P75 Aleph A B C E Psi   5 33 81 218 323 467 483 614 623 927 920-C 945 1175 1311 1739 1827 1838.
Von Soden indicates: Most Egyptian mss, I a1 (D? 88 181 915 917 1829 1874 1898), I b1 (206 242 429 522 536 1758 1831 1891), I b2 (216 440 2298), I c1 (1108 1245 1518 1611 2138), I c2 (257 913 1765 2147).
Old Latin? Vulgate Syriac: (Peshitta) (Harclean); Coptic: Bohairic; (Ethiopic).
Chrysostom, Constantinople, 407.

ACTS 9:38
AV CR   they sent unto him two men
HF RP   omits "two men"
Geneva Bishops   Steph. Beza Elz.
P45 P74 Aleph A B C E Psi   36 323 614 945 1175 1739 many others.
Von Soden indicates. Most Egyptian mss, I a1 (D? 88 181 431 915 917 1829 1874), I b1 (206 242 429 522 1758 1831 1891), I b2 (2298), I c1 (1108 1245 1518 1611 2138), I c2 (255 257 385·913 1610 1765).
Old Latin; Vulgate; Syriac; Coptic.
Basil, Cappadocia, 379   Chrysostom, Constantinople, 407.

ACTS 10:6
AV   he shall tell thee what thou oughtest to do
HF RP CR   omits entire passage
Tyndale Great Geneva Bishops   Steph. Beza Elz.
69-mg. 1611 others.
Vulgate: Clementine demid; Ethiopic.
Theophylact, Bulgaria, 1017.
Von Soden cites a Greek variant which considerably expands the KJV reading: 88 251 461 915.

ACTS 10:21
AV   the men which were sent unto him from Cornelius
HF RP CR   the man...
Tyndale Great Geneva Bishops   Steph. Beza Elz.
H 69 2495 others.
Von Soden does not cite.
Old Latin (W).
Theophylact, Bulgaria, 1017.

ACTS 10:39
AV   whom they slew and hanged on a tree
HF RP CR whom they also slew...
Tyndale Great Geneva Bishops   Steph. Beza Elz.
33 2147 many others.
Vulgate : Clementine fuld; Syriac: Peshitta; Coptic: Sahadic Bohairic.
Irenaeus, Lyons, Latin, 178   Cosmas , Indicopleustes, 550.
The "also" gives a secondary sense to our Lord's death.

ACTS 13:23
AV CR   a Saviour, Jesus
HF RP   omits "Jesus"
Tyndale Great Geneval Bishops Steph. Beza Elz.
Aleph A B C (D) E P Psi   5 81 94 103 181 242 307 429 440 453 489 614 623 945 1145 1522 1739 1829 1838 2143 many others.
Von Soden indicates: Most Egyptian mss, I a1 Andreas mss. (36 610), I c1 (1108 1245 1518 1611

2138), I c2 (255 385 614).
Old Latin? Vulgate Syriac: Peshitta Harclean; Coptic: Sahadic Bohairic;
Armenian.
Athanasius, Alexandria, 373   Chrysostom, Constantinople, 407   Theodoret, Cyrus, 466
Theophylact, Bulgaria, 1077.

ACTS 13:41

AV CR   for I work a work in your days, a work which
HF RP   omits "a work"
Geneva Bishops   Steph. Beza Elz.
P74 Aleph A B C I Psi   5 33 36 81 181 226 255 431 453 467 623 945 1175 1522 1739 1765 1827
1875* 1898 2143.
Von Soden indicates: Most Egyptian mss, I a1 Andreas mss (36 307 453 610), I b1 (206 242 429
522 1891), I b2 (2298).
Vulgate; Coptic: Sahadic Bohairic; Armenian; Ethiopic.
Theophylact, Bulgaria, 1017.

ACTS 13:43

AV CR   who, speaking to them, persuaded them to continue
HF RP   omits "to them"
Tyndale Great Geneva Bishops   Steph. Beza Elz.
Aleph B C D I   81 209 547 642 808 1311 1837 1845-c 2180 many others.
Von Soden indicates: Most Egyptian mss, I a1 (E 88 181 431 915 1829 1898) 1898), I a2 (5 467
489 623 927 1827 1838 1873 2143), I b1 (206 242 429 522 536 1750 1831 1891), I b2 (216 323
440 1739 2290), I c1 (1108 1245 1518 1611 2138), I c2 (255 257 383· 305 614 913 1765 2147), K c
(42 57 223 479 483 582 1405 2115), K r (201 480 664).
Many of the versions.
Chrysostom, Constantinople, 407   Theophylact, Bulgaria, 1017.

ACTS 14:3

AV   unto the word of his grace, and granted signs
HF RP CR   omits "and"
Tyndale Great Geneva Bishops   Steph. Beza Elz.
C L   104 181 257 323 467 913 915 945 1145 1739 1838 1845-c 1898 many others.
Von Soden indicates: I b1 (206 242 429 522 536 1758 1831 1891), I b2 (216 440 2298).
Armenian; Ethiopic.
Theophylact, Bulgaria, 1077.

ACTS 14:17

AV   and gave us rain from heaven
HF RP CR   ...you...
Tyndale Great Geneva Bishops   Steph. Beza Elz.
88 209 226 255 256 337 383 460 547 614 794 808 915 917 1108 1611 1827 2147 2180 many
others
Von Soden indicates: I b1 (206 242 522 536 1831).

Coptic: Bohairic.

ACTS 15:11
AV   Lord Jesus Christ
HF RP CR   Lord Jesus
Tyndale Great Geneva Bishops   Steph. Beza Elz.
C D Psi   33 36 69 453 945 1175 1739 many others.
Von Soden indicates: I a1 Andreas ms, (610), I b1 (206 522 536 1758 1831 1891), I b2 (1739 2298).
Old Latin; Vulgate: Clementine; Syriac: Peshitta; Coptic: Bohairic-pt; Armenian; Ethiopic.
Irenaeus, Lyons, Latin, 178   Origen, Alexandria, Caesarea, Latin 254
Augustine, Hippo, Latin, 430   Theophylact, Bulgaria, 1077

ACTS 17:5
AV   the Jews which believed not, moved with envy, took
HF RP   the Jews which believed not, took
CR   the Jews, moved with envy, took
Tyndale, Great, Geneva Bishops   Steph. Beza Elz.
441 many others.
Theophylact, Bulgaria, 1077.
After citing evidence for the removal of "moved with envy", von Soden then
gives the evidence in its favour. He then cites evidence for three possible
placements of "which believed not". If he means this to be in addition to the
other half of the reading, then the support for the KJV translation is quite considerable.

ACTS 17:19
AV   Then certain philosophers of the Epicureans
HF RP CR Then also certain...
E many cursives ,
Von Soden indicates: I a1 (88 181 431 915 1898), I c1 (1108 1245 1510 1611 2138), I c2 (255 257 383 385 614 913 1610 2147).
Old Latin? Vulgate; Syriac: Harclean; Coptic: Sahadic Bohairic; Armenian; Ethiopic.
Theophylact, Bulgaria, 1077.

ACTS 17:19
AV   preached unto them Jesus, and the resurrection
HF RP CR   omits "unto them"
Tyndale Great Geneva Bishops   Steph. Beza Elz.
Aleph-c A E   1 33 36 69 81 88 104 181 218 326 337 460 483 1311 1522 1845 1898 many others.
The above and following witnesses include minor variants.
Von Soden indicates: I a2 (5 467 489 623 927 1827 1838 2143), I b1 (206 242 429 522 536 1758 1831 1891), I b2 (216 323 440 1739 2298), I c1 (1108 1245 1518 1611 2138), I c2 (203 255 257 383 385 614 913 1765 2147).
Old Latin; Syriac: Peshitta; Coptic: Bohairic.

ACTS 20:8
AV   The upper chamber, where they were gathered together
HF RP CR   ...we...
Tyndale Geneva Bishops   Steph. Beza Elz.
1 209 489 1518 others.
Coptic: Bohairic; Ethiopic.
Theophylact, Bulgaria, 1077.

ACTS 20:28
AV CR   to feed the church of God
HF RP   ...of the Lord and God
Tyndale Geneva Bishops   Steph. Beza Elz.
Aleph B 056 0142   4 104 218 312 424 441 459 614 629 917 1175 1505 1522 1758 1831 1877 2298 2414 2495 others.
Von Soden indicates: I c1 (1108 1245 1518 1611 2138), I c2 (255 383 385 913 1610 2147).
Lectionaries 60 368 598 603 611 1021 1291 1439.
Old Latin: ar c; Vulgate: am ful tol demid; Syriac: Peshitta Harclean;
Coptic: an early Bohairic ms; Georgian.
Caelestinus, Rome, Latin, IV   Basil, Cappodocia, 379   Orsisus, Egypt, 380
Ambrose, Milan, Latin, 397   Epiphanius, Cyprus, 403   Chrysostom, Constantinople, 407
Theodore, Mopsuestia, 428   Cyril, Alexandria, 444   Pseudo-Athanasius, VI
Primasius, Adrumentum, Latin, 552   Antiochus, Ptolemaais, 614 Theophylact, Bulgaria, 1077.

ACTS 20:34
AV   Yea, ye yourselves know
HF RP CR omits "Yea"
Great Geneva Bishops   Steph. Beza Elz.
Cursives.
Von Soden does not cite.
Syriac: (Peshitta); Coptic: Bohairic; (Ethiopic).
A Greek variant would read with the KJV.

ACTS 21:11
AV   bound his own hands and feet
HF RP CR   ...feet and hands
Tyndale Geneva Bishops   Steph. Beza Elz.
A 5 69 206 241 323 522 623 (642) 1898 many others.
Von Soden indicates: I c1 (1108 1245 1518 1611 2138), I c2 (257 383 385 506 614 913 1610 2147).
Coptic: Sahadic Bohairic; Ethiopic.
Origen, Alexandria, Caesacea , 254   Chrysostom, Constantinople, 407.
Alford mentions that it would be more natural to bind the hands first.

ACTS 21:20
AV CR   and said unto him, Thou seest
HF RP   omits "and"

Tyndale Great Geneva Bishops   Steph. Beza Elz.
P74 (Aleph) A B (E) H L P Psi   36 209 257 (307) 453 483 489 623 642 many others. The above and following include minor variants.
Von Soden indicates: I a1 (431 915 917 1829 1874), I b1 (206 242 429 522 536 1758 1831), I b2 (216 440 1739 2298).
Vulgate; Syriac: Peshitta; Coptic: Sahadic Bohairic.
Theophylact, Bulgaria, 1077.

ACTS 21:29
AV CR   For they had seen before with him in the city Trophimus
HF RP   omits "before"
Geneva Bishops   Steph. Beza Elz.
Aleph A B C D E   5 181 614 623 920 927 1845-C 1873 1898 2147.
Von Soden indicates: Most Egyptian mss., I a1 Andreas mss. (36 307 453 610), I bl (206 242 429 522 536 1758 1831 1891), I b2 (216 323 440 1739 2298), I c1 (1108 1245 1518 1611 2138).
Old Latin: gig.

ACTS 23:29
AV CR   but to have nothing laid
HF RP   omits "but"
Tyndale Great Geneva Bishops   Steph. Beza Elz.
Aleph A B E H   69 209* 483 642 808 1837 1845 many others.
Von Soden indicates: Most Egyptian mss, I a1 (181 431 1829 1898), I a2 (5 467 489 623 927 1827 1838 1873 2143), I b1 (206 242 429 522 536 1738 1831 1891, I b2 (1739 2298), I c1 (1108 1245 1518 1611 2138), I c2 (255 383 385 639 913 2147).
Old Latin? Vulgate; Coptic: Sahadic Bohairic; Syriac: (Peshitta) Harclean; Armenian; (Ethiopic).
Theophylact, Bulgaria, 1077.

ACTS 24:9
AV   And the Jews also assented
HF RP CR   ... joined in the attack
Tyndale Great Geneva Bishops   Steph. Beza Elz.
(33) 216 323 440 614 1522 many others.
Old Latin: (E); (Vulgate)   Syriac: (Peshitta) Harclean ,
The Greek for "joined" in the attack is not found elsewhere in the N. T.

ACTS 24:20
AV   let these same *here* say, if they have found any evil.
HF RP CR   omits "if"
Tyndale Great Geneva Bishops   Steph. Beza Elz.
Many cursives.
Old Latin; Vulgate; Syriac: Harclean; Ethiopic.

ACTS 26:17
AV   unto whom now I send thee
HF RP CR   omits "now"
Tyndale Great Geneva Bishops   Steph. Beza Elz.
1518   many cursives,
Von Soden indicates: I a1 (88 181 431 915 917 1829 1874 1898), I a2 (5 467 489 623 927 1827 1838 1873 2143).
Old Latin.

ROMANS 2:5
AV CR   and revelation of the righteous judgment of God
HF RP   and revelation and righteousness of God
Tyndale Great Geneval Bishops Steph. Beza Elz.
Aleph* A B D* F G   1 81 255 323 876 919 1506 1610 many others.
Old Latin: including d e g; Vulgate; Syriac: Peshitta; Coptic.
Origen, Alexandria, Caesarea, 254   Eusebius, Caesarea, 3:39.

ROMANS 11:19
AV   The branches were broken off
HF RP CR   omits "The"
Tyndale Great Geneva Bishops   Steph. Beza Elz.
D*   88 216 241 385 440 547 630 823 917 1149 1311 1319 1518 1610 2495 many others.
Theodoret, Cyrus, 466   Antiochus, Ptolemais, 614   Theophylact, Bulgaria, 1077.

ROMANS 14:6
AV   He that eateth, eateth to the Lord
HF RP CR   And he...
Tyndale Great Geneva Bishops   Steph. Beza Elz.
P46   241 623 others.
Clement, Alexandria, 215.

ROMANS 14:23
AV [CR]   The chapter ends at 14 :23
HF RP   The chapter ends at 14:26, with 16:25-27 being placed here
Tyndale Great Geneva Bishops   Steph. Beza Elz.
Aleph B C D D-abs G 048   81 256 263 296 365 429 436 623 630 1319 1739 1837 1852 1962 2127
Old Latin: ar d* e f r1 x z;
Sahadic Bohairic; Ethiopic.
Marcion, 130   Clement, Alexandria, 215   Origen, Alexandria, Caesarea, Latin and Greek, 254 Ambrosiaster, Latin, 384.

ROMANS 15:8
AV   Now I say that Jesus Christ was a minister
HF RP   ...Christ Jesus...

CR   ...Christ...
Tyndale Great Geneva Bishops   Steph. Beza Elz.
D E F G 104 216 241 257 296 440 462 1108 1311 1611.
Old Latin d e f g; Vulgate: harl; Syriac: Peshitta Harclean.

ROMANS 16:24, 25-27

AV   place the doxology after 16:24
HF RP   places the doxology after 14:23
CR   places the doxology after 16:23 (omitting 16:24)

Support for the inclusion of 16:24:

Tyndale Great Geneva Bishps   Steph. Beza Elz. HF.
D E F (G) L Psi The vast majority of cursive mss. including 88 181 326 330 451 614 629 (630) 1241 1877 1881 1984 1985 2492 2495.
Old Latin: ar d dem (e) (f) (g) gig (x); Vulgate: Clementine tol harl demid; Syriac: Harclean; (Gothic).
Chrysostom, Constantinople, 407   Euthalius, Sulci, 458   Theodoret, Cyrus, 466.

Support for the doxology being placed at the end of Romans:

P61 Aleph B C D D-abs 5 81 88 256 263 296 365 436 623 630 1319 1739 1838 1962 2127 2464 others.
Old Latin: a ar b d e f gig x 2; Vulgate: am fuld demid harl tol others; Syriac: Peshitta; Coptic: Sahadic Bohairic; Ethiopic.
Clement, Alexandria, 215   Origen, Alexandria, Caesarea, Greek and Latin, 254
Ambrosiaster, Latin, 354.
Thus there is strong support for both the inclusion of 16:24, and the doxology being placed at the end of the Epistle. How could it be anywhere else? The standard printed editions do not, however, clarify the question as to how many Greek mss actually combine both of these factors. The Latin mss do! Origen, in his commentary on the Epistle claimed that confusion in the Greek mss can be traced to the influential heretic, Marcion, who removed chapters 15 and 16 from his edition of Romans. The God-given sequence was retained in the Latin West.

1 CORINTHIANS 1:29

AV   That no flesh should glory in his presence
HF RP CR   ...glory before God
Tyndale Great Geneva Bishops   Steph. Beza Elz. ,
(Aleph-2nd cor) C* Psi 88 330 623 629 1241 many others.
Old Latin: f; Vulgate; Syriac: Peshitta Harclean; Armenian.
Marcion, 130   Origen, Alexandria, Caesarea, 254   Ambrosiaster, Latin, 384
Ambrose, Milan, Latin, 397 "Dialogue against the Marclonites," (no date)
Severian, Syria, 408   Theodoret, Cyrus, 466.

1 CORINTHIANS 6:5
AV   ...is not a wise man...
HF RP CR   ...not one wise...
Geneva Bishops   Steph. Beza Elz.
P11 D E F G   6 69 104 365 462 630 1739 1881 1926 many others
Old Latin? Vulgate?
Athanasius, Alexandria, 373.

1 CORINTHIANS 6:10
AV CR   Nor thieves, nor covetous
HF RP   Nor covetous, nor thieves
Tyndale Great Geneva Bishops   Steph. Beza Elz.
(P46) Aleph A B C D* E P   5 35 38 51 69 177 206 218 221 241 255 256 263 330 385 429 467 623 635 1319 1610 1738 1758 1838 2127 2298 many others.
Von Soden indicates: Most Egyptian mss, I a1 (88 181 915 917 1836 1898 1912).
Old Latin: d e f; Vulgate; Coptic: Bohairic; Armenian; Ethiopic.
Irenaeus, Lyons, Latin, 178   Clement, Alexandria, 215   Origen, Alexandria,Caesarea, Latin, 254
Cyprian, Carthage, Latin, 258   Methodius, 312   Julian?, Italy, Latin, 454

1 CORINTHIANS 7:34
AV   There is a difference *also*
HF RP   There is a difference also
CR   And there is a difference also
Tyndale Great Bishops   Steph. Beza Elz.
The Greek text of the KJV omits "kai" (translated: "and", "also") both before and after "there is a difference". The vast majority of mss. omit the first "kai"; the second is omitted in:
D* E 203 506 others.
Lectionary majority.
Vulgate: ful demid; Syriac: Peshitta; Coptic: Bohairic; Armenian.
Tertullian, N. Africa, Latin, 220   Athanasius, Alexandria, 373   Ambrosiaster, Latin, 384
Ambrose, Milan, Latin, 397   Jerome, Latin, 420 Augustine, Hippo, Latin, 430.
The resultant translation is practically the same.

1 CORINTHIANS 7:39
AV   but if her husband be dead
HF RP CR   ...*her* husband...
Tyndale Great Geneva Bishops   Steph. Beza Elz.
D E F G L I   5 33 88 104 206 241 257 296 323 330 462 467 623 794 913 1610 1739 1758 1835 1867 2004 many others.
Old Latin; Vulgate; Syriac: Peshitta Harclean Coptic: Bohairic; Armenian; Ethiopic.
Tertullian, N. Africa, Latin, 220 Origen, Alexandria, C.aesarea, 254
Ambrosiaster, Latin, 384   Ambrose, Milan, Latin, 397   Chrysostom, Constantinople, 407
Augustine, Hippo, Latin, 430   John, Damascus, 749   Theophylact, Bulgaria , 1077.

1 CORINTHIANS 10:30
AV   For if I by grace be a partaker
HF RP CR omits "For"
Tyndale Great Geneva Bishops   Steph. Beza Elz.
P46 242 others.
Theodoret, Cyrus, 466 Oecumenius, Thrace, VI.

1 CORINTHIANS 12:2
AV   Ye know that ye were Gentiles
HF CR   ...that when ye were...
Tyndale Great Geneva Bishops   Steph. Beza Elz.
F G K M-mg 1 2 38 88 177 216 319 330 337 629 635 639 642 823 1827 1836 1867 1898 2093 2138 2298 many others.
Old Latin: a b d e; Vulgate: early mss, D-Latin; Syriac: Peshitta; Coptic: Bohairic; Armenian?
Ambrosiaster, Latin, 384   Pelagius, Latin, 412.

1 CORINTHIANS 15:39
AV   one *kind of* flesh of men
HF CR   omits "flesh"
Tyndale Great Geneva Bishops   Steph. Beza Elz.
Many cursives.
Syriac: Peshitta; Coptic: Bohairic; Armenian?
"Dialogue Against Marcionites"

2 CORINTHIANS 1:6,7
There are four component parts in this passage which may be set out thusly:

AV   consolation and salvation
which is effectual in the enduring of the same sufferings which we also
        suffer.
 or whether we be comforted
 it is for your consolation and salvation
        and our hope of you is steadfast, knowing
HF RP   consolation and salvation
        which is effectual in the enduring of the same suffering which we also
        suffer.
        and our hope of you is steadfast
        or whether we be comforted
        it is for your consolation and salvation
        knowing
CR   consolation and salvation
        whether we be comforted
        it is for your consolation ("salvation" is omitted)
        Which is effectual in the enduring of the same suffering which we also suffer
        and our hope of you is steadfast

knowing

The KJV sequence is supported by Tyndale (Great) Geneva Bishops Steph. Elz. though no ms evidence is cited in the manuals. However, the KJV is a composite of those elements in the sequence which do have the best support. Namely:

"And our hope of you is steadfast" seems clearly to introduce the conclusion and is supported by the CR.   The HF RP agrees with the KJV except it transposes this phrase into the first half of the passage.

Studying the passage in its context convinces us that the KJV sequence is right. The Reformation editors and translators certainly thought so.

2 CORINTHIANS 1:11
AV CR   thanks may be given by many on our behalf

HF RP   ...on your behalf

Tyndale Great Geneva Bishops   Steph. Beza Elz.

P46-c Aleph A C D G M Psi 0121a 0243   33 38 81 104 181 206 218 241 256 263 296 326 330 429 436 451 489 913 919 927 999 1319 1739 1758 1837 ,1873 1877 1881 1962 1984 1985 2127 2143 2492 2495 many others.

Von Soden indicates: Most Egyptian mas, I c1 (1108 1245 1611 2005).

Old Latin: ar d dem e f g r1 x z; Vulgate: incuding am ful others; Syriac: Peshitta Harc1ean; Coptic: Sahadic Bohairic; Gothic; Armenian.

Ambrosiaster, Latin, 384   Chrysostom, Constantinople, 407   Euthalius, Sulci, 458 Theodoret, Cyrus, 466.

2 CORINTHIANS 2:17
AV CR   For we are not as many

HF RP   ...as others

Tyndale Great Geneva Bishops   Steph. Beza Elz.

P46 Aleph A B C K P Psi 0243   1 5 69 88 203 206? 216 221 226 241 242 256 257 263 330 385 436 440 489 506 547 623 639 917 1319 1518 1610 1739 1835 1837 1867 1873 1912 2004 2127 2143 2298 many others.

Von Soden indicates: Most Egyptian mss.

Old Latin: including d e f (g); Vulgate; Coptic: Sahadic Bohairic; Ethiopic.

Irenaeus, Lyons, Latin, 178   Basil, Cappodocia, 379   Ambrosiaster, Latin, 304 Didymus, Alexandria, 398   Euthalius, Sulci, 458   John, Damascus, 749.

2 CORINTHIANS 2:17
AV   *of* your ready mind

HF RP CR ...our...

Tyndale Great Geneva Bishops   Steph. Beza Elz.

(D) F (E) others.

Old Latin: d.

The collection which Paul was gathering was not to be a demonstration of *his* "ready mind" but of those from whom he was gathering it, the Corinthians.

2 CORINTHIANS 8:24
AV   Wherefore shew ye to them, and before the churches
HF RP CR   omits "and"
Geneva   Steph. Elz.
263 (Tischendorf's 132 134) others.
This and the previous verse show that the grace of giving was to be demonstrated to two parties, the messengers and the churches.

2 CORINTHIANS 11:31
AV RP   The God and Father of our Lord Jesus Christ
HF CR   omits "Christ"
Tyndale Great Geneva Bishops   Steph. Beza Elz.
C D E M P 0121   1 2 5 6 38 69 181 206 216 219 241 263 296 323 326 429 436 440 462 489 547 623 642 823 919 1518 1610 1758 1827 1836 1837 1845 1867 1891 many others.
Old Latin: d e f; Vulgate: including ful demid others, F-Latin;
Syriac: Peshitta; Coptic: Bohairic; Armenian; Ethiopic.
Ambrosiaster, Latin, 384   Augustine, Hippo, Latin, 430   Euthalius, Sulci, 458
Theodoret, Cyrus, 466,   other fathers.

EPHESIANS 1:10
AV   things in Christ, both which are in heaven...earth
HF RP CR   omits "both"
Tyndale Great Geneva Bishops   Steph. Beza Elz.
Aleph-c   69 323 462 945 1831 cursives.
Victorinus, Rome, Latin, 362   Ambrose, Milan, Latin, 397   Epiphanius, Cyprus, 403
Cyril, Alexandria, 444.

EPHESIANS 1:18
AV   The eyes of your understanding being enlightened
HF RP CR   ... eyes of your heart...
Tyndale Great Geneva Bishops   Steph. Beza Elz.
Cursives.
Cyril, Jerusalem, 386   Theodoret, Cyrus, 466   Oecumenius, Thrace, VI.
The "eyes of the heart" occurs nowhere else in the Bible. The phrase doesn't set well with Scriptural truth, and probably comes from the heathen philosophers. Plato spoke about the "eyes of the soul"; and Ovid, speaking of Pythagoras said: "with his mind he approached the gods, though far removed in heaven, and what nature denied to human sight, he drew forth with the eyes his heart (*Vincents Word Studies*, p. 848).

EPHESIANS 3:9
AV   what *is* the fellowship of the mystery
HF RP CR   ...administration...
Tyndale Great Geneva Bishops   Steph. Beza Elz.
31-mg 69-mg others.
"fellowship" fits the context better than "administration". See verse 6. Keep in mind that the

non-citing of evidence on these passages by von Soden and others does not, mean that it is lacking but rather that there is a lack of interest on their part. Their chief concern is the gathering of material which shows some affinity with codices Aleph and B for the reconstruction of the NT Text. The last thing on their minds is the defence of the King James Bible. Thus, until someone is able to gather evidence for these passages from all of the extant items, we will have to be content with these few bits of information. This wait will not affect our confidence in God's preservation of the Scriptures at every point as we have it in the AV.

EPHESIANS 4:6
AV   and through all, and in you all
HF RP   ...and in us all
CR   ...and in all
Tyndale Great Geneva Bishops   Steph. Beza Elz.
489 other cursives.
Chrysostom, Constantinople, 407   Theodoret, Cyrus, 466   Oecumenius, Thrace, VI
Theophylact, Bulgaria, 1077.

EPHESIANS 4:32
AV CR   even as God for Christ's sake hath forgiven you
HF RP   ...hath forgiven us
Tyndale Great Geneva Bishops   Steph. Beza Elz.
P46 Aleph A F G P   6 35 38 69 81 177 218 221 326 330 365 383 547 614 629 1149 1245 1319 1827 1898 2127 2298 2492 many others.
Von Soden indicates: Most Egyptian mss.
Old Latin: ar c d dem e f g mon t x; Vulgate: Clementine ful demid tol others;
Coptic: Sahadic Bohairic; Gothic Ethiopic.
Clement, Alexandria, 215   Tertullian, N. Africa, Latin, 220
Origen, Alexandria, Caesarea, Latin, 254   Victorinus, Rome, Latin, 362
Ambrosiaster, Latin, 384   Chrysostom, Constantinople, 407 Pelagius, Latin, 412
Jerome, Latin, 420   Euthalius, Sulci, 458 Oecumenius, Thrace, VI.

PHILIPPIANS 3:3
AV   Which worship God in the spirit
HF RP CR   Which worship in the spirit of God
Tyndale Great Geneva Bishops   Steph. Beza Elz.
Aleph-2nd cor C D* P Psi   88 365 436 1175 1319 1837 1962 (1984) 2127 many others.
Old Latin: ar c d dem div e f m x 61; Vulgate: including D-Latin F-Latin;
Syriac: Peshitta Harclean; Gothic, Armenian, Ethiopic.
Origen, Alexandria, Caesarea, Greek and Latin, 254   Victorinus, Rome, Latin, 362
Ambrosiaster, Latin, 384   Ambrose, Milan, 397, citation of Latin mss
Chrysostom, Constantinople, 407   Theodore, Mopsuestia, Latin, 428
Augustine, Hippo, 430, citation of Greek and Latin mss   Theodoret, Cyrus, 466
"Speculum", Pseudo-Auqustine , Latin, V.
A Greek variant reads with the KJV.

PHILIPPIANS 3:8
AV CR   Yea doubtless, and I count all things *but* loss
HF RP   Yea indeed...
Tyndale Great Geneva Bishops   Steph. Beza Elz.
P46 Aleph A P   5 33 38 51 69 88 203 216 218 256 257 263 296 330 436 440 462 467 489 506
623 642 927 1319 1827 1831 1845? 1912 2005 2127 many others.
Von Soden indicates: Most Egyptian mss.
Basil, Cappodocia, 379   Didymus, Alexandria, 398   Cyril, Alexandria, 444
Euthalius, Sulci, 458   Theodoret, Cyrus, 466   John, Damascus, 749
Theophylact, Bulgaria, 1077.

PHILIPPIANS 4:3
AV   And I intreat thee also
HF RP CR   Yes I intreat...
        Steph. Beza Elz.
103 other cursives.
Ambrosiaster, Latin, 384.

1 THESSALONIANS 2:2
AV   But even after that we had suffered before
HF RP CR   omits "even"
(Tyndale Great Geneva Bishops ?)   Steph. Beza, Elz.
Many cursives.
Old Latin: d e; Vulgate: D-Latin.

1 THESSALONIANS 4:8
AV   who hath also given unto us his holy Spirit
HF RP CR   unto you...
Tyndale Great Geneva Bishops   Steph. Beza Elz.
A 6 177 337 365 547 917 1518 1611 1739 1881 1912 2005 many others.
Old Latin: a f m t; Vulgate: Clementine demid harl; Syriac: Harclean; Ethiopic.
Ambrosiaster, Latin, 384   Ambrose, Milan, Latin, 397   Didymus, Alexandria, 398
Chrysostom, Constantinople, 407   "Speculum", Pseudo-Augustine, Latin, V
Theodoret, Cyrus; 466   Theophylact, Bulgaria, 1077.

1 THESSALONIANS 4:13
AV   But I would not have you to be ignorant
HF RP CR   But we would not...
Tyndale Great Geneva Bishops   Steph. Beza Elz.,
1 104 203 506 614 630 642 794 1908 2138 apparently many others
Vulgate: early mss; Syriac: Peshitta Harclean; Coptic; (Armenian?).
Alexandria, Caesarea, 254   Eusebius,Caesarea, 339   Basil, Caesarea, 379
Chrysostom, Constantinople, 407   Augustine-pt., Hippo, Latin, 430   Theodoret, Cyrus, 466.

2 THESSALONIANS 3:6

AV the tradition which he received of us
HF RP CR   ...they...
Great Geneva Bishops Steph. Beza Elz.
5 76 218 234 1962 others
Syriac: Peshitta.
Basil, Cappadoeia, 379. Oecumenius, Thraee, VI.

1 TIMOTHY 6:12

AV whereunto thou art also called
HF RP CR   omits "also"
Great Geneva Bishops Steph. Beza Elz
2 69 81 177 226 296 440 462 467 642 919 1311 1319 1835 1872 1891 apparently many others.
Syriac: Harclean-with asterisk.
Ambrosiaster, Latin, 384 Oecumenius, Thrace, VI Theophylact, Bulgaria, 1077.

2 TIMOTHY 2:19

AV Let everyone that nameth the name of Christ
HF RP CR   ...name of the Lord
Tyndale Great Geneva Bishops Steph. Beza Elz.
1518 other cursives ,
The second half of the verse links the title "Christ" to God, thus declaring His deity. This is weakened and made less distinct by substituting "Lord".

TITUS 2:8

AV having no evil thing to say of you
HF RP CR   ...of us
Tyndale Great Geneva Bishops Steph. Beza Elz.
A 5 many others.
Old Latin: a; Vulgate: early mss; Coptic: Bohairic,
Ephraem, Syria, 373 Theodoret, Cyrus, 466.

PHILEMON 6

AV every good thing which is in you in Christ Jesus
HF RP CR   ...in us...
Tyndale Great Geneva Bishops Steph. Beza Elz.
P61 Aleph C F G P 5 33 35 69 104 177 226 256 263 296 323 337 365 436 441 462 467 489 618 642 823 999 1739 1827 1835 1837 1867 1877* 1881 1908 1984-c (apparently) 2004 2492 many others.
Von Soden indicates: I c1 (1245 1518 1611 2005 2138).
Old Latin: ar div f g x 61; Vulgate: including Clementine; Syriac: Peshitta Harclean;
Coptic: Sahadic Bohairic; Armenian.
Chrysostom, Constantinople" 407 Jerome, Latin, 420 Primasius, Adrumentum, Latin, 552
Cassiodorus, Latin, 580 Oecumenius, Thrace, VI Theophylact, Bulgaria, 1077.

HEBREWS 3:1
AV   the Apostle and High Priest of our profession, Christ Jesus
HF RP   ...Jesus Christ
CR   ...Jesus
Tyndale Great Geneva Bishops   Steph. Beza Elz.
Cursives.
The titles which precede show that the emphasis is upon Christ Jesus.

HEBREWS 8:11
AV   And they shall not teach every man his neighbour
HF RP CR   ...his fellow citizen
Tyndale Great Geneva Bishops   Staph. Beza Elz.,
C (according to von Soden) P 35 38 81 104 206 218 226 257 326 365 429 436 483 547 629 630
642 1149 1311 1518 1758 1867 1912 1985 2464 many others.
Old Latin: ar c dem div f z 61; Vulgate; Syriac: Harclean-mg; Ethiopic.
Chrysostom, Constantinople, 401 Cyril, Alexandria, 444 Euthalius, Sulci, 458
Theophylact, Bulgaria, 1077.

HEBREWS 9:38
AV   so Christ was once offered
HF RP CR so Christ also was...
Tyndale Great Geneva Bishops   Steph. Elz.
216 others.
Normally the inclusion of an "also" would indicate that someone else has performed the same act. Here the word detracts from the once and for all, and totally unprecedented fact of our Saviour's death.

HEBREWS 11:13
AV   having seen them afar off, and were persuaded of *them*
HF RP CR   omits "and were persuaded of them"
Tyndale Great Geneva Bishops   Steph. Beza Elz.
1518 other cursives.

HEBREWS 12:20
AV   it shall be stoned, or thrust through with a dart
HF RP CR   omits "or thrust through with a dart"
Tyndale Great Geneva Bishops   Steph. Beza Elz.
2 440 823 other cursives.
Exodus 19:13, to which this passage refers, reads: "he shall surely be stoned, or shot through".

JAMES 2:5
AV   chosen the poor of this world
HF CR   omits "this"
Tyndale Great Geneva Bishops   Steph. Beza Elz.

61 1831 others.
Ethiopic.
Oecumenius, Thrace, VI.
A Greek variant. reads with the KJV; also the NASV translates the CR as the KJV. Von Soden
seems to indicate that "this" is in many of the Koine (Byzantine) mss.

JAMES 4:2
AV   yet ye have not, because ye ask not
HF RP CR omits "yet"
(Tyndale Great Geneva Bishops: may have left the word untranslated)   Steph. Beza Elz.
36 945 1241 1739 2298 others.
A well attested Greek variant could translate as the KJV.

JAMES 4:12
AV RP   who art thou that judgest another
HF CR   but who art thou...
Tyndale Great Geneva Bishops   Steph. Beza Elz.
216 429 462 614 630 1505 2495 many others.
Von Soden indicates: I c1 (1108 1245 1518 1611 2138).
Syriac: Harclean with asterisk; Coptic: Sahadic Bohairic-pt; Armenian.
Oecumenius, Thrace, VI.

JAMES 4:13
AV CR Today or tomorrow
HF RP Today and tomorrow
Geneva Beza   Elz.
P74 Aleph B Psi   5 33 81 181 255 322 323 429 623 927 945 1241 1739 2298 many others.
Von Soden indicates: Most Egyptian mss.
Old Latin; Vulgate; Syrialc: Peshitta; Coptic: Sahadic Bohairic; Ethiopic.
Jerome, Latin, 420 Hesychtius, Jerusalem, 450.

JAMES 5:9
AV   brethren, lest ye be condemned
HF RP CR   ...judged
Tyndale Great Geneva Bishops   Steph. Beza Elz.
209* other cursives.
Oecumenius , Thrace, VI.
There is only a marginal difference in the translation. The HF RP CR has the non-intensified
form of the word which is usually translated "judged". Though on four occasions it is translated
"condemned".

JAMES 5:11
AV CR that the Lord is very pitiful
HF RP that he...
Tyndale Great Geneva   Steph. Beza Elz.

Aleph A (B) P Psi 5 33 81 101 255 429 614 623 630 927 945 1739 1827 2298 2495 others.
Von Soden indicates: I c1 (1108 1245 1611 1852 2138).
Old Latin: ff1; Vulgate; Syriac.

1 PETER 1:12
AV   but unto us they did minister these things
HF RP CR   ...you...
Tyndale Great Geneva Bishops   Steph. Beza Elz.
K 945 1241 many others.
Vulgate: early mss; Syriac: (Peshitta); Coptic: Bohairic; Armenian.
Jerome, Latin, 420 Cyril, Alexandria, 444   Theophylact, Bulgaria, 1077
Oecumenius, Thrace, VI.

1 PETER 2:6
AV   Wherefore also it is contained in the sciptures
HF RP CR   omits "also"
          Steph. Beza Elz.
Cursives.
Oecumenius, Thrace, VI.

1 PETER 2:21
AV   leaving us an exaxple
HF RP CR   ...you...
Tyndale Great Geneva Bishops   Steph. Beza.
2 4 90 94 102 205 242 336 429 614 629 1243 1505 2412 2495 others.
Old Latin: r; Syriac: Peshitta; Coptic: Bohairic.
Augustine, Hippo, Latin, 430   John, Damascus, 749.

1 PETER 3:18
AV   that he might bring us to God
HF RP CR   ...you...
Tyndale Great Geneva Bishops   Steph. Beza Elz.
Aleph-2nd cor A C K L 056 0142 5 33 81 88 104 218 241 242 256 337 436 460 462 483 489
547 614 623 629 630 642 808 915 919 920 927 945 1175 1311 1319 1518 1739 1835 1837 1830
1873 1881 1891 2127 2412 many others.
Von Soden indicates: I a1 Andreas mss (36 307 453 610), I b2 (323 935 2298), I c2 (255 378
385 913 1765 2147).
Lectionary majority.
Old Latin: ar c dem div pt; Vulgate; Syriac: Harclean-mg; Coptic: Sahadic Bohairic.
Clement, Alexandria, 214 Cyprian, Carthage, Latin, 259   Peter, Alexandria, 311
Didymus, Alexandria, 444 Oecumenius, Thrace, VI Theophylact, Bulgaria, 1077.

1 PETER 3:20
AV   when once the long-suffering of God waited
HF RP CR omits "once"

Great Geneva Bishops   Steph. Beza Elz.,
K 69 (apparently) 467 917 1319 1874 others.
Origen, Alexandria, Caesarea, 254   Oecumenius, Thrace, VI.

1 PETER 5:8
AV   Be sober, be vigilant; because your adversary
HF RP CR   omits "because"
Tyndale Great Geneva Bishops   Steph. Beza Elz.
P72 Aleph-2nd cor L Psi 049-c   33 69 323 429 614 623 630 945 1175 1241 1505 1739 1758 1831 1838 1874 2495 many others.
Von Soden indicates: I b2 (935 2298), I c1 (1108 1245 1518 1611 1852 2138), I c2 (378 383 305 2147).
Old Latin; Vulgate; Syriac: Peshitta Harclean; Coptic; Armenian; Ethiopic.
Origen, Alexandria, Caesarea, 254   Cyprian, Carthage, Latin, 258
Cassidorus, Latin, 580   Antiochus, Ptolemais , 614   Oecumenius, Thrace, VI.

1 PETER 5:10
AV   who hath called us unto his eternal glory
HF RP CR   ...you...
Great Geneva Bishops   Steph. Elz.
K 0206   489 1518 1873 1881 many others.
Old Latin: q t; Vulgate: including am ful; Syriac: Peshitta; Coptic: early Bohairic mss.
Didymus, Alexandria, 398   Oecumenius , Thrace, VI.

2 PETER 1:4
AV   exceeding great and precious promises
HF RP CR exceeding precious and great promises
Geneva   Steph. Beza Elz.
Cursives.
A well attested Greek variant would translate as the KJV, supported by: (A) C P Psi   1 5 33 69 81 85 218 467 623 915 945 1241 1739 1845 1873.
Old Latin-pt; Vulgate.
Didymus, 370.
Also, von Soden indicates: I al Andreas mss. (36 307 453 610), I b2 (35 491 823 935 1149 1739 1872 2298).

2 PETER 2:2
AV   And many shall follow their pernicious ways
HF RP CR   ...sensual...
Tyndale Great Geneva Bishops   Steph. Beza Elz.
Cursives.
Coptic.
Oecumenius, Thrace, VI.
The KJV reading gives the all-inclusive term and fits the context better. The more limited issue of sensuality is not dealt with until later in the chapter.

2 PETER 3:2
AV   and of the commandments of us the apostles
HF RP CR   ...of your apostles
Tyndale Great Geneva Bishops   Steph. Beza Elz.
Psi   5 36 88 241 337 489 614 623 630 808 915 927 1505 1827 1835 1837 1852 1873 2298 2464 2495 others.
Von Soden indicates: I b1 (206 429 522 1758 1831), I c1 (1245 1611 1852 2138), I c2 (255 383 385 614 1765 2147).
Oecumenius, Thrace, VI.

1 John 1:4
AV   that your joy may be full
HF RP CR ...our...
Great Geneva Bishops   Beza Elz.
A -2nd cor. (apparently) K P 056 0142   5 33 81 88 104 177 206 218 241 323 330 337 429 451 460 467 547 614 623 629 630 642 808 915 945 1505 1525 1739 1758 1831 1835 1873 1877 1881 2143 2412 2495 many others.
Von Soden indicates: I a1 Andreas mss (36 307 453 610), I b2 (935 1739 2298), I c1 (1245 1518 1611 1852 2138), I c2 (255 378 385 1765).
Lectionaries: 598 1021.
Old Latin: ar c dem div (t); Vulgate: including Clementine demid; Syriac: Harclean Palestinian; Coptic: Bohairic; Armenian; Ethiopic.
Augustine, Hippo, Latin, 430 Oecumenius, Thrace, VI   Bede, England, Latin, 735
Theophylact, Bulgaria, 1077.
A Greek variant supports the usage of the second person pronoun.

1 JOHN 3:1
AV CR   the world knoweth us not
HF RP   ... you...
Bishops   Steph. Beza Elz.
P74 Aleph-2nd cor A B C Psi   5 33 88 206 218 241 323 429 467 547 614 623 630 642 808 915 945 1505 1739 1831? 1838 1845 2495 many others.
Von Soden indicates: Most Egyptian mss, I a1 Andreas mss, (36 307 453 610), I b2 (935 2298), I c1 (1245 1518 1611 1852 2138), I c2 (378 383 385 1765 2147).
Old Latin-pt; Vulgate; Syriac: Peshitta Harclean; Coptic: Sahadic Bohairic; Armenian; Ethiopic.
Augustine, Hippo, Latin, 430   Bede, England, Latin, 735.

1 JOHN 3:23
AV CR   as he gave us commandment
HF RP   omits "us"
Bishops Steph. Beza Elz.
Aleph A B C Psi 0245   5 33 69 81 206 255 323 378 429 467 614 623 630 1241 1311 1611 1739 1758 1831 1837 1838 2138 2495 many others.
Von Soden indicates: Most Egyptian mss, I a1 Andreas mss, (36 307 453 610), I b2 (935 2298).

Old Latin; Vulgate; Syriac; Coptic.
Lucifer, Cagliari, Latin, 370   Augustine, Hippo, Latin, 430   Oecumenius,Thrace, VI
Theophylact, Bulgaria, 1077.
A well attested Greek variant reads with the KJV.

1 JOHN 4:2
AV CR   Hereby know ye the Spirit of God
HF RP   ...he knows...
Tyndale Great Geneva Bishops   Steph. Beza Elz.
Aleph-2nd cor A B C L Psi   1 5 33 337 378 .436 460 467 614 623 913 945 1311 1739 1829 1838
1852 1874 1881 1891 2298 many others.
Von Soden indicates: Most Egyptian mss, I a1 Andreas mss, (36 307 453 610).
Syriac: Harclean; Coptic: Sahadic Bohairic; Ethiopic.
Irenaeus, Lyons, Latin, 178   Lucifer, Cagliari, Latin, 370.

1 JOHN 5:7, 8

See the special study in Chapter 6

3 JOHN 11
AV   but he that doeth evil hath not seen God
HF RP CR omits "but"
Tyndale Great Geneva Bishops   Steph. Beza Elz.
L 69 242 913 1852 many others.
Vulgate: eary mss; Coptic: Bohairic; Armenian; Ethiopic.
Didymus, Alexandria, 398   Oecumenius, Thrace, VI   John, Damascus, 749
Theophylact, Bulgaria, 1077.

See Chapter 4.

REVELATION 1:4
AV   Grace be unto youl, and peace, from him which is
HF RP   ...from God which is
Tyndale Great Geneva Bishops   Steph. Beza Elz.
61-mg 429 617 1934.
About 8 of Hoskier's cursives.
The well-attested CR reading translates as the KJV

REVELATION 1:8
AV   saith the Lord
HF RP CR saith the Lord God
Tyndale Great Geneva Bishops   Steph. Beza Elz.
429 1894.
About 5 of Hoskier's cursives.
Armenian: an early ms.

WHEN THE KJV DEPARTS FROM THE MAJORITY TEXT

REVELATION 1:9
AV   I John, who also am your brother
HF RP CR omits "who also am"
Geneva   Steph. Beza Elz.
About 7 of Hoskier's cursives.
Ethiopic.

REVELATION 1:11
AV   I am Alpha and Omega, the first and the last
HF RP CR   omits the entire phrase
Tyndale Great (Geneva) Bishops Steph. Beza Elz.
P 1 42 61* 104 336 628 2019 2020 2023 2057, most of the Andreas mss.
About 57 of Hoskier's cursives. Von Soden indicates: I a (181 296 432 598 743 2026 2031 2033 2054 2055 2056 2060 2064 2067 2068 2069), I b2 (104 459 922).
Andreas, Cappadocia, 614.
Many of the above witnesses have minor variations. This serves to demonstrate that they are not copies of each other but represent individual and long lines of transmission.

REVELATION 1:11
AV   and sent *it* unto the seven churches which are in Asia
HF RP CR   omits "which are in Asia"
Tyndale Great Geneva Bishops Steph. Beza Elz.
296 1894 2066.
About 10 of Hoskier's cursives.
Vulgate: Clementine; Coptic: Bohairic; Armenian; Arabic.
Bede, England, Latin, 735.

REVELATION 1:17
AV   saying unto me, Fear not
HF RP CR omits "unto me"
Tyndale Great Geneva Bishops Steph. Beza Elz.
About 18 of Hoskier's cursives. Von Soden indicates: I a5 (2028 2029 2033 2054 2068 2069).
Armenian: 3 early mss; Ethiopic.

REVELATION 1:19
AV   Write the things which thou hast seen
HF RP CR Write therefore the...
Geneva Steph. Beza Elz.
1 498 620 628 1894 2020 2023 2050 2066 others, part of tha Andreas mss.
About 30 of Hosldar's cursives. Von Soden indicates: I a5 (2054 2068 2069).
Coptic: Bohairic; Armenian: 3 early mss.
Arethas, Cappodocia, 914.

REVELATION 2:1
AV   Unto the angel of the church of Ephesus write

HF RP CR   ...the church in Ephesus...
Tyndale Great Geneva Bishops   Steph. Beza Elz.
296 1894.
About 11 of Hoskier's cursives.
Old Latin: (gig); Syriac: (Peshitta); Coptic: (Bohairic).

REVELATION 2:3
AV   and hast patience, and for my name' s sake hast laboured
HF RP CR   omits second "and"
Tyndale Great Geneva Bishops   Steph.BezaElz.
About 11 of Hoskier's cursives.
Each of the four "ands" are required in this verse.

REVELATION 2:3
AV   hast laboured, and hast not fainted
HF RP CR   ...and hast not grown weary
Tyndale Great Geneva Bishops   Steph. Beza Elz.
296 2066.
Hoskier seems to indicate about, 55 cursives.

REVELATION 2:13
AV CR   and hast not denied my faith, even in those days
HF RP   omits "even"
Tyndale Great Geneva Bishops   Steph. Beza Elz.
A C 1854 1957 2050 2053 2329 2344.
About 14 of Hoskier's cursives.
Old Latin: a ar c div gig haf z (apparently) 61; Vulgate; Syriac: Peshitta; Coptic: Sahadic Bohairic; Ethiopic.
Bede, England, Latin, 735   Haymo, Halberstadt, Latin, 841.

REVELATION 2:15
AV   the doctrine of the Nicolaitanes, which thing I hate
HF RP CR   "which thing I hate" is changed to "in the same way"
Tyndale Great Geneva Bishops   Stepha Beza Elz.
1 61-mg 2037.
About 22 of Hoskier's cursives, including 11 which have a variant that translates as the KJV.
Armenian.
Andreas, Cappadocia, 614.
The HF RP CR reading does not make good sense. This may have been an attempt of early scribes to link Nicolaitanism with the sins of 2:14 in order to escape the suspicion that a hierarchal form of church government was in view.
Many other mss. have the words "which I hate", but in conjunction with "in the same way".

REVELATION 2:19
AV   I know thy works, and charity, and service , and faith

HF RP CR ...and faith and service
Tyndale Great Geneva Bishops   Steph. Beza Elz.
1.
About 15 of Hoskier's cursives. Von Soden indicates: I a2 (296 1894 2066).

REVELATION 2:19
AV   and thy works; and the last *to be* more than
HF RP CR   omits the second "and"
Geneva Steph. Beza Elz.
1 218.
About 14 of Hoskier's cursives. Von Soden indicate: I a2 (296 1894 2066).

REVELATION 2:20
AV   I have a few things: against thee
HF RP CR omits "few things"
Tyndale Great Geneva Bishops   Steph. Beza Elz
1 296 1894 2066.
About 39 of Hoskier's cursives.
Vulgate: Clementine.
Haymo, Halberstadt, Latin, 841.

REVELATION 2:20
AV CR   that woman Jezebel
HF RP   thy wife Jezebel
Tyndale Great Geneva Bishops   Steph. Beza Elz.
Aleph C P 1 104 205 468* 620 2019 2020 2038 2040 2050 2057 2329, most of the Andreas mss.
About 58 of Hoskier's cursives. Von Soden indicates: Most Egyptian mss., I a (35 181 209 296 598 1894 2026 2028 2029 2031 2033 2053 2054 2056 2059 2060 2066 2068 2069 2081), I b(459 628 922 1778 2080).
Old Latin: gig; Vulgate; Coptic: Bohairic; Armenian: including 2 early mss; Ethiopic.
Tertullian, N. Africa, Latin, 220   Epiphanius, Cyprus, 403 "Quaestions", Latin
Andreas, Cappadocia 614 Haymo, Halberstadt, Latin, 841.

REVELATION 2:21
AV   And I gave her' space to repent, of her fornication and she repented not
HF RP CR   And I gave her space to repent and she did not wish to repent
of her fornication
Tyndale Great Geneva Bishops   Steph. Beza Elz.
1, part of the Andreas mss.
About 17 of Hoskier's cursives. Von Soden indicates: I a2 (296 1894 2066), I a5 (2028 2033 2054 20682069).

REVELATION 2:22
AV   except they repent of their deeds

HF RP CR   except they repent of her deeds
Tyndale Great Geneva Bishops   Steph. Beza Elz.
A   1 (35*) 61-mg 181 205 468 632 1854 2019 2023* 2036 2037 2038 2057 2065 2067 2073
2081 2329 2344, many of the Andreas mss.
About 61 of Hoskier's cursives. Von Soden indicates: I a (209 296 598 743 1876 1894 2014 2015
2026 2031 2043 2055 2056 2059 2066 2286).
Old Latin: ar c dem div haf t; Vulgate: Clementine demid harl-with asterisks;
Syriac: Philoxenian; Armenian: including 3 early mss.; Coptic: Bohairic; Ethiopic.
Cyprian, Carthage, Latin, 258   Ambrosiaster, Latin, 384 "Quaestions", Latin
Primasius, Adrumentum, Latin, 552   Andreas, Cappadocia, 614.

REVELATION 2:24
AV   and unto the rest in Thyatira
HF RP CR omits "and"
Tyndale Great Geneva Bishops   Steph. Beza Elz.
61-mg 1894.
About 20 of Hoskier's cursives,
Vulgate: Clementine har 1 tol.
"Quaestions", Latin   Haymo, Halberstadt, Latin, 841   Arethas, Cappadocia, 919.
A Greek variant would read with the KJV.

REVELATION 2:24
AV   as many as have not. this doctrine, and which have not
HF RP CR   omits "and"
Tyndale Great Bishops   Steph. Beza Elz.
2066.
About 7 of Hoskier's cursives.
Vulgate: Clementine.
"Quaestions", Latin.

REVELATION 3:2
AV   that are ready to die
HF RP   that are ready to be cast away
CR   that were ready to die
Tyndale Great Geneva Bishops   Steph. Beza Elz.
296 1894 2066.
About 7 of Hoskier's cursives.
Ethiopic.
Vigilius, Thapsus, Latin, 484.
Thus the AV has support from HF RP for "are ready", and from CR for "to die". Hoskier lists 6
main variants and numerous sub-variants for this passage.

REVELATION 3:4
AV   Thou hast
HF RP CR But thou hast

Tyndale (Great) Geneva Bishops   Steph. Beza Elz.
1 181 205 209 1778 1894 2026 2031 2045 2049 2056 2057 2059 2060 2081 2186 2286 2302, part of the Andreas mss.
Von Soden indicates: I a1 (598 2065), I a2 (1 2066), I a3 (35).
Armenian.
Apringius, Portugal, Latin, 551   Andreas, Cappadocia, 614.

REVELATION 3:4
AV   a few names even in Sardis
HF RP CR   omits "even"
Geneva   Steph. Beza Elz.
1 2059 2066 2001, part of the Andreas cursives.
About 22 of Hoskier's cucsives. Von Soden indicates: I a5 (2028 2033 2054 2068 2069).

REVELATION 3:7
AV   and no man shuttetlh; and shutteth, and no man openeth
HF RP   shall shut it except he who opens, and no man openeth
CR   shall shut, and shutteth, and no man openeth
Tyndale Great Geneva Bishops   Steph. Beza Elz.

Support for the three parts of the KJV reading.

1.   and no man shutteth
1 61-mg 205 314 632* 1611 1854 2016 2019 2023 2037 2038 2053 2067 many others.
Old Latin gig;   Vulgate   Coptic: (Bohairic);   Syriac: Philoxenian Harclean;
Armenian.
Hippolytus, Portus, 235   Tyconius, Latin, 380   Primasius, Adrumentum, Latin, 552

2.   and shutteth
C 61-mg 2016 others.
Old Latin: gig; Vulgate; Syriac: Philoxenian: Armenian.
Irenaeus, Lyons, Latin, 178   Origen, Alexandria, Caesarea, 254
Haymo,Halberstadt, Latin, 841.

3.   and no man openeth
A C P 61-mg. 205 1611 1854 2019 2037 2038 2053 2067 others.
Old Latin: gig; Vulgate; Syriac: Philoxenian Harclean.
Hippolytus, Portus, 235   Origen, Alexandria, Caesarea, 254 Tyconius, Latin, 380
Primss.eus, Adrumentum, Latin, 552   Andreas, Cappodocia, 614.
The HF apparatus lists 10 variants (with sub-variants in Hoskier). The well attested CR (except for the awkward future tense) reads nearly as the KJV. The HF RP is left hanging. The three parts of the KJV are well supported but it is difficult to derive from Hoskier or von Soden the amount of support for the entire reading.

REVELATION 3:8
AV   and no man can shut it
HF RP CR which no man...
Tyndale Great Geneva Bishops   Steph. Beza Elz.
1 61-mg 1611 2037 2067, part of the Andreas mss.
About 25 of Hoskier's cursives. Von Soden indicates: I a2 (296 1894 2066), I a5 (2028 2029 2033 2054 2068 2069).
Ethiopic.
Andreas, Cappadocia, 614.

REVELATION 3:11
AV   Behold, I come quickly
HF RP CR omits "Behold"
Tyndale Great Geneva Bishops   Steph. Beza Elz.
468* 1894 2014 2015 2019 2036, part of the Andreas mss.
About 18 of Hoskier's cursives. Von Soden indicates: I a4 (1876 2043).
Old Latin: a; Vulgate: Clementine ful demid harl; Armenian; Ethiopic.
Tyconius, Latin, 380   Pacianus, Barcelona, Latin, 392   Apringius, Portugal, Latin, 551
Bede, England, Latin, 735.

REVELATION 3:14
AV   And unto the angel of the church of the Laodiceans write
HF RP CR   ...of the church in Laodicea...
Geneva   Steph. Beza Elz.
About 7 of Hoskier's cursives.
Armenian: 2 early mss.
The first of the seven messages is to "the church of Ephesus", the last is the "the church of the Laodiceans". The other five are to "the church in...". This was the church "of the Laodiceans"; it belonged to them, Christ stood outside.

REVELATION 3:16
AV   neither cold nor hot
HF RP CR   ...hot nor cold
Tyndale Great Geneva Bishops   Steph. Beza Elz.
A P 205 209 296 (2050).
About 13 of Hoskier's cursives.
Old Latin: a; Vulgate; Syriac: Philoxenian; Coptic: Sahadic.
Victorinus, Pettau, Latin, 304   Apringius, Portugal, Latin, 551.

REVELATION 3:18
AV   and anoint
HF RP   that you may anoint
CR   to anoint...
Tyndale Great Geneva Bishops   Steph. Beza Elz.
P 1 35 94 110 469 517 598 1854 2023 2028 2029 2033 2054 2057 2059 2068 2069 2073 2074

2081 2186 2254 2286 (cited by Hoskier), most Andreas mss.
Syriac: Philoxenian.
The CR could translate as the KJV, as would also a number of the variants Hoskier cites.

REVELATION 4:3
AV   And he that sat was to look upon like a jasper
HF RP   omits "And he that sat was"
CR   And he that sat *was* to...
Tyndale Great Geneva Bishops   Steph. Beza Elz.
About 7 of Hoskier's cursives.
Except for the "was" which must be supplied in the translation, the CR is the
same as KJV. It is supported by Aleph A P 046 0169 and 26 of Hoskiers cursives.
Support for the general reading also comes from the Latin, Syriac, Coptic, Ethiopic, Armenian
and Origen, Tyconius, Andreas, Arethas.

REVELATION 4:4
AV   and they had on their heads crowns of gold
HF RP CR   and on their heads...
Tyndale Great Geneva Bishops Steph. Beza Elz.
2066.
About 7 of Hoskier's cursives.
Old Latin: gig; Armenian: an early mss.
The HF RP CR reading could quite naturally translate as the KJV.

REVELATION 4:5
AV   lightnings and thunderings and voices
HF RP CR lightnings and voices and thunderings
Tyndale Great Geneva Bishops   Steph. Beza Elz.
1 385 2020 2040 2329.
About 22 of Hoskier's curives. Von Soden cites: I a1 (2060 2081 2086) , I a2 (296 2059 2066),
I a6 (743 2055 2064 2067), I bl (1778 2080).
It is more natural to link lightning and thunder together; but see 11:19 wherethe "voices" are
likely more prominent than the "thunderings". Certainly the KJV reading cannot be accused of
"parallelism".

REVELATION 4:5
AV CR   seven lamps of fire burning before the throne
HF RP   ...before his throne
Tyndale Great Geneva Bishops   Steph. Beza Elz.
Aleph A P I 632* 2019 2020 2038 2050 2067, part of the Andreas mss.
About 47 of Hoskier's cursives.
Old Latin: gig; Vulgate; Coptic: Bohairic; Armenian; Ethiopic.
Primasius, Adrumentum, 552   Andreas, Cappadocia, 614.

REVELATION 4:6
AV   And before the throne *there was* a sea of glass
HF RP CR   ...as a sea of glass
Tyndale Great Geneva Bishops   Steph. Beza Elz.
1 201 2053, part of the Andreas mss.
About 50 of Hoskier's cursives. Von Soden indicates: I a2 (296 2059) , I a5 (2028 2029 2033 2054 2068).
Syriac: Philoxenian; Coptic: Sahadic; Armenian Ethiopic.
Tyconius, Latin, 380   Primasius, Adrumentum, Latin, 552.

REVELATION 4:11
AV   Thou art worthy, O Lord
HF RP   ...O Lord and our God, the Holy One
CR   ...O Lord and our God
Tyndale (Great) Geneva Bishops   Steph. Beza Elz.
P 1 1820 1054 2020, many of the Andreas mss.
Von Soden indicates: I a (35 181 209 296 598 743 1876 1894 2014 2015 2026 2028 2029 2031 2033 2036 2043 2054 2055 2056 2059 2060 2064 2068 2069 2081 2286), I b (104 449 628 922 1778 2080).
Old Latin: gig; Vulgate; Syriac: Harclean; Armenian.
Note: von Soden seems to glve considerably more support to the KJV reading than does Hoskler.
Lord, Lord God, Lord our God (once 19:1), *Lord God Almighty* are used in Revelation. The manner and combinations of the titles used in the HF RP and CR variants are unique.

REVELATION 5:1
AV CR   a book written within and on the backside
HF RP   ...within and without
Tyndale Great Geneva Bishops   Steph. Beza Elz.
A 1 69 1820-mg 2057 2059 2081 2329 2344, part of the Andreas mss.
About 18 of Hoskier's cursives. Von Soden indicates: Most Egyptian mss., I a1 (598 2060 2286), I a2 (181 296 1894 2059 2066), I a3 (35 2031 2056).
Old Latin-pt; Syriac: including Harclean.
Origen, Alexandria, Caesarea, 254 Cyprian, Carthage, Latin, 258
Epiphanius, Cyprus, 403   Cassiodorus, Latin, 580.

REVELATION 5:5
AV   to open the book, and to loose the seven seals thereof
HF RP CR   omits "to loose"
Tyndale Great Geneva Bishops   Steph. Beza Elz.
Aleph   296 2026 2066 2067 2344.
About 13 of Hoskier's cursives. Von Soden indicates: 1 a6 (743 2055 2064).
Vulgate: Clementine demid; Syriac: Philoxenian; Armenian: 3 early mss.
Hippolytus, Portus, 235   Origen, Alexandria, Caesarea, 254   Cyprian, Carthage, Latin, 258
Jerome, Latin, 420   Apringius, Portugal, Latin, 551 Andreas, Cappadocia, 614

Haymo, Halberstadt, Latin, 841.
Generally a seal would be "loosed" not "opened".

REVELATION 5:6
AV   And I beheld, and, lo, in the modst of the throne
HF RP CR   omits "and, lo"
Tyndale Great Geneva Bishops   Steph. Beza Elz.
(A) 172 296 1006 1828 1841 2018 2065.
About 25 of Hoskier's cursives.
Old Latin-pt; Vulgate: including am ful.
Tyconius, Latin, 380.

REVELATION 5:7
AV   he came and took the book out of the right hand
HF RP CR   ...took *it* out of...
Tyndale Great Geneva Bishops   Steph. Beza. Elz.
1* 104 205 209 620 1006 1841 2019 2050.
About 28 of Hoskier's cursives. Von Soden indicates: I b (459 628 922 1772 2080) •
Old Latin-pt including gig; Vulgate: Clementine and early mss; Syriac: Philoxenian;
Coptic: Sahadic Bohairic.
Hippolytus, Portus, 235   Cyprian, Carthage, Latin, 258   Maternus (?) 348
Primasius, Adrumentum, Latin, 552.
A variant in which Hoskier cites 25 cursiveswould probably translate as the KJV. The solemnity
of the: event requires inclusion of "the book ".

REVELATION 5:10
AV   And hast made us unto our God
HF RP CR   ...them...
Tyndale Great Geneva Bishops   Steph. Beza Elz.
2066.
About 10 of Hoskier's cursives.
Old Latin: gig; Vulgate: Clementine demid ful harl lipss tol; Coptic: Sahadic;
Armenian: 3 early mss.
Cyprian, Carthage, Latin, 258   Maternus (?) 348   Fulgentius, N. Africa, Latin, 533 Primasius,
Adumentum, Latin, 552   Andreas-pt, Cappadocia, 614 Beatus, Libana, Latin, 786
Arethas, Cappadocia, 914.
There is no previous mention as to who "them" would be; "us" refers to the 24 elders
representing the church before the throne.

REVELATION 5:10
AV   and we shall reign on the earth
HF RP CR ...they...
Tyndale Great Geneva Bishops   Steph. Beza Elz
296 2049 2066 2432.
About 6 (apparently) of Hoskier's cursives.

Old Latin: dem; Vulgate: Clementine demid lipss; Armenian: 3 early mss.
Maternus (?) 348 Tyconius, Latin, 380 Primasius, Adrumentum, Latin, 552
Bede, England, Latin, 735 Haymo, Halberstadt, Latin, 841 Arethas, Cappadocia, 914.
Again, there is no previous indication as to who "they" would be.

REVELATION 5:11
AV CR And I beheld, and I heard the voice of many angels
HF RP ...I heard as the voice...
Tyndale Great Geneva Bishops Steph. Beza Elz.
A P 046* 1 69 205 1611* 2023 2036 2329 2053 2351, many of the Andreas mss.
About 48 of Hoskier's cursives.
Old Latin: gig; Vulgate; Coptic: Bohairic; Armenian: including 2 early mss; Ethiopic.
Origen, Alexandria, Caesarıea, 254 Tyconius, Latin, 380 Primasius, Adrumentwn, Latin, 552.
There is no question of symbolism here, John heard angels!

REVELATION 5:13
AV CR for ever and ever
HF RP for ever and ever. Amen
Tyndale Great Geneva Bishops Steph. Beza Elz.
Aleph A P 69 104 172 201 205 250 1006 1611 1841 1854 2018 2020 2050 2053 2329 2344 2351.
About 40 of Hoskier's cursives. Von Soden indicates: Most Egyptian mss., I a (1 35 181 296 598
743 1876 2014 2015 2026 2028 2029 2031 2033 2036 2043 2054 2055 2056 2059 2060 2064
2066 2067 2068 2069 2081 2286).
Old Latin: gig; Vulgate; Syriac: Philoxenin Harclean; Coptic: Armenian: including 2 early mss.
Origen, Alexandria, Caesarlia, 254 Primasius, Adrumentum, Latin, 552.

REVELATION 5:14
AV And the four *and* twenty elders
HF RP CR And the elders
Tyndale Great Geneva Bishops Steph. Beza Elz.
296 2026 2066.
About 7 of Hoskier's cursives.
Vulgate: Clementine demid harl lipss; Armenian.
Primasius, Adrumentum, Latin, 552 Haymo, Halberstadt, Latin, 841.
Coming to the close of this chapter with its grand ascription of worship, we would expect the
elders to be given their full (as is usually the case) designation. The beasts are enumerated, so
should also the elders be.

REVELATION 5:14
AV and worshipped him that liveth for ever and ever
HF RP CR omits "him that liveth for ever and ever"
Tyndale Great Geneva Bishops Steph. Beza Elz.
296 2045 2049 (cited by Hoskier).
Vulgate: Clementine lipss.
Primasius, Adrumentum, Latin, 552 Haymo, Halberstadt, Latin, 841.

As this worship is directed to the Lamb (vs. 13), a key statement about Christ's eternal being is removed from the HF RP CR text.

REVELATION 6:1
AV   one of the seals
HF RP CR one of the seven seals
Tyndale Great Geneva Bishops   Steph. Beza Elz.
P   1 205 314 325 456 2015 2016 2023 2036 2038 2057 2344, many of the Andreas mss.
About 46 of Hoskier's cursives. Von Soden indicates: I a (35 181 209. 296 598 743 1876 1894 2014 2026 2031 2043 2056 2059 2064 2031 2286).
Coptic: Sahadic Bohairic;   Armenian: an early ms.
Andreas, Cappadocia, 614.

REVELATION 6:1,2
AV   Come and see. (2) And I saw, and behold
HF RP   Come and see. (2) And behold
CR   Come (2) And I saw, and behold
Tyndale Great Geneva Bishops   Steph. Beza Elz.

The two parts of the KJV reading

1.   Come and see
Strongly supported tnough with a slight variation in the Greek which does not affect the translation:
Aleph 046, over 120 of Hoskier's cursives.
Old Latin: gig; Vulgate; Syriac: Philoxenian Harclean; Coptic: Bohairic; Ethiopic.
Victorinus, Pettau, Latin, 304   Primasius, Adrumentum, Latin, 552.

2.   And I saw, and behold
Aleph A C P, nearly 100 of Hoskier's cursives.
Old Latin: gig; Vulgate: Clementinc am hail-with asterisks lipss; Syriac: Harclean;
Coptic: Bohairic; Gothic Armenian.
Andreas, Cappadocia, 614.
The two component parts of the KJV reading are strongly supported. They join up in Aleph and a number of the Versions. From Hoskier they appear to combine
in about 23 cursives. These would probably be 42 104 205 205-abs 209 367 459 468 469 620 628 680 743 935 1918- 2029 2045 2051 2064 2071.
Would the cherubim call for the Antichrist to come, as in the CR reading!

REVELATION 6:3,4
AV   Come and see. (4) And there went out another horse
HF RP CR   omits "and see"...
Tyndale Great Geneva Bishops   Steph. Beza Elz., •
Aleph   122 209 296 743 1828 2055 2064 2066 2067.
About 40 of Hoskiar's cursives (including those with the variant mentioned in 6: 1).

Old Latin: gig; Vulgate: Clementine demid harl lipss tol; Coptic: Bohairic; Armenian; Ethlopic.
Victorinus, Pettau, Latin, 304 Tyconius, Latin, 380 Primasius, Adrumentum, Latin, 552.

REVELATION 6:5
AV   Come and see. And I beheld, and lo a black horse
HF RP   omits "And I beheld"
CR   omits "and see"
Tyndale Great Geneva Bishops   Steph. Beza Elz.

The two parts of the KJV reading.

1.   Come and see
Aleph 046.
About 120 of Hoskiers cursives (including the variant mentioned above).
Vulgate: Clementine demid had lipss tol; Syriac: Harclean; Coptic: Bohairic; Armenian
Ethiopic; Arabic.
Victorinus, Pettau, Latin, 304   Primasius, Adrumentum, Latin, 552
Andreas, Cappadocia, 614   Arethas, Cappadocia, 914.

2.   And I beheld and lo
Aleph C P.
About 80 of Hoskier's cursives.
Vulgate: ful; Syriac: Harclean,
Primasius, Adrumentum, Latin, 552 Andreas, Cappadocia, 614.
Along with Aleph, a number of the Versions, Andreas and others, the two parts seem to join in
many cursives including: 110 205 205-Abs. 209 743 469 2051 2055 2064 2067.

REVELATION 6:7,8
AV   Come and see. (8) And I looked, and behold a pale horse.
HF RP   omits "and I looked"
CR   omits "and see"
Tyndale Great Geneva Bishops   Steph. Beza Elz.

The two parts of the KJV reading.

1.   Come and see
Aleph 046.
About 120 of Hoskiers cursives (including the variant).
Old Latin: gig; Vulgate: Clementine demid tol;   Syriac: Harclean;
          Coptic: Bohairic; Ethiopic.
Primasius , Adrumentum, Latin, 552 Andreas, Cappadocia, 614
Haymo, Halberstadt, Latin, 841 Arethas, Cappadocia, 914.

2.   And I looked, and behold
Aleph A C P.

About 100 of Hoskier's cursives.
Vulgate: am ful; Syriac: Copitc: Bohairic; Armenian.
Andreas, Cappadocia, 614.
Along with Aleph, a number of the Versions, Andreas and others, the two parts seem to join in many cursives including: 35 149 201 205 205-Abs. 209 368 386 469 743 1597 2045 2051 2055 2064 2071 2013 2254 (also Hoskiers #206).

REVELATION 6:8
AV CR   And power was given unto them
HF RP   ...unto him
Tyndale Great Geneva Bishops   Steph. Beza Elz.
Aleph A C P   1 35 104 468 2015 2023 2036 2037 2038 2057 2067 many of the Andreas mss.
About 52 of Hoskier's cursives. Von Soden indicates: Most Egyptian mss. I a (60 181 296 598 743 1876 2014 2026 2031 2043 2055 2056 2060 2064 2065 2066 2081 2286), I b1 (1778 2080).
Andreas, Cappadocia, 914

REVELATION 6:9
AV CR   the testimony which they held
HF RP   the testimony of the Lamb which they held
Tyndale Great Geneva Bishops   Steph. Beza Elz.
Aleph A C P   1 241 632 1778 2015 2016 2019 2020 2036 2037 2038 2057, many of the Andreas mss.
About 50 of the Hoskier's cursives. Von Soden indicates: Most Egyptian mss., I a (181 296 598 743 1876 2014 2026 2029 2031 2043 2055 2056 2059 2060 2064 2065 2066 2068 2069 2081 2286), I b2 (104 459 628 922).
Old Latin: gig; Vulgate Coptic: Bohairic; Armenian.
Cyprian, Carthage, Latin, 258   Primasius, Adrumentum, Latin, 552
Andreas, Cappadocia, 614   Haymo, Halberstadt, 841.

REVELATION 6:11
AV   unto everyone of them
HF RP   unto them
Tyndale Great Geneva Bishops   Steph. Beza Elz.
296 2066.
About 20 of Hoskier's cursives (including 3 variants, one of which is supported by Syriac: Philoxenian Harc:lean; Coptic: Bohairic; Ethiopic).
The CR reading translates as the KJV and is supported by Aleph A C P, about 101 of Hoskiers cursives, Coptic: Sahadic; an early Armenian mss. Also with minor variation: Old Latin: gig; Vulgate.

REVELATION 6:11
AV   white robes
HF RP CR a white robe
Tyndale Great Geneva Bishops   Steph. Beza Elz.

57 141 218 296 2066.

Vulgate: including harl; Armenian: an early ms; Ethiopic; Arabic.

Cyprian, Cathage, Latin, 258   Victorinus, Pettau, Latin, 304   Fulgentius, N. Africa, Latin, 533   Primasius, Adrumentum, Latin, 552   Beatus, Libana, Latin, 786.

The impressive parallelism is broken in the revised reading (6:9,11), "Souls...white robes", becomes "souls...a white robe."

REVELATION 6:11
AV RP   killed as they *were*, should be fulfilled
HF   ...they should fulfil it
Tyndale Great Geneva Bishops   Steph. Beza Elz.
296 2029 2033 2049.

Arethas, Cappadocia, 914.

The CR (also Oxford 1025 TR) reads with the KJV. Supported by: A C 385 2344.

Old Latin: gig; Vulgate; Syriac: Phyloxenian; Coptic: Bohairic; Armenian;   Ethiopic.

Cyprian. 258   Fulgentius, 553.

The HF RP introduces a very questionable element into the passage. Do the martyrs fulfil their own martyrdom? Is it not much more in line with the spirit of Scripture to put the subject of martyrdom in the passive rather than active tense?

REVELATION 6:12
AV   and, lo, there was a great earthquake
HF RP CR omits "lo"
Tyndale Great Geneva Bishops Steph. Beza Elz.
A 296 2066.

About 17 of Hoskier's cursives.

Old Latin: c haf; Vulgate: Clementine harl lipss.

Primasius, Adrumentum, Latin, 552.

As "behold" or "lo" introduces most of the other Seal judgements; when we come to the awe filled conclusion we would expect to see it there also.

REVELATION 6:15
AV   and the rich men, and the chief captains
HF RP CR   ...chief captains...rich men
Tyndale Great Geneva Bishops   Steph. Beza Elz.
1 254 598 743 1778 1678 2019 2020 2026 2028 2029 2038 2049 2051 2052 2057 2059 2060 2064 2065 2067 2080 2081 2083 2085 2286 2302, most of the Andreas mss.

Von Soden indicates: I a1 (296 1894· 2014 2033 2036 2054 2055 2066 2068) , I b2 (104 459 628 922).

Andreas, Cappadocia, 614.

REVELATION 7:14
AV   Sir, thou knowest
HF RP CR My sir (or "lord"), thou knowest
Tyndale Great Geneva Bishops   Steph. Beza Elz.

A   1 181 209 205 296 1611* 2066.
Hoskier seems to cite about 18 cursives.
Old Latin-pt. including a gig; Vulgate: Clementine, early mss; Coptic: Sahadic, an early
Bohairic ms; Armenian: an early ms; Ethiopic.
Cyprian, Carthage, Latin, 258   Primasius, Adrumentum, Latin, 552   Beatus, Libana, Latin 786.

REVELATION 8:7
AV   and the third part of the trees
HF RP CR and the third part of the earth was burnt up, and the third part of the trees
Tyndale Great Geneva Bishops: Steph. Beza Elz.
1 1854 2018.
About 21 of Hoskier's Cursives.
Coptic: Bohairic; Armenian: 2 early mss.
If, as the revised reading states, "a third part of the earth burns up", why would the other "third
parts" be mentioned? If they are in addition to the "third part of the earth" then it is more than
a third part, of the trees which burn. Also, "all the green grass burning up" conflicts with "a
third of the earth burning."

REVELATION 9:10
AV   and there were stings in their tails
HF RP CR   and stings, and in there tails
Tyndale Great Geneva Bishops Steph. Beza Elz.
296 2066.
About 5 of Hoskier's cursives.
Vulgate: Clementine ful clemid harl-with asterisks, lipss.
Haymo, Halberstadt, Latin, 841.
A variant, translates practically the same as the KJV. Supported by 77 of Hoskiers cursives, Old
Latin: gig; Vulgate: am tol; Armenian Ethiopic.
Tyconius 380,   Andreas 614.

REVELATION 9:11
AV   And they had a king over them
HF RP CR omits "And"
Tyndale Great Geneva Bishops   Steph. Beza Elz.
P 1 172 250 1828? 1854 2351.
Hoskier cites three families of cursives which contain "and",' P-pt. 21 34. Von Soden indicates:
I a (60 181 296 432 598 1876 1994 2014 2015 2023 2028 2029 2033 2036 2043 2054 2059
2061 2066 2068 2069 2081).
Vulgate; Syriac; Armenian; Ethiopic.
Primasius, Andrumentum, Latin, 552   Andreas, Cappadocia; 614.

REVELATION 9:15
AV CR and a day
HF RP and unto the day

Tyndale Great Geneva Bishops   Steph. Beza Elz.
P 47 A P 35 205 2037 2038 2057 2067 2329.
About 50 of Hoskd er's cuesives. Von Soden indicates: Most Egyptian mss I a (1 60 181 209 432 598 743 1876 2014 2015 2023 2026 2029 2031 2033 2036 2043 2054 2055 2056 2059 2060 2061 2064 2065 2066 2068 2069 2081 2286).
Old Latin: gig; Vulgate.
Cyprian, Carthage, Latin, 258 Tyconius, Latin, 390 Primasius, Adrumentum, Latin, 552
Andreas, Cappadocia, 614   other fathers.

REVELATION 9:16
AV CR   two hundred thousand thousand
HF RP   thousands of thousands
Tyndale Gtreat Geneva Bishops   Steph. Beza Elz.
P47 Aleph A P   296 1894 (these and the following include variants).
About 60 of Hoskier's cursives.
Coptic: early Sahadic mss Bohairic; Armenian: an early ms.
Origen, Alexandria, Caesarea, 254   Cyprian, Carthage, Latin, 258
Primasius, Adrumentum, Latin, 552 Andreas, Cappadocia, 614 Beatus, Libana, Latin, 786
Arethas, Cappadocia, 914.

REVELATION 9:16
AV   and I heard the number of them
HF RP CR   omits "and"
Tyndale Great Geneva Bishops   Steph. Beza Elz.
296 2049 2066.
Vulgate: Clementine harl lipss.
Epiphanius, Cyprus, 403   Arethas, Cappadocia, 914.
Without the "and" the final sentence of the verse is abrupt, and intrusive. See the NASV. In the KJV it is a statement of John's reflection over the vastness of the army.

REVELATION 9:18
AV   By these three
HF RP CR By these three plagues
Tyndale Great Geneva Bishops   Steph. Beza Elz.
1 35 150 181 2020 2038 2056 2059, part of the Andreas mss.
About 17 of Hoskier's cursives. Von Soden indicates: I a1 (598 2026 2060 2286).
Armenian: (an early ms.); (Ethiopic).
Andreas, Cappadocia, 614.

REVELATION 10:1
AV CR And I saw another mighty angel
HF RP   omits "another"
Tyndale Great Geneva Bishops   Steph. Beza Elz.
P47 Aleph A C 172 2105 250 2018 2019 2020 2038 2057 2067, part of the Andreas mss.
Hoskier cites 21 cursives (including two supporting variants) and one family of cursives.

Von Soden indicates I a (181 209 296 598 2026 2028 2029 2031 2033 2054 2056 2059 2060 2065 2066 2068 2069 2081 2286), I b (104 459 628 922 1778 2080), I o1 (424 1828 1862).
Old Latin: gig; Vulgate; Syriac: Philoxenian Harclean; Coptic: Sahadic Bohairic; Armenian; Ethiopic; Arabic.
Tertullian, N. Africa, 220 Origen, Alexandria, Caesarea, 254 Victorinus, Pettau, Latin, 304
Tyconills, Latin, 380 Primasius, Adrumentum,. Latin, 552 Cassidorus, Latin, 580
Andreaas, Cappadocia, 614 Beatus, Libana, Latin, 786 Arethas, Cappadocia, 914.

REVELATION 10:4

AV   And when the seven thunders had uttered their voices
HF RP CR   ...had spoken
Tyndale Great Geneva Bishops   Steph. Beza Elz.
(172) 254 296 429-c 628 (664) (1094) (2042) 2066.
Old Latin: c div haf Z-c: (Z*); Vulgate: Clementine harl lipss.
Haymo, Halberstadt, Latin, 841

REVELATION 10:4

AV   I heard a voice from heaven saying unto me
HF RP CR   omits "unto me"
Tyndale Great Geneva Bishops   Steph. Beza Elz.
296 2049 2066.
Vulgate: Clementine, early mss; Coptic: Bohairic.
This is not a general statement, but directed to John personally. See 1:17 5:5 7:13, 14 10:9,11 11:1 14:13 17:1, 7, 15 19:9, 10 21:5, 6, 10 22: 1, 6, 8, 9, 10.

REVELATION 10:5

AV   lifted up his hand to heaven
HF RP CR   ...his right hand...
Tyndale Great Geneva Bishops   Steph. Beza Elz.
A 1 35 181 296 598 2019 2026 2038 2049 2057 2059 2065 2081 2186 2286, many of the Andreas mss.
Von Soden indicates: I a (60 432 2015 2023 2028 2029 2033 2054 2061 2068 2069).
Vulgate: including harl; Syriac: Philoxenian; Coptic: early Bohairic mss.
Andreas, Cappadocia, 614.

REVELATION 11:8

AV   where also our Lord was crucified
HF RP CR   ...their Lord...
Tyndale Great Geneva Bishops   Steph. Beza Elz.
1 296 2049.
"their Lord" is rare in Scripture narration.

REVELATION 11:9

AV   not suffer their dead bodies to be put in graves
HF RP CR   ...in a grave

Tyndale Great Geneva Bishops   Steph. Beza Elz.
Aleph - 2nd cor   205 205-Abs 209 522 1611 1678 1778 2049 2080 (these and the following include a supportive variant).
Von Soden indicates: I a2 (181 296 1894 2066).
Vulgate; Syriac: Philoxenian Harclean; Coptic: Sahadic Bohairic; Armenian: 2 early mss; Ethiopic.
Primasius, Adrumentum, Latin, 552, other fathers.
It would be more likely for them to contemplate putting "bodies" (plural) into "graves" (plural).

REVELATION 11:12
AV CR   And they heard...saying unto them
HF RP   And I heard...saying unto them
Tyndale Great Geneva Bishops   Steph. Beza Elz.
Aleph* A C P   250 296 429* 467* 1862 2020 2049 2053 2066 2081 2256.
Vulgate: including am ful, most early mss; Syriac: Philoxenian; Armnian.
Tyconius, Latin, 380 Haymo, Halberstadt, Latin, 841, other fathers.
A variant supported by 1678 1778 2020 2080 2321 reads with the KJV. The voice was directed to the Two Witnesses, not John.

REVELATION 11:13
AV CR   the same hour was there a great earthquake
HF RP   ...day...
Tyndale Great Geneva Bishops   Steph. Beza Elz.
Aleph A C P 1 205 1828 2019 2037 2040 2057 2351
About 49 of Hoskier's cursives. Von Soden indicates: I a (181 209 296 2026 2028 2029 2031 2033 2054 2056 2059 2060 2065 2066 2068 2069 2081 2286) I b1 (1778 2080).
Vulgate; Syriac: Philoxenian Harclean; Coptic: Bohaidc; Armenian: including 3 early mss: Ethiopic.
Origen, Alexandria, Caesarea, 254 Tyconius, Latin, 380 Primasius, Adrumentum, Latin, 552 Andreas, Cappadocia, 614 Beatus, Libana, Latin, 786.

REVELATION 11:15
AV   the kingdoms of this world are become *the kingdoms* of our Lord
HF RP CR   ...kingdom...*kingdom*...
Tyndale Great Geneva Bishops   Steph. Beza Elz.
1 104 205 205-Abs 209 459 598 680 2019 2028 2029 2038 2044 2045 2049 2054 (2057) 2059 2060 2065 2069 2069 2081 2083 2091 2186 2286 2302.
Von Soden indicates: I a1 (2026), I a2 (181 296 2066), I a5 (2033 2068) I b2 (629 922).
Armenian: including 2 early mss.
Is there only one kingdom on earth today? Will there only be one kingdom that becomes the Lord's at His Second Coming? When Christ returns, He will destroy kingdoms (Dan. 2: 44)! The HF RP CR reading is an attack upon Premillennialism.

REVELATION 11:17
AV   which art, and wast, and art to come
HF RP CR   omits "and art to come"
Tyndale Great Geneva Bishops   Steph. Beza Elz.
051   35 296 1006 1841 1894 1957 2015 2019 2023 2026 2036 2037 2040 2041 2065 2066,
some of the Andreas mss.
About 65 of Hoskier's cursives. Von Soden indicates: I a3 (2031 2056), I a4 (1876 2014 2043),
I a7 (60 432 2061).
Vulgate: Clementine, early mss; Coptic: (Bohairic); Armenian.
Tyconius, Latin, 390   Andreas, Cappadocia, 614   Beatus, Libana, Latin, 796.

REVELATION 11:19
AV CR lightnings, and volces, and thunderings, and an earthquake
HF RP   omits "and an earthquake"
Tyndale Great Geneva Bishops   Steph. Beza Elz.
Aleph A C P 1 35* (181) 205 2015 2019 2020 2023 2036 2040 2329
2351, most of the Andreas mss.
About 70 of Hoskier's cursives (13 others have the plural). Von Soden indicates: I a (181 209
296 598 743 1876 2014 2026 2029 2029 2031 2043 2054 2055 2056 2059 2060 2064 2065
2066 2068 2069 2081 2286), I b2 (104 459 628 922), I 01 (172 424 1828 1862).
Old Latin: including f1 gig; Vulgate; Syriac: Philoxenian Harclean; Armenian : including 2 early
mss; Ethiopic.
Origen, Alexandria, Caasarea , 254   Tyconius, Latin, 380   Primasius, Adrumentum, Latin, 552
Andreas, Cappadocia, 614.

REVELATION 12:12
AV   Woe to the inhabitants of the earth and of the sea
HF RP CR omits "the inhabitants of"
Tyndale Great Geneva Bishops   Stepha Beza Elz.
1 254 296 20282029 2033 2037 2044 2046 2049 2054 2066 2068 2069 2186, part, of the
Andreas mss.
Andreas, Cappadocia, 614.

REVELATION 12:17
AV   and have the testimony of Jesus Christ
HF RP CR   omits "Christ"
Tyndale Great Geneva Bishops   Stepha Beza Elz.
296 2049 2066.
Vulgate: Clementine lipss tol; Armenian: 2 early mss.
Primasius, Adrumentum, Latin, 552.
The full title is necessary. Christ's name is here linked to God. The translation: "The
commandments of God and the testimony of Jesus", could be construed to put our Lord on a
lower plain.

REVELATION 13:1

AV   having seven heads and ten horns

HF RP CR   ...ten horns and seven heads

Tyndale Great Geneva Bishops   Stepha Beza Elz.

2066.

About 14 of Hcskier's cursives.

Vulgate; Armenian: including 2 early. mss.

It is in accord wlth the context to mention the beast's heads before its horns as the more prominent. In verse 3, John's attention is centered on one of these heads. The horns are not explained until Ch. 17. It is noteworthy that Erasmus' first edition placed the horns first but was changed in subsequent editions on what he obviously felt were good reasons.

REVELATION 13:3

AV   And I saw one of his heads

HF RP CR   omits "I saw"

Tyndale Great Geneva Bishops   Stepha Beza Elz.

203 296 506 1006 1841 2040 2049 2065 2066 2067.

Vulgate: Clementine ful dem lipss; Armenian: Including 1 early ms.

Tyconius, Latin, 380   Pseudo-Ambrose, Latin, VI   Andreas, Cappadocia, 614

Beatus, Libana, Latin, 786   Haymo, Halberstadt, Latin, 841.

The emphasis of the first three verses is on what John saw. The NASV translators felt it necessary to supply these words.

REVELATION 13:5

AV CR   a mouth speaking...blasphemies

HF RP   ...blasphemy

Tyndale Great Geneva Bishops   Stepha Beza Elz.

P47 Aleph C   18 39 201 206 386 582 620 628 866 1006 1611 1841 1918 2020 2040 2066 2344, part of the Andreas mss.

About 33 of Hoskier's cursives.

Old Latin: a; Vulgate: Clementine demid ful lipss tol;   Syriac: Harclean;

Coptic: (Bohairic); Armenian: 2 early mss; Ethiopic.

Dionysius, Alexandria, 265   Rufinus, Aquileia, Latin, 410   Haymo, Halberstadt, Latin, 841.

REVELATION 13:10

AV   He that leadeth into captivity shall go into captivity

HF RP   He that holds captive, goes *into captivity*

Tyndale Great Geneva Bishops   Steph. Beza Elz.

2059 2081.

Arethas, Cappadocia, 914.

The extant mss. have many variations. About 15 of Hoskier's cursives would translate as the KJV, and probably also the CR (supported by A and early Vulgate mss).

The HF RP reading is scarcely translatable. Metzger says it must be regarded as a scribal blunder (*Textual Commentary*).

REVELATION 13:18

AV RP CR for it is...and his number is
HF   omits "and"
Tyndale Great Geneva Bishops   Steph. Beza Elz.
A C P 046   1 35 60 94 205 432 632 1957 2015 2020 2023 2036 2037 2038 2040 2041 2067.
About 95 of Hoskier's cursives.
Old Latin: gig; Vulgate; Syriac: Harclean; Coptic: Bohairic including 2 early mss. Ethiopic.
Primasius, Adrunentum, Latin, 552.

REVELATION 14:1

AV   have his Father's name written in their foreheads
HF RP CR   ...his name and his Father's name...
Tyndale (Great) Geneva Bishops   Steph. Beza Elz.
P   1 296 2049 2053 2065 2256-mg.
Armenian: early mss.
There is but one name of Deity on their foreheads. See 7:3 9:4, also 3:12 John 5:40.

REVELATION 14:5

AV   in their mouth was found no guile
HF RP CR   ...no lie
Tyndale Great Geneva Bishops   Steph. Beza Elz.
1 296 582-mg. 2028 2029 2033 2037 2044 2046 2049 2054 2068 2069? 2083, part of the
Andreas mss.
Von Soden indicates: I a2 (181 296 2066).
Armenian: an early ms.
Andreas, Cappadocia, 614.
"Guile" is the more descriptive, all-inclusive word.

REVELATION 14:5

AV   they are without fault before the throne
HF RP CR   omits "before the throne"
Tyndale Great Geneva Bishops   Steph. Beza Elz.
296 2049 2066.
Old Latin: several mss; Vulgate: Clementine demid lipss; Armenian : an early ms.
The scribes who altered the words probably could not understand how the 144,000 could be in
heaven at this point in time. A fuller understanding of 12:4 gives the answer.

REVELATION 14:6

AV CR And I saw another anqel
HF RP omits "another"
Great Geneva Bishops   Steph. Beza Elz.
Aleph-c A C P 051 35 218 250 1006 1611 1841 1957 2018 2023 2036 2037 2040 2053 2065 2066
2073* 2329 2344 1841 2432.
About 64 of Hoskier's cursives . Von Soden indicates: Most Egyptian mss, I a3 (2031 2056) ,
I a4 (1876 2014 2015 2043), I a6 (743 2055 2064 2067), I a7 (60 2061), I 01 (172 424 1828

1862).
Old Latin: ar c dem div gig haf t z 61; Vulgate; Syriac: Philoxenian. Harclean; Coptic: Bohairic;
Armenian; Ethiopic.
Cyprian, Carthage, Latin, 258   Maternus (?) 348 Tyconius, Latin, 380
Vigilius, Thapaus , Latin, 484   Primasius, Adrumentum, Latin, 552
Cassiodorus, Latin, 580   Pseudo-Ambrose, Latin, VI Andreas, Cappadocia, 614
Beatus, Libana, Latin, 786 Haymo, Halberstadt, Latin, 841.
A Greek variant reads with the KJV.

REVELATION 14:8
AV   there followed another angel
HF RP CR   another, a second angel
Tyndale Great Geneva Bishops   Steph. Beza Elz.
61 69 296 598 2038 2049 2066 2286.
Old Latin: a ar c dem div haf Z 61; Vulgate: including harl; Ethiopic.
Victorinus, Pettau, Latin, 304   Tyconius, Latin, 380 Pseudo-Ambrose, Latin, VI.
The HF RP CR readings are awkward and amount to tautology.

REVELATION 14:8
AV   Babylon that great city
HF RP CR   omits "city"
Tyndale Great Geneva Bishops   Steph. Beza Elz.
296 1894 2049 2066.
Ethiopic.
Arethas, Cappadocia, 914.
This is the first mention of latter day and prophetic Babylon in the New Testament. It is
necessary to state that an actual city is in view.
A Greek variant supports the KJV.

REVELATION 14:8
AV   because she made all nations drink of the wine
HF RP   she made...
CR   she who made...
Tyndale Great Geneva Bishops   Steph. Beza Elz.
1 2019 2037 2067, part of the Andreas mss.
About 30 of Hoskiers cursives. Von Soden indicates: I a (181 296 743 1894 2026 2028 2029
2033 2054 2055 2059 2064 2066 2068 2069 2081 2286).
Andreas, Cappadocia, 614   Arethas, Cappadocia, 914

REVELATION 14:9
AV   And the third angel followed them
HF RP CR   ...another, a third angel...
Tyndale Great Geneva Bishops   Steph. Beza Elz.
296 2049 2066 2077.
About 10 (apparently) of Hoskier's cursives.

Vulgate: Clementine am demid lipss; Ethiopic.
Cyprian, Carthage, Latin, 258 Primasius, Adrumentum, Latin, 552 Arethas, Cappadocia, 914.
As in 14:8, there is an awkwardness in the revised reading which is not seen elsewhere in Scripture enumeration.

REVELATION 14:15
AV   for the time is come for thee to reap
HF RP CR   omits "for thee"
(Tyndale Great Geneva Bishops ?)   Steph. Beza Elz.
104 620.
About 10 of Hoskier's cursives.
A variant supported by: E, 20 of Hoskiers cursives (Andreas mss.), translates as the KJV.
It is expressly time for Christ to reap.

REVELATION 15:2
AV   victory...over his mark, and over the number of his name
HF RP CR   omits "over his mark"
Tyndale Great Geneva Bishops   Steph. Beza Elz.
051 1 35 42 172 181 205 205-Abs. 209 241 250 367 424 468 598 616 743 1704 1732 1828 1849
1862 1876 1888 2004 2014 2015 2018 2019 2026 2028 2029 2031 2033 2034 2036 2037 2042
2043 2044 2045 2046 2047 2051 2054 2055 2056 2057 2059 2060 2064 2065 2067 2060
2069 2071 2073 2074 2075 2076 2077 2078 2079 2091 2082 2083 2084 2091 2186 2254 2256
2286 2302 (here is one of the few places where Hoskier directly cites the mss. supportive of the
KJV reading).
Armenian.
Andreas, Cappadocia, Latin, 614   Arethas, Cappadocia, 914.

REVELATION 15:3
AV   just and true *are* thy ways, thou King of saints
HF RP CR   ...King of nations
Tyndale Great Geneva Bishops   Steph. Beza Elz.
296 2049 2066.
Victorinus, Pettau, Latin, 304   Tyconius, Latin, 380 Apringius, Portugal, Latin, 551
Cassiodorus, Latin, 580.
At the time of the statement, Christ is King of saints. He has not yet returned; the nations have
not yet acknowledged his kingship.

REVELATION 15:5
AV   I looked, and, behold, the temple of the tabernacle
HF RP CR   omits "behold"
Tyndale Great Geneva Bishops   Steph. Beza Elz.
296 2049 2066 2344?
Old Latin-pt; Vulgate; Coptic: Bohairic; Armenian: an early ms; Arabic.
Tyconius, Latin, 380   Primasius, Adrumentum, Latin, 552   Pseudo-Ambrose, Latin, VI
Cassiodorus, Latin, 580   Beatus, Libana, Latin, 796.

John sees heaven opened. The fuller expression of his awe is the appropriate reading.

REVELATION 15:6
AV CR   And the seven angels...clothed
HF RP   ...they were clothed
Tyndale Great Geneva Bishops   Steph. Beza Elz.
P41 Aleph A C P   1 35* 2040 2057 2329, many of the Andreas mss.
About 57 of Hoskier's cursives. Von Soden indicates: 1 a (60 181 296 432 598 743 1876 1894 2014 2015 2029 2031 2033 2036 2043 2054 2055 2056 2059 2060 2064 2065 2066 2067 2068 2081 2086), I b1 (1779 2080).
Old Latin: including gig; Vulgate; Syriac: Philoxenian; Coptic: Bohairic; Armenian: an early mss.
Tyconius, Latin, 380   Primasius, Adrumentum, Latin, 552.

REVELATION 16:5
AV   Thou art righteous, O Lord
HF RP CR   omits "O Lord"
Tyndale Great Geneva Bishops   Steph. Beza Elz.
296 2049.
Vulgate: Clementine lipss; Coptic: Bohairic; Ethiopic.
It is out of harmony with the other ascriptions of praise to describe our Lord's attributes without first addressing His Person.

REVELATION 16:5
AV   which art, and wast, and shalt be
HF RP CR   ...the Holy One
Elz 1633, Beza 1582, 89, 98. Beza in his 1598 edition wrote, "ex vetusto bonae fidei manuscripto codice restitui."

Jeffrey Khoo quotes Beza concerning the reading "*and shalt be*" being seen in an ancient MS: "But with John there remains a completeness where the name of Jehovah (the Lord) is used, just as we have said before, 1:4; he always uses the three closely together, therefore it is certainly "and shall be", for why would he pass over it in this place? And so ***without doubting the genuine writing in this ancient manuscript, I faithfully restored in the good book what was certainly there, shall he***"(Cited by Khoo from Thomas Holland, *Manuscript* Evidence, emphasis added).

Khoo adds: "Besides the ancient Greek manuscript that Beza had, it ought to be noted that Beatus of Liebana in the eighth century, in his compilation of commentaries on the Book of Revelation has the Latin phrase, **qui fuisti et futures es,** for Revelation 16:5 which was found in the commentary of Tyconius which goes back to the fourth century. It is entirely possible that there were either early Greek manuscripts or Old Latin versions as early as the fourth century which contained the reading **esomenos.**" (*Dean Burgon Society eNews*, 89, emphasis added).

Herman Hoskier cites "and shalt be" in the Ethiopic Version with the following Latin translation: *...Justus es, Domine, et Rectus qui fuisti et eris* ("and will be", *Text of the Apocalypse*. Alerted to by Jack McElroy).

The KJV reading is in harmony with the four other places in Revelation where this phrase is found.

1:4 "him which is, and which was, and which is to come"

1:8 "the Lord, which is, and which was, and which is to come, the Almighty"

4:8 "Lord God Almighty, which was, and is, and is to come"

11:17 "Lord God Almighty, which art, and wast, and art to come"

Indeed Christ is the Holy One, but in the Scriptures of the Apostle John the title is found only once (1 John 2:20), and there, a totally different Greek word is used. The Preface to the Authorised Version reads: "with the former translations diligently compared and revised".

The translators must have felt there was good reason to insert these words though it ran counter to much external evidence. They obviously did not believe the charge made today that Beza inserted it on the basis of "conjectural emendation." They knew that they were translating the Word of God, and so do we. Later the the Elzivers clearly thought the same by placing it in their edition of the Received Text. The logic of faith should lead us to see God's guiding providence in a passage such like this.

REVELATION 16:9

AV CR   And men were scorched with great heat, and blasphemed

HF RP   ...and men blasphemed

Tyndale Great Geneva Bishops   Steph. Baza Elz.

Aleph A C P   1 205 2019 2020 2036 2037 2038 2040 2057 2067 2329, many of the Andreas mss.

About 60 of Hoskier's cursives. Von Soden indicates: Most Egyptian mss, I a (181 209 296 598 743 1876 2014 2015 2026 2031 2043 2055 2056 2059 2060 2064 2065 2066 2081 2286), I b2 (1778 2080).

Old Latin: gig; Vulgate; Syriac: Philoxenian; Coptic: Sahadic Bohairic; Armenian: including 3 early mss; Ethiopic.

Tyconius, Latin, 380   Primasius, Adrumentum, Latin, 552   Andreas, Cappadocia, 614   Beatus, Liberia, Latin, 786

REVELATION 16:14

AV   unto the kings of the earth and of the whole world

HF RP CR   omits "of the earth"

Tyndale Great Geneva Bishops   Steph. Beza Elz.

1 2037 2059.

About 22 of Hoskier's cursives.

Andreas, Cappadocia, 614.

REVELATION 16:18

AV   voices, and thunders, and lightnings

HF RP   lightnings, and thunders, and voices

CR   lightnings, . and voices, and thunders

Tyndale Great Geneva Bishops   Steph. Beza Elz.

1 2037, part of the Andreas mss.

About 14 of Hoskier's cursives. Von Soden indicates: K c (920 1859 1872 2027 2040).

Andreas, Capadocia, 614.

REVELATION 17:4
AV CR   arrayed in purple and scarlet colour, and decked with gold
HF RP   omits the 2nd "and"
Tyndale Great Geneva Bishops   Steph. Beza Elz.
Aleph A   1 42 104 250 424 (620) 1087 1611 1779 1854 2018 2019 2020 2022 2037 2060 2062 2069 2286 2329.
About 44 of Hoskier's cursives. Von Soden indicates: I a2 (1 181 296 2066).
Old Latin: including gig; Vulgate; Syriac: including Harclean; Coptic:Bohairic;
Armenian: including 2 early mss; (Ethiopic).
Cyprian, Carthage, Latin, 258   Tyconius, Latin, 380   Primasius, Adrumentum, Latin, 552
Andreas, Cappadocia, 614.

REVELATION 17:8
AV   when they behold the beast that was, and is not, and yet is
HF RP CR   ...and is not, and will come
Geneva Bishops   Steph. Beza Elz.
2049.
Keep in mind that the context of the reading is the future Tribulation (not John' s day). It strains the sense to be looking at something that "will come". "Those who dwell on the earth will wonder...when they see the beast that...will come" (NASV). When the world looks at him he "is", not "shall be".
A variant (kai paresti) read by Aleph-c, about 31 Andreas type mss, and the Syriac Sinaitic can translate virtually the same as the KJV.
Aleph* 1854 2014 2034, an early Armenian ms would also translate about the same.

REVELATION 17:10
AV   five are fallen, and one is
HF RP CR   omits "and"
Tyndale Great Geneva Bishops   Steph. Beza Elz.
1 296 2049 2058 2066 2070 2305.
Vulgate: lipss; Syriac: Philoxenian; Coptic: Bohairic; Armenian; Ethiopic.
A variant would read with the KJV., supported by 468 2041 Hippolytus, 220   Primasius, 552.

REVELATION 17:13
AV   and shall give...to the beast
HF RP CR   and give...
Tyndale Great Geneva Bishops   Steph. Beza Elz.
296 2049.
The "shall" here is in harmony with the two "shalls" of verse 14.
Two variants translate "shall give". Read by: 15 of Hoskiers cursives, Vulgate: Clementine demid ful lipss tol; Coptic: Sahadic Bohairic; Ethiopic; Hippolytus, 235   Tyconius, 380 Primasius, 552.

REVELATION 17:16
AV   the ten horns which thou sawest upon the beast, these shall hate
HF RP CR   ... sawest, and the beast, these...
Tyndale Great Geneva Bishops   Steph. Beza Elz.
209 296 2049 2066.
Vulgate: Clementine lipss;. Syriac; Armenian.
Arethas, Cappadocia, 914.
Verses 15,16 return to the overall composite entity, i.e. the beast with the ten horns (13:1, 17:3,7). The HF RP CR reading confuses the beast which arises out from among the 10 horns with the beast which bears the ten horns.

REVELATION 18:2
AV   And he cried mightily with a strong voice
HF RP CR   omits "strong"
Tyndale Great Geneva Bishops   Steph. Beza Elz.
(209) 468 2038-c 2055 2060.
About 40 of Hoskiers cursives. Von Soden indicates: I a1 (598 2026 2065 2081), I a2 (1 181 296 2059 2066), I a5 (2028 2029 2033 2054 2068 2069), I b1 (1778 2080).
Old Latin: (gig).
Hippolytus, Portus, Latin, 235   Primasius, Adrumentum, Latin, 552.

REVELATION 18:9
AV   the kings...shall bewail her
HF RP CR   omits "her"
Tyndale Great Geneva Bishops   Steph. Beza Elz. [Omitted in Scrivener]
P 046 051   1 35 205 1854 2036 2037 2057 2067, part of the Andreas mss.
At least 16 of Hoskier's cursives, plus 3 of his family groupings. Von Soden indicates:I a (181 209 296 598 743 1894 2014 2015 2026 2028 2029 2031 2033 2043 2054 2055 2056 2059 2060 2064 2065 2066 2068 2069 2081 2086).
Syriac: Philoxenian; Ethiopic.
Andreas, Cappadocla, 614.
A Greek variant translates as the KJV.

REVELATION 18:17
AV   and all the company in ships
HF RP CR and all who sail everywhere
Tyndale Great Geneva Bishops   Steph. Beza Elz.
1 296 2029 2029 2033 2037 2044 2046 2049 2054 2069 2069 2083 2196.
Von Soden shows substantial support for the two parts of the KJV reading.
Coptic: Bohairic.
Hippolytus, Portus, Latin, 235   Andreas, Cappadocia, 614.

REVELATION 18:20
AV   and *ye* holy apostles and prophets
HF RP CR and *ye* saints and apostles and prophets

Tyndale Great Geneva Bishops   Steph. Beza Elz.
C E 051   1 35 41 2057 2329, most of the Andreas mas.
30 of Hoskier's cursives, plus 3 of his family groupings. Von Soden indicates: I a (181 209 296
598 743 2026 2028 2029 2031 2033 2054 2055 2056 2059 2060 2065 2069 2081).
Old Latin: a gig; Vulgate: Clementine demid lipss tol; Armenian: including 2 early mss.
Apringius, Portugal, Latin, 551   Andreas. Cappadocia, 614   Beatus, Libana, Latin, 786
Haymo, Halberstadt, 841.

REVELATION 19:1
AV   I heard a great voice of much people in heaven
HF RP CR   I heard as it were a great voice...
Tyndale Great Geneva Bishops   Steph. Beza.
051* 1 94 104 181 241 336 620 632 1006 2020 2038 2053 2057 2062 2064 2067, most of the
Andreas mss.
About 58 of Hoskier's cursives. Von Soden indicates: I a (209 296 599 743 1994 2026 2028
2029 2031 2033 2054 2055 2056 2059 2060 2066 2068 2069 2081 2286), I b2 (459 628 922).
Old Latin: gig; Syriac: Philoxenian Harclean; Armenian.
Tyconius, Latin, 380   Primasius, Adrumentum, Latin, 552 Andreas, Cappadocia,614.
There is no question of symbolism here. John heard many people (see 5:11).

REVELATION 19:1
AV   and glory, and honour, and power
HF RP   and power, and glory
CR   and glory, and power
Tyndale Great Geneva Bishops   Steph. Beza Elz.
1 209 632-c 2019 2081 2329, part of the Andreas mss.
About 33 of Hoskier's cursives. Von Soden indicates: I a2 (181 296 2059), I a5 (2028 2029
2033 2054 2068 2069), I a6 (743 2055 2064 2067).
Syriac: including (Harclean); Coptic: Sahadic Bohairic; Armenian: including an early ms;
Arabic.
Andreas, Cappadocia, 614.

REVELATION 19:1
AV   unto the Lord our God
HF RP CR   unto our God
Tyndale Great Geneva Bishops   Steph. Beza Elz.
1 296 2028 2029 2033 2037 2044 2046 2049 2054 2068 2069 2083 2186,
part of the Andreas mas.
Andreas, Cappadocia, 614.

REVELATION 19:5
AV   and ye that fear him, both small and great
HF RP CR   omits "both"
Tyndale Great Geneva Bishops   Steph. Beza Elz.
1 69 172 181 296 628 2023 2028 2037 2046 2081 2186, part of the Andreas mss.

One of Hoskier's cursive families.
Armenian: an early ms.
Andreas, Cappadocia, 614.

REVELATION 19:6
AV   for the Lord God omnipotent reigneth
HF RP [CR] ...Lord our God...
(Tyndale) (Geneva) Bishops   Steph. Beza Elz.
A 1 254 792 1006 1841 2023 2040 2065 2070 2186 2432.
Von Soden indicates: I a1 (1 296 1894 2066).
Old Latin: t; Syriac: Philoxenian-c; Coptic: Sahadic Bohairic; Ethiopic; Armenian: 2 early mss.
Cyprian, Carthage, Latin, 258.

REVELATION 19:8
AV   arrayed in fine linen, clean and white
HF RP   ...white and clean
CR   ...clean *and* white
Tyndale Great Geneva Bishops Steph. Beza Elz.
1 254 296 2019 2026 2028 2037 2046 2057 2067, part of the Andreas mss.
Two of Hoskier's cursive families. Von Soden indicates: I a1 (59B 2060 2081 2286), I a7 (60 432 2023 2061)
Syriac: Philoxenian; Armenian.
Andreas, Cappadocia, 614.
A variant supported by E and 32 of Hoskiers cursives could translate as the KJV. The CR is close.

REVELATION 19:15
AV CR out of his mouth goeth a sharp sword
HF RP   ...a sharp two edged sword
Tyndale Geneva Bishops   Steph. Beza Elz.
Aleph A E P 046 1 35* 94 181 209 254 296 598 2014 2019 2020 2026 2031 2036 2037 2046 2053 2057 2059 2060 2062 2073 2081 2186 2254 2329, many of the Andreas mss.
Four of Hoskiers cursive families (in addition to the above citations). Von Soden indicates: Most of the Egyptian mss., I a (1 35 181 209 296 598 1876 1894 2015 2029 2033 2043 2056 2065 2066 2068 2069 2286). I b1 (1778 2080).
Old Latin: gig; Vulgate: am dem ful; Syriac: Philoxenian; Coptic: Sahadic Bohairic; (Armenian); Ethiopic.
Irenaeus, Lyons, 178 Origen, Alexandria, Caesarea, 254 Jerome, Latin, 420
Apringius, Portugal, Latin, 551 Pseudo-Ambrose, Latin VI Cassiodorus, Latin, 580
Andreas, Cappadocia, 614 Beatus, Libana,Latin, 786.

REVELATION 19:17
AV   Come and gather yourselves
HF RP CR Come, assemble yourselves
Tyndale Great Geneva Bishops   Steph. Beza Elz.

296 2066.
About 7 of Hoskier's cursives.
Vulgate: Clementine lipss.
Haymo, Halberstadt, Latin, 841.
The HF RP CR reading could probably translate as the KJV.

REVELATION 19:17
AV   gather yourselves unto the supper of the great God
HF RP CR   ...the great supper of God
Tyndale Great Geneva Bishops   Steph. Beza Elz.
E 051   1 101 209 337 598 1732 1876 2014 2019 2023 2026 2028 2029 2031 2033 2034 2036
2037 2038 2044 2045 2046 2049 2054 2057 2059 2068 2069 2073-mg. 2074 2081 2003 2091
2186 2286, many of the Andreas mss.
Vulgate: lipss; Armenian: including an early ms; (Ethiopic); Arabic.
Andreas, Cappadocia, 614.

REVELATION 20:3
AV   cast him into the bottomless pit, and shut him up
HF RP CR   ...and shut it
Tyndale Great (Geneva) Bishops   Steph. Beza Elz.
1 296 2066.
About 10 of Hoskier's cursives.
Coptic: Bohairic; Ethiopic.
Satan's judgement is magnified by the repetition of "him". "And cast him into the bottomless
pit, and shut him up, and set a seal upon him, that he... This stress is broken in the HF RP CR
reading.

REVELATION 20:12
AV   And I saw the dead, small and great
HF RP CR   ...the great and the small
Bishops   Steph. Beza Elz.
About 7 of Hoskier's cursives. Von Soden cites (may be among the supporting variants) 046 31
250 296 2016 2066.
About 18 cursives (from Hoskier) with variation could translate as the KJV.
Also Coptic: Bohairic; Andreas, 614 Arethas, 914.

REVELATION 20:12
AV   stand before God
HF RP CR   stand before the throne
Tyndale Great Geneva Bishops   Steph. Beza Elz.
1 181 296 522 1894 2028 2037 2046 2049 2059 2067 2081 2186.
Von Soden indicates: I a6 (743 2055 2064) .
Andreas, Cappadocia, 614.
As "the Father judgeth no man, but hath comitted all judgement unto the Son" (John 5:22), the
reading as it stands in the KJV declares the deity of Christ. This truth is lost when "God" is

changed to "throne". Partial support can be claimed from a variant which reads "throne of God".

REVELATION 20:12
AV   and the books were opened
HF RP   and they opened the books
Tyndale Great Geneva Bishops   Steph. Beza Elz.
35 104 181 205 432 617 632-c 1957 2016 2020 2023 2037 2038 2050 2066, most of the Andreas mss.
Supported by about 24 cursives in the HF listing (p xlvi). The Hoskier material was too diffuse to be usuable. Von Soden indicates: I a1 (598 2026 2060 2065 2081 2286), I a3 (209 2031 2056), I a5 (2028 2029 2033 2054 2068 2069).
Andreas, Cappadocia, 614   Arethas, Cappadocia, 914.
The well attested CR reading translates as the KJV, supported by: A P 046, about 23 cursives. Other variants would read as the KJV.

REVELATION 20:14
AV   cast into the lake of fire. This is the second death
HF RP CR   ...This is the second death, the lake of fire.
Tyndale Great Geneva Bishops   Steph. Beza Elz.
051 1 94 201 296 452 2016 2021 2053 2062 2066, manyof the Andreas mss.
Old Latin: a; Vulgate: Clementine lipss; Coptic: Bohairic; Armenian.
Augustine, Hippo, Latin, 430 "Promissionibus de", Latin, 453
Primasius, Adrumentum, Latin, 552 Andreas, Cappadocia, 614
Haymo, Halberstadt, Latin, 841.
The HF RP CR is clearly wrong in repeating "the lake of fire".

REVELATION 21:2
AV   And I John saw the holy city
HF RP CR omits "I John"
Tyndale Great Geneva Bishops   Steph. Beza Elz.
296 2049 2066.
Vulgate: Clementine lipss.
This is the second of three places where the phrase "I John" is found in Revelation, and is completely appropriate here.

REVELATION 21:3
AV   and God himself shall be with them, *and be* their God
HF   and shall be with them
RP CR   and God himself shall be with them.
Tyndale Great Geneva Bishops   Steph. Beza Elz.
A P 051-supplied 35* 175 181 205 296 598 617 1854 2016 2026 2036 2037 2038 2057 2065 2066 2080 2329, many of the Andreas mss. (the above' and following include minor variations).
About 44 of Hoskier's cursives. Von Soden indicates: . I a3 (209 2056), I a4 (1876 2014 2015

2043), I a6 (743 2064 2067).
Vulgate Syriac: Philoxenian Harclean.
Irenaeus, Lyons, Latin, 178   Tyconius, Latin, 380   Ambrose, Milan, Latin, 397
Apringius, Portugal, Latin, 551   Andreas, Cappadocia, 614   Beatus, Libana, Latin, 786.

REVELATION 21:4
AV   And God shal wipe away all tears from their eyes
HF RP CR omits "God"
Tyndale Great Geneva Bishops   Steph. Beza Elz.
A   1 172 1006 1841 2055 2065 2067 2081, part of the Andreas mss.
About 27 of Hoskier's cursives. Von Soden indicates: I a2 (1 296 1894 2059), I a5 (2028 2029
2033 2054 2068 2069).
Vulgate.
Tertullian, N. Africa, Latin, 220   Tyconius, Latin, 390   Augustine, Hippo, Latin,430
Apringius, Portugal, Latin, 551   Primasius, Adrumentum, Latin, 552   Andreas, Cappadocia, 614
Why is the name "God" removed in these latter readings (20:12 21:3)?

REVELATION 21:6
AV   It is done. I am Alpha and Omega
HF RP   omits "I am"
Tyndale Great Geneva Bishops   Steph. Beza Elz.
296 1779 1918 2020 2065 2066 2080.
About 17 of Hoskier's cursives.
Old Latin: gig; Vulgate; Coptic: Bohairic; Ethiopic.
Origen, Alexandria, Caesarea, 254   Cyprian, Carthage, Latin, 258   Tyconius, Latin, 380
Primasius, Adrumentum, Latin, 552.
The CR reading has "I am" (though proceeded by "they are done") supported by A 1006 1841
2053 2062. Some 67 of Hoskiers cursives with Aleph B E P read "I" by itself. This would most
naturally be translated as the KJV.

REVELATION 21:7
AV RP   shall inherit all things
HF   I will give to him these things
CR   shall inherit these things
Tyndale Great Geneva Bishops   Steph. Beza Elz.

The two parts of the KJV reading

1.   shall inherit (with variants)
Aleph A E P   1 35 104 205 241 325 432 632-c 1951 1957 2020 2023 2036 2037 2038 2050
2067.
About 106 of Hoskier's cursives.
Old Latin: gig; Vulgate; Coptic: Sahadic Bohairic; Ethiopic.
Cyprian, Carthage, Latin, 258   Tyconius, Latin, 380   Fulgentius, N. Africa Latin, 593

Primasius, Adrumentum, Latin, 552.

2. all things
1 2037.
About 20 of Hoskiers cursives. Von Soden indicates: I a5 (2029 .2033 2054 2068 2069).
Apringius,Portugal, Latin, 551   Andreas, Cappadocia, 614.
Part of the Andreas mss. support the entira reading.

REVELATION 21:8
AV CR   and unbelieving
HF RP   and unbelieving and sinners
Tyndale Great Geneva Bishops   Steph. Beza Elz.
Aleph A P 1 2023 2036 2037 2038 2050 2057.
About 50 of Hoskier's cursives. Von Soden indicates: Most Egyptian mss, I a (60 181 296 598 1876 1894 2014 2015 2026 2031 2043 2056 2059 2060 2065 2066 2081 2286), I b1 (1778 2090).
Old Latin: gig; Vulgate; Coptic: Sahadic Bohairic; Armenian; Ethiopic.
Tertullian, N. Africa, Latin, 220 Tyconius, Latin, 380   Primaaius, Adrumentum, Latin, 552
Andreas, Cappadocia, 614.
Some early scribes may have wrongly thought that unbelief and fearfulness were insufficient to damn the soul to hell.

REVELATION 21:9
AV   And there came unto me one of the seven angels
HF RP CR   omits "unto me"
Tyndale Great Geneva Bishops   Steph. Beza Elz.
296 506 2049 2066.
Vulgate: lipss; Armenian: including 2 early mss; Arabic.
The angel did in fact "come to John".

REVELATION 21:10
AV RP   that great city, the holy Jerusalem
HF CR omits "that great"
Tyndale Great Geneva Bishops   Steph. Beza Elz.
E 051   1 35 175·205 250 617 1854 1957 2016 2023 2030 2036 2037 2039 2041 2067 2377, many of the Andreas mss. (the above and following citations include a minor variant).
About 105 of Hoskier's cursives.
Armenian.
Andreas, Cappadocia, 614.

REVELATION 21:11
AV   and her light *was* like unto a stone most precious
HF RP CR omits "and"
Tyndale Great Geneva Bishops   Steph. Beza Elz.
1 104 172 205 1862 2067 2080 2081 2329, many of the Andreas mss.

About 49 of Hoskier's cursives. Von Soden indicates: I a2 (1 181 296 1894 2059 2066), I a5 (2028 2029 2033 2054 2068 2069).
Old LatinI t; Vulgate I Clementine demid l1pss; Syriac', Philoxenian; Coptic: (Bohairic); Armenian: including an early ms; Ethiopic; Arabic.
Primasius, Adrumentum, Latin, 522 Andreas, Cappadocia, 614
Haymo, Halberstadt, Latin,841   Arethas, Cappadocia, 914.

REVELATION 21:13
AV   on the north three gates
HF RP CR and on...
(Geneva Tyndale, Great, Bishops ??)   Steph. Beza Elz.
051 1 205 1611 2037 2038 2057 2067 2329, many of the Andreas mss.
Von Soden indicates: I a (181 209 296 598 743 1876 1894 2014 2015 2016 2028 2029 2031 2033 2036 2043 2054 2055 2056 2059 2060 2064 2067 2068 2069 2081 2286).
Old Latin: t; Vulgate: ful demid lipss tol; Armenian: including 2 early mss.
Tyconius, Latin, 380   Primasius, Adrumentum, Latin, 552   Andreas, Cappadocia,614
Beatus, Libana, Latin, 796.

REVELATION 21:13
AV   on the south three gates
HF RP CR and on...
Witnesses are virtually the same as those above.

REVELATION 21:14
AV   and in them the names
HF RP CR and on them the names
Tyndale Great Geneva Bishops   Steph. Beza. Elz.
296 2049. (Von Soden does not cite).
Old Latin: gig; Vulgate.
Pseudo-Ambrose VI.
The translation is probably not affected. "epi" is translated "in" with regard to the seal or mark in 9:4 13:16 14:1 20:4.

REVELATION 21:14
AV   the names of the twelve apostles
HF RP CR the twelve names of the twelve apostles
Tyndale Geneva   Steph. Beza Elz.
1* 104.
About 20 or less of Hoskier's cursives.
Vulgate: lipss; Coptic: Sahadic Bohairic; Armenian; Ethiopic.
Primasius, Adrumentum, Lat!n, 552.
Repeating "twelve" three times in the HF RP CR reading amounts to tautology.

REVELATION 21:24
AV   And the nations of them which are saved shall walk in the light

HF RP CR   omits "of them which are saved"
Tyndale Great Geneva Bishops   Steph. Beza Elz.
1 2049.
Von Soden apparently cites 2054 2069.
A variant contains the words "which are saved" and is supported by part of the Andreas tradition mss.
Erasmus does not have the words in his editions, though the Aldus printed text of 1518 does. This indicates that evidence came to light as the sixteenth century progressed which convinced the later editors in favor of the readings inclusion.
After many millenniums of the contrary, the Scriptures here state that there will be *saved nations.*

REVELATION 22:1
AV RP   a pure river of water of life
HF CR   omits "pure"
Tyndale Great Geneva Bishops   Steph. Beza Elz.
E 051-supplied   1 35 104 175 205 209 218 242 250 506 617 1934 1957 2016 2017 2020 2023 2030 2036 2037 2038 2041 2067 2377, many of the Andreas mss. (the above and following include a minor variant).
About 110 of Hoskiers cursives.
Syriac; Armenian; Arabic.
Andreas, Cappadocia,614   Arethas, Cappadocia, 914.

REVELATION 22:8
AV   I John saw these things,and heard *them*
HF RP CR   ...heard...saw
Tyndale Great Geneva.Bishops   Steph. Beza Elz.
1 296 2066.
About 10 of Hoskiers cursives.
A variant supported by Aleph, 66 of Hoskier'scursives, Syriac Philoxenian, Coptic Bohairic, Dionysius, 265 Andreas, 614 Arethas, 914 would probably translate as the KJV.

REVELATION 22:11
AV   and he that is righteous, let him be righteous still
HF RP CR   ...let him practice righteousness still
Tyndale Great Geneva Bishops   Steph. Beza Elz.
296 2020 2036· 2066, some of the Andreas mss.
About 26 of Hoskier's cursives.
Von Soden indicates: I a4 (1876 2014 2015 2036 2043).
Old Latin t; Vulgate: Clementine lipss; Coptic: (Bohairic); Armenian: including (1 early ms.); Ethiopic.
Augustine, Hippo, Latin, 430.

REVELATION 22:12
AV   And behold, I come quickly

HF RP CR omits "And"
Tyndale Great Geneva Bishops   Staph. Beza Elz.
1 191 254 296 598 743 1611-supplied 2026 2030 2031 2038 2045 2051 2055 2056 2057 2059 2060 2064 2067 2073 2081 2186 2254 2286, many of the Andreas mss.
Vulgate: early mss; Ethiopic.
Tyconius, Latin, 380   Andreas, Cappadocia, 614.

REVELATION 22:15
AV   For without are dogs
HF RP CR omits "For"
Tyndale Great Geneva Bishops   Steph. Beza Elz.
110? 296 1994 2049 2066.
Vulgate: lipss; Syriac: Philoxenian; Coptic: Sahadic Bohairic; Armenian; Arabic.
Fulgentius, N. Africa, Latin, 533   Primasius, Adrumentum, Latin, 552.

REVELATION 22:16
AV   the bright and morning star
HF RP CR   omits "and"
(Tyndale Great Geneva Bishops ??)   Steph. Beza Elz.
296 (apparently) 2066.
About 17 of Hoskier's cursives.
Haymo, Halberstadt, Latin, 841.
Two variants read by A, 11 of Hoskiers cursives, Old Latin gig, Vulgate, Apringius 551, Primasius 552, Pseudo-Ambrose VI, Beatus 786.

REVELATION 22:17
AV   And let him that is athirst come. And...let
HF RP CR   omits   the second "And"
Tyndale Great Geneva Bishops   Steph. Beza Elz.
209 218 254 296 1894 2049 2050 2066 2075-supplied 2321.
Vulgate: Clementine ful lipss; Syriac: including Harclean; Coptic: Sahadic; Armenian: including an early ms; Arabic.
Primasius, Adrumentum, Latin, 552   Arethas, Cappadocia, 614.

REVELATION 22:18
AV   For I testify unto every man
HF RP CR omits "For"
Geneva   Steph. Beza Elz.
2066.
About 8 of Hoskier's cursives (including variants).
Vulgate: Clementine lipss; Coptic: Bohairic; Ethiopic.
Tyconius, Latin, 380   Haymo, Halberstadt, Latin, 841.
"For" is a necessary connective here.

REVELATION 22:19
AV   God shall take away his part out of the book of life
HF RP CR   ...the tree of life
Tyndale Great Geneva Bishops   Steph. Beza Elz.
296 2049 2067-mg.
Vulgate: Clementine ful lipss; Coptic: Bohairic; Arabic.
Ambrose, Milan, Latin, 397 Speculum, Pseudo-Augustine, Latin, V
Primasius, Adrumentum, Latin, 552 Andreas, Cappadocia, 614 Haymo,
Halberstadt, Latin, 941.
Each person has his own individual "part in the book of life". But what are we to make of a man's "part in the tree of life"? The revised reading lessens the impact of the last warning in the Bible. Also, a parallel is intended "...this book...the book of life".
Hoskier doubts that Erasmus copied this from the Vulgate, suggesting instead that he followed Codex 2049 (Hills *KJVD* p. 202).

REVELATION 22:19
AV   and *from* the things which are written in this book
HF RP CR   tree...and from the holy city, which...
Tyndale Great Geneva Bishops   Steph. Beza Elz.
296 2049.
Old Latin: (gig); (Vulgate); (Arabic).
Apringius, Portugal, Latin, 551 Haymo, Halberstadt, Latin, 941.
The blessings and prospects of the entire book of Revelation are now summed up as the believers portion. The HF RP CR reading in effect limits this portion to the final two chapters.

REVELATION 22:21
AV   The grace of our Lord Jesus Christ
HF RP omits "our"
CR   omits "our" and "Christ"
Tyndale Great Geneva Bishops   Steph. Beza Elz.

The two parts of the KJV reading

1._   Inclusion of "our"
149 205 205Abs. 254, 296 429 468 582 1719 1948 2021 2049 2057 2058 2067 2078 2082 2258.
Old Latin: ar c dem div gig haf; Vulgate; Syriac: Philoxenian Harclean; Coptic: Sahadic (Bohairic); Armenian; Ethiopic.
Pseudo-Ambrose, Latin, VI Andreas, Cappadocia, 614 Beatus, Libana, Latin, 786.

2._   Inclusion of "Christ"
046.
About 162 of Hoskier's cursives.
Old Latin: ar c dem div gig haf; Vulgate; Syriac: Philoxenian Harclean; Coptic: Bohairic; Armenian; Ethiopic.
Pseudo-Ambrose, Latin, VI Andreas, Cappadocia, 614 Beatus, Libana, Latin, 786.

With the exception of II Cor. 13:14, this closing benediction always has "the grace of <u>our</u> Lord Jesus <u>Christ</u>".

REVELATION 22:21

AV   with you all
HF RP   with all the saints
CR   with all
Tyndale Great Geneva Bishops   Steph. Beza Elz.
296 2050 2066.
About 15 of Hoskier's cursives.
Old Latin: c dem div haf; Vulgate: Clementine demid ful lipss; Ethiopic.
Pseudo-Ambrose, Latin, VI.
The HF RP reading would be unique in the New Testament. The closest to it is II Cor. 13:13, Phil. 4:22.

The words of the LORD are pure words: as silver tried in a furnace of earth, purified seven times. Thou shalt keep them, O LORD, thou shalt preserve them from this generation for ever.

(Psalms 12:6-7)

CHAPTER 6

THE MOST FAMOUS
"MINORITY" PASSAGE—I JOHN 5:7,8

The passage as it stands is the strongest statement in the Bible on the Holy Trinity. It is not surprising that it should be the subject of debate and we believe an object of Satan's attack. It is sad to observe how readily modern christians will surrender this and other passages on "textual grounds" without taking the time to look more closely at the evidence.

Modern textual criticism, and here Bruce Metzger, unites in telling us:

1. The passage is absent from every known Greek manuscript except four, and these contain the passage in what appears to be a translation from a late recension of the Latin Vulgate. These four are:

    61, a 16th century MS formerly at Oxford, now at Dublin.

    88, a 12th century MS at Naples, which had the passage written in the margin by a modern hand.

    629, a 14th or 15th century MS in the Vatican.

    635, an 11th century MS which has the passage written in the margin by a 17th century hand.

2. The passage is quoted by none of the Greek Fathers, who, had they known it, would most certainly have employed it in the Trinitarian controversies (Sabellian and Arian). Its first appearance in Greek is in a Greek version of the (Latin) Acts of the Latern Council in 1215.

3. The passage is absent from the MSS of all ancient versions. (Syriac, Coptic, Armenian, Ethiopic, Arabic. Slavonic) except the Latin.

    It is not found in the Old Latin in its early form (Tertullian, Cyprian, Augustine).

    It is not found in the Vulgate as issued by Jerome (codex Fuldensis, copied 541-46; codex Amiatinus, copied before A.D. 716). Nor in the revision by Alcuin (first hand of codex Vercellensis, 9th century).

    The earliest instance of the passage being quoted as a part of the actual text of 1 John is a fourth century Latin treatise entitled *Liber Apologeticus*, attributed either to the Spanish

141

heretic Priscillian (died about 385) or to his follower Bishop Instantias. Apparently the gloss arose when the original passage was understood to symbolize the Trinity (through the mention of three witnesses; the Spirit, the water, and the blood), an interpretation which may have been written first as a marginal note and afterwards found its way into the text.

In the 5th century the gloss was quoted by Latin Fathers in North Africa and Italy as part of the text of the Epistle, and from the 6th century onwards it is found more and more frequently in MSS of the Old Latin and Vulgate.

4. As regards transcriptional probability, if the passage were original, no good reason can be found to account for its omission, either accidently or intentionally, by copyists of hundreds of Greek MSS, and by translators of ancient versions.

5. As regards intrinsic probability, the passage makes an awkward break in the sense (Metzger, *Textual Commentary*, pp 715-17).

There you have it! These are the standard arguments that have been tirelessly repeated. In fact, Metzger seems to repeat this almost verbatim from the *International Critical Commentary* of 1920. Their case sounds convincing. But is it really as open and shut as Metzger and most others would have us believe? And, is the entire story being told?

INTERNAL EVIDENCE

If the passage is removed from the Greek text, the two loose ends will not join up grammatically. A problem arises which has to do with the use of the participle (a kind of verbal adjective). Being an adjective it modifies nouns and must agree with them in gender.

With the full passage set out, it becomes apparent how this rule of grammar is violated when the words are omitted. The disputed words are enclosed in square brackets. The underlined words form a participle.

- vs. 6 *And it is the Spirit* (neuter) *that beareth witness* (neut) *because the Spirit* (neut.) *is truth.*

- vs. 7 *For there are three* (masculine) *that bear record* (masc) [in heaven, the Father (masc.), the Word (masc.), and the Holy Ghost (neut): and these three (masc) are one (masc).

- vs. 8 And there are three (masc) that bear witness (masc) in earth] the Spirit (neut) and the water (neut), and the blood (neut): and these three (masc) agree in one.

If one wants to remove the words within the brackets, the following problems must be addressed:

1. Why after using a neuter participle in line one is a masculine participle used in line three? Especially so if this second participle must now modify three neuter nouns - *Spirit, water, blood*?

2. How can the masculine (1) numeral, (2) article (in the Greek), and (3) participle (i.e. three masculine adjectives) of line three be allowed to directly modify the three neuter nouns: *Spirit, water, blood*?

3. What phenomena in Greek syntax would cause these three neuter nouns *Spirit, water, blood* to be treated as masculine by *these three* ?

There is not a good answer! And perhaps this is the reason why such leading Greek scholars as Metzger, Vincent, Alford, Vine, Wuest, Bruce, Plummer, do not make the barest mention of the problem when dealing with the passage. The *International Critical Commentary* devotes twelve pages to the passage but says nothing about the mismatched genders.

As for the third point, Hills mentions an attempt toward an answer.

> The words spirit, water, and blood are neuter in gender, but in I John 5:8 they are treated as masculine. If the Johannine comma is rejected, it is hard to explain this irregularity. It is usually said that In I John 5:8 the spirit, the water, and the blood are personalized and that this is the reason for the adoption of the masculine gender. But it is hard to see how such personalization would involve the change from the neuter to the masculine. For in verse 6, the word spirit plainly refers to the Holy Spirit, the ·third person of the trinity. Surely in this verse, the word spirit is "personalized," and yet the neuter gender is used (i.e., in the participle). Therefore, since personalization did not bring about a change of gender in verse 6, it cannot fairly be pleaded as the reason for such a change in verse 8. If, however, the Johannlne comma is retained, a reason for referring to the neuter nouns spirit, water, and blood in the masculine gender becomes readily apparent. It was due to the influence of the nouns Father and Word, which are masculine (*KJVD* pp 211,12).

It is this principle of influence and attraction in Greek grammar which is the key here. What influence would cause: *that bear record* in line three and *these three* at the end to suddenly become masculine? The answer can only be the inclusion of <u>the Father</u> and <u>the Word</u>, to which the beginning and ending of the passage are attracted.

Robert Dabney describes this process:

> The masculine article numeral and participle HOI TREIS MARTUROUNTES, are made to agree directly with three neuters,an insuperable and very bald grammatical difficulty. If the disputed words are allowed to remain, they agree with two masculines and one neuter noun HO PATER, HO LOGOS, KAI TO HAGION PNEUMA and, according to the rule of syntax, the masculines among the group control the gender over a neuter connected with them. Then the occurance of the masculines TREIS MARTUROUNTES in verse 8 (i.e. the second occurance of "three that bear witness") agreeing with the neuters PNEUMA, HUDOR and HAIMA may be accounted for by the power of attraction, well known in Greek syntax. (An extract from "Dabneys Discussions

Evangelical and Theological," reprinted by the Trinitarian Bible Society).

Matthew Henry's commentary puts forward a second grammatical argument:

> If we admit v. 8 in the room of v. 7, it looks too much like a tautology and repetition of what was included in *v*, 6, "This is he that came by water and blood, not by water only, but by water and blood; and it is the Spirit that beareth witness. For there are three that bear witness, the spirit, the water, and the blood."

A third grammatical argument in the passage's favor concerns the final sentence of verse 8:

> ...*and these three agree in one.*

It is not merely that the *spirit, water* and *blood* agree among themselves; that would go without saying. But they appear to be in agreement with something else that had been previously mentioned. This is confirmed in the Greek.

Dabney says:

> If the words are omitted, the concluding words at the end of verse 8 contain an unintelligible reference. The Greek words KAI HOI TREIS EIS TO HEN EISIN mean precisely - "and these three agree to that (aforesaid) One." If the 7th verse is omitted "that One" does not appear.

Gaussen in his famous book on inspiration quotes Bishop Middleton to the same effect:

> To this Bishop Middleton devotes eighteen pages in his beautiful work on the Doctrine of the Greek Article (1828). "I cannot conceive", says he in conclusion, "how this word, that ONE (TO HEN) can be reconciled with the taking away of the preceeding words" (*The Inspiration of the Holy Scriptures* p. 193).

Finally we quote again from Dabney who gives an excellent summary of the passage:

> John has asserted in the previous 6 verses that faith is the bond of our spiritual life and victory over the world. This faith must have a solid warrant, and the truth of which faith must be assured is the Sonship and Divinity of Christ. See 5:5, 11, 12, 20. The only faith that quickens the soul and overcomes the world is (verse 5) the belief that Jesus is God's Son, that God has appointed Him our Life, and that this Life is true God.
>
> God's warrant for this faith comes:
>
> FIRST In verse 6, in the words of the Holy Ghost speaking by inspired men.
>
> SECOND In verse 7, in the words of the Father, the Word and the Spirit, asserting and confirming by miracles the Sonship and unity of Christ with the Father.
>
> THIRD In verse 8, in the work of the Holy Ghost applying the blood and water from Christ's pierced side for our cleansing.
>
> FOURTH In verses 10, in the spiritual consciousness of the believer himself, certifying to him that he feels within a divine change.
>
> How harmonious is all this if we accept the 7th verse as genuine, but if we omit it the very keystone of the arch is wanting, and the crowning proof that the warrant of our faith is divine (verse 9) is struck out.

Thus, there are very strong internal reasons for retaining I John 5:7.

Gaussen says it best:

> Remove it, and the grammar becomes incoherent.

EXTERNAL EVIDENCE

(1) GREEK MANUSCRIPTS

The Nestle-Aland 26th edition lists the following as having the passage:

61	XVI
88 mg	XII
221 mg	X
429 mg	XIV
629	XIV
635 mg	XI cited by Metzger and UBS-1, but not N-A
636 mg	XV
918	XVI
2318	XVIII

The N.A. apparatus states that other Greek MSS contain the reading in the margin. It was from MS 61 that Erasmus brought the passage into his third edition (1522). The Complutenslan (1514) containing the passage was a spur to Erasmus eventually inserting it. It is asserted that a number of the above MSS are merely copies of the Vulgate at I John 5:7.

Metzger says:

> ...these [referring to four MSS] contain the passage in what appears to be a translation from a late recension of the Latin Vulgate (*Textual Commentary*).

This is by no means certain, and Metzger's statement stops short of certainty. Matthew Henry's Commentary in discussing certain aspects of the Complutensian's treatment of the passage, concludes:

> ...which seems to show that that edition depended upon some Greek authority, and not merely, as some would have us believe upon the authority either of the vulgar Latin or or Thomas Aquinas.

Thus, the list of Greek MSS presently known to contain the passage is not long, but it is certainly longer (and growing) than what many have told us. Plummer in his disdain for the passage and desire to rule out any early Greek evidence virtually admits in the following statement that some does exist:

> Again, It has been urged that the Greek Synopsis of Holy Scripture printed in some editions of the Greek Fathers,· and also the so-called Disputaion wth Arius, "seems to betray an acquaintance with the disputed verse." Even if this "seeming" could be shown to be a reality, the fact would prove no more than that the interpolation existed in a Greek as well as a Latin form about the fifth century (*The Epistles of St. John, The Cambridge Bible for Schools and Colleges*, p 205).

A fifth century Greek witness (probably about 450 AD) is in fact quite early, when one considers that MSS such as Aleph and B are only 75-100 years older! Thus though missing in most Greek manuscripts, <u>the passage nevertheless leaves in them its *footprint*</u>! And this, with the mismatched genders that result when the words are removed.

(2) OTHER EASTERN WITNESSES

Available evidence indicates a paucity of support for the passage in the Greek speaking East, and among the Fathers and Versions associated with that part of the Roman Empire.

Metzger, however, goes too far when he says:

> The Passage is absent from the MSS of all ancient versions except the Latin (*Textual Commentary*).

In his *Plain Introduction* (1883), Scrivener mentions the following as containing I John 5:7, 8:

1. In 1569, utilizing several Syriac Peshitta MSS, Immanuel Tremellius prepared the second printed edition of the Syriac New Testament. (The first had been printed in 1555 by Albert Widmanstadt who had used two MSS). Tremellius placed 1 John 5:7,8 in the margin of his edition.
2. Giles Guthier, using two MSS published a Syriac edition at Hamburg in 1664. This edition places the passage in the text.
3. The first printed edition of the Armenian Bible was published in 1666 by Bishop Uscan. It was based primarily on an Armenian MS dated 1295. This first Armenian Bible contains the passage.
4. The Armenian edition of John Zohrob (1789) mentions that 18 MSS (Armenian) were consulted for the Epistle of 1 John. One of these contained 1 John 5:7,8.
5. The first printed Georgian Bible, published at Moscow in 1743 contains 1 John 5:7,8.

   Of this edition Voobus says:

   > It is interesting that this edition was not based upon the revised text but upon Georgian MSS which reflect an older type (Arthur Voobus, *Early Versions of the New Testament*, Stockholm, 1954, p. 206).

6. Scrivener mentions a "few recent" Slavonic MSS as having the passage.

Regarding the Gothic Version, no portion of Acts, and Hebrews to Revelation has been known to survive. As for the early eastern Fathers silence on the passage; they are silent on just about everything else, for the simple reason that their literary works have not survived.

The point made by Sturz would apply here:

> ...there are no earlier Antiochian Fathers than Chrysostom (died 407) whose literary remains are extensive enough so that their New Testament quotations may be analyzed as to the type of text they support (Harry A. Sturz, *The Byzantine Text Type and New Testament Textual Criticism*).

As for the eastern Fathers from Chrysostom onwards we would like to see some hard factual evidence as to how thorough the search has been, and the same for the Versions also. With the exception of Michael Maynard's massive *A History Of The Debate Over 1 John 5:7-8,* the textual scene has given very little attention to the passage. Nevertheless, it is good to know that a number of the key printed editions which reached great numbers of people in the East, contain the passage.

(3) EARLY LATIN WITNESSES

Practically all of the extant Latin Vulgate MSS contain the "Three Heavenly Witnesses," though a few early copies omit it (Fuldensis - 546, Amiatinus - 716). The following gives some of the testimony for the disputed words in the Latin West before 550:

1. A passage in the writings of Tertullian (died 220) has been cited as indicating that this Father knew of the words. Many deny this, and say that Tertullian's statement is to be limited to John 16:14 and 10: 30.

    > He saith, "He shall take of mine," even as He Himself of the Father. Thus the connexlon of the Father in the Son, and of the Son In the Paraclete, maketh Three that cohere together one from the other: which Three are one Substance, not one Person; as it is said, "I and My Father are one," in respect to unity of essence, not to singularity of number (*adv. Praxean*, c. 25).

2. Cyprian of Carthage (died 258) refers plainly to the disputed words:

    > The Lord saith, "I and the Father are one;" and again it is written concerning the Father, Son and Holy Spirit, "And three are one" (*de Catholicae ecclesiae unitate*, c. 6).

    Critics have argued that Cyprian was merely giving a Trinitarian interpretation to verse 8.

    > the spirit, and the water, and the blood: and these three agree in one.

    The answer to this is obvious; the figures of verse 8 cannot naturally be interpreted as the <u>Persons</u> of the Holy Trinity.

    It is further argued that Facundus (c550), a bishop of Cyprian's church, interpreted verse 8 as refering to the Trinity and quotes Cyprian's statement as supporting his view. This is countered by pointing out that Fulgentius of the same church who wrote a little earlier quotes Cyprian as refering to verse seven.

3. Priscillian, a Spanish christian executed on a charge of heresy in AD 385, quotes the words in his *Liber Apologeticus.*

    Two other works quoting the passage may be as early if not earlier than Priscillian.

4. The *Speculum,* a treatise which contains the Old Latin text, records the words. The work was written not later than the first half of the fifth century. However, the manner in which

the passage is worded points to a date earlier than Priscillian (i.e. certainly for the passage, if not the *Speculum* itself).

5. A creed known as *Expositio Fidei* quotes the passage. Of this work the *International Critical Commentary* in I John says:

> The evidence of the "Exposltio Fidei" published by Caspari from the Ambroslan MS...is also important. The close agreement of this with Priscillian's quotation is evident...Caspari, its editor, regards the creed as African, of the fifth or sixth century. Dom Morin would attribute it to Isaac the Jew and the times of Damasus (372). Kunstle regards it as clearly antl-Prlscillianist... (pp 158, 59).

6. The passage is found in r, an Old Latin MS of the 5th or 6th century.

7. The words are quoted in a confession of faith drawn up by Eugenius, Bishop of Carthage in 484. This was presented by the bishops of North Africa to the vandal King Hunnerich. The Confession is found in *Historia Persecutionis*, a 7th century work.

8. Two works either by, or associated with, Vigilus of Thapsus, in North Africa (490) give the passage. These are vol. I of *de Trinitate*, and *Contra Varimadum*.

9. Fulgentius of Ruspe in North Africa (died 533) quotes the passage in *De fide Catholica adv. Pintam*.

10. Though the early Vulgate MS (Fuldensis, 546) does not have the passage, it is quoted in the manuscript's prologue to the General Epistles.

11. Cassiodorus (480-570) of Italy quotes the passage.

Therefore, <u>early</u> testimony for this key Trinitarian verse does exist. It must be borne in mind that the above do not merely formulate the words for a treatise or creed, but quote them as an actual part of the text of I John.

ERASMUS AND 1 JOHN 5:7,8

It has often been asserted that Erasmus said he would insert the passage only if someone could show him a Greek manuscript containing the words, to which a manuscript was hastily prepared for that purpose. A letter from the Erasmian scholar H. J. de Jonge to Michael Maynard in 1995 puts the matter in a different light. Quoting Erasmus in his dispute with Edward Lee, de Jonge says:

> Erasmus first records that Lee had reproached him with neglect of the manuscripts of I John. Erasmus (according to Lee) had consulted only one manuscript. Erasmus replies that he had "certainly not used only one manuscript, but many copies, first in England, then in Brabant, and finally in Basle. He cannot accept, therefore, Lee's reproach of negligence and impiety."

"Is it negligence and impiety, if I did not consult manuscripts which were not within my reach? I have at least assembled whatever I could assemble. Let Lee produce a Greek MS which contains what my edition does not contain and let him show that that manuscript was within my reach. Only then can he reproach me with negligence in sacred matters."

From this passage you can see that Erasmus does not challenge Lee to produce a manuscript etc. What Erasmus argues is that Lee may only reproach Erasmus with negligence of MSS if he demonstrates that Erasmus could have consulted any MS in which the Comma Johanneum figured. Erasmus does not at all ask for a MS containing the Comma Johanneum. He denies Lee the right to call him negligent and impious if the latter does not prove that Erasmus neglected a manuscript to which he had access. (Michael Maynard, *A History of the Debate over I John 5:7,8*, p. 383).

Jeffrey Khoo points out:

Yale professor Roland Bainton.... agrees with de Jonge, furnishing proof from Erasmus' own writing that Erasmus' inclusion of I John 5:7 was not due to a so-called "promise" but the fact that he believed "the verse was in the Vulgate and must therefore have been in the Greek text used by Jerome." (*Kept Pure in all Ages*, p.88; cited in D.W. Cloud, *The Bible Version Question/Answer Database*, p.343). See also *And These Three are One* by Jesse Boyd, Wake Forest, 1999.

A POSSIBLE REASON FOR THE OMISSION OF I JOHN 5:7 FROM THE GREEK MANUSCRIPTS

Edward Hills gives the following:

...during the second and third centuries (between 220 and 270, according to Harnack) the heresy which orthodox Christians were called upon to combat was not Arianism (since this error had not yet arisen), but Sabellianism (so named after Sabellius, one of its principal promoters), according to which the Father, the Son, and the Holy Spirit were one in the sense that they were identical. Those that advocated this heretical view were called Patripassians (Father-sufferers), because they believed that God the Father, being Identical with Christ, suffered and died upon the cross; and Monarchians, because they clalmed to uphold the Monarchy (sole-government) of God.

It is possible, therefore, that the Sabellian heresy brought the Johannine comma into disfavour with orthodox christians. The statement, "these three are one," no doubt seemed to them to teach the Sabellian view that the Father, the Son, and the Holy Spirit were identical. And if during the course of the controversy manuscripts were discovered which had lost this reading..., it is easy to see how the orthodox party would consider these mutilated manuscripts to represent the true text and regard the Johannine comma as a heretical addition. In the Greek-speaking East especially the comma would be unanimously rejected, for there the struggle against Sabellianism was particularly severe.

Thus it is not impossible that durlnq the 3rd century, amid the stress and strain of the Sabellian controversy, the Johannine comma lost its place in the Greek text but was preserved in the Latin texts of Africa and Spain, where the influence of Sabellianism was probably not so great. To suppose this, at any rate, is strictly in accord with the principles of believing Bible study. For, although the Greek New Testament text was the special object of God's providential care, nevertheless, this care also extended, in lesser degree, to the ancient versions and to the usage not only of Greek-speaking christians, but also of the other branches of the christian church. Hence, although the Traditional text found in the vast majority of the Greek manuscripts is a fully trustworthy reproduction of the divinely Inspired original text, still it is possible that the text of the Latin Vulgate, which really represents the long-established usage of the Latin Church, preserves a few genuine readings not found In the Greek manuscripts. And hence, also, it is possible that the Johannine comma is one of these exceptional readings which, we may well believe, were included in the Textus Receptus under the direction of God's special providence (*KJVD*, p 212, 13).

The fate of this passage in the Greek East does indeed parallel the many times Satan in OT days sought to destroy the line through which Christ the Living Word would come. We are reminded of Athaliah cutting off all of the seed royal—except for Joash! The passage has been strongly defended by men who hallow the words of Scripture. It has the ring of truth. And it is the Holy Spirit *who guides into all truth* (John 16: 13) who has given it that "ring".

Michael Maynard's monumental work on the disputed passage will, I think, demonstrate that this has not been a debate over "thin air". His book chronicles the fact that <u>defence of the faith and defence of this passage has frequently gone hand in hand</u>.

SUMMARY AND CONCLUSION

We come to the end of our inquiry into the Hodges-Farstad, Robinson-Pierpont *"Majority", Byzantine* editions of the Greek New Testament Text. The editions represent a textual "half-way house" for those who while seeing the fallacy of Westcott and Hort, have still *at this late date* not come to a finalized and perfected Text. They do not recognize as we do that this once inspired and preserved Text is that which underlies our 400 – year Standard Bible, the Authorized Version.

Their editions have three fundamental flaws:

1. The editors do not go a great deal further than the critical editors in declaring faith in God's promise to verbally preserve the Scriptures.

2. *HF* claims to be a *majority* text but is based almost entirely on the research of Hermann von Soden. Von Soden did not collate anything approaching a majority of the manuscripts. Those he consulted on an even remotely consistant basis total only about 414. The number of specific manuscripts to which *RP* appeals is considerably less.

3. Though using a somewhat different approach, the great number of changes *HF* and *RP* introduce into the text of Revelation is based on their choice of the 046 MSS rather than the Andrean. And, this despite the fact that the Andrean Text can be shown to be

older, more cohesive, and has been the traditionally printed text for the Apocalypse. Further, *HF* greatly misrepresented the relative numbers of the Andreas and 046 MSS.

A great deal of valuable material is presented in the *HF* and *RP* editions, but at this late date their Text by their own acknowledgement is only *tentative* and *provisional*. We are convinced further inquiry will not change this conclusion.

It is with thankfulness to God that when an inquiry of this kind is made, the Authorized Version and its underlying Text is shown to be more than equal to the challenge. It can be tested and proven at every point. <u>We will continue to hold to every Word of our Standard Bible.</u>

Concerning thy testimonies, I have known of old that thou hast founded them for ever.

(Psalms 119:152)

APPENDIX 1

PLACES WHERE THE OXFORD 1825 TR USED BY THE HF EDITORS DEPARTS FROM THE KJV TEXT

It is surprising that Hodges and Farstad editon did not use one of the more standard editions of the Textus Receptus as the basis of comparison with their "majority" text. They instead used the Oxford 1825 edition.

Regarding this choice Andrew Brown says:

> This Oxford edition is not an accurate copy of any of the early editions and differs from Stephanus 1550 in approximately 125 passages in matters of spelling or wording. As a result the Hodges-Farstad footnotes attribute to "TR" 56 readings which belong not to Stephanus 1550, but to the 1825 reprint (Including a number of undoubted errors, such as GENOMENOS for LEGOMENOS In Mk. 15:7. Similarly they adopt non-Stephanus readings In their text without any accompanying footnote (*Trinitarian Bible Society Quarterly Record*, January .1983, p 16).

In the Manuscript Digest, I have assumed that AV readings are accurately reflected by *The Greek Text Underlying the English Version of 1611*, edited by F.H.A. Scrivener. The following KJV readings do not deviate from the "majority" text, as implied in the *HF* apparatus. It is with the 1825 TR that they disagree.

Mt. 9:18 there came a certain ruler
10:10 neither shoes, nor yet staves
11 :21 Bethsaida
20:15 Is thine eye evil
23:13 But woe unto you, scribes
23:14 Woe unto you, scribes
26:9 given to the poor
Mk. 4:18 these are they which are sown among thorns
6:29 laid it in a tomb
13:14 standing
15:7 *one* named Barabbas
15:29 Ah, thou that destroyest
Lk. 12:20 Thou fool
15:26 one of the servants
17:1 but that offences will come
22:47 and drew near
24:9 and told all these things.
Jhn. 5:5 thirty and eight years
6 :28 what shall we do
18:16 which was known
Acts 2:36 that God hath made that same Jesus

4:25 mouth of thy servant David
7:44 Our fathers had the tabernacle
8:13 beholding the miracles and signs
8:13 wondered...which were done
21:4 And finding disciples
24:18 Whereupon certain Jews
27:3 to go unto his friends
1 Cor. 11:32 chastened of the Lord
2 Cor. 5:4 not for that we would be unclothed
Gal. 6:13 may glory in your flesh
Eph. 1:6 accepted in the beloved
6:7 as to the Lord
Phil. 4:12 I know both
1 Thess. 1:8 and Achaia
1:9 we had unto you
2:15 have persecuted us
2 Tim. 2:8 was raised from the dead
Heb. 9:1 the first *covenant*
1 Pet. 1:4 reserved in heaven for you
3:16 they speak evil of you
2 Pet. 1:21 holy men of God
2:12 beasts, made
1 Jhn. 1:5 the message
Rev. 2: 14 Balac
7:2 ascending from the east
9:19 is in their mouth
14:7 and the sea
16:14 which go forth
16:14 to the battle
17:4 the woman was arrayed
17: 8 The beast
18:5 her sins have reached unto heaven
19:16 a name written
19:18 both free and bond
20:4 his image

Total – 56

APPENDIX 2

KJV PASSAGES WHICH WOULD NOT BE AFFECTED BY THE DIVERGENT GREEK OF THE "MAJORITY" TEXT

In the current debate we will seek at every point to defend the underlying Text and English wording of the Authorized Version. Variant readings in the Greek text which do not affect that Translation, though a concern, are not in this study our inmediate concern.

The underlying Text of the AV in the following passages is indicated by *HF* to have "minority" support. However, if the "majority" reading were used, the translation would remain the same. An*asterisk indicates that the translation process would be somewhat more complex, but the passage would still be rendered as the KJV. Two-thirds of the changes Hodges and Farstad would introduce have no material effect on our English Bible.

As shown, it is not necessarily true that the underlying Text of the KJV in these passages is "minority". Along with the passages we have examined in the Manuscript Digest, a vast amount of evidence could also be gathered for them. Readings which are only now shown to be "majority" and have not in previous generations been acknowledged by God's people by being placed into one of the printed editions should be viewed with suspicion.

Matthew

5 :23 and there rememberest
5:28 to lust after her
5:44 do good to them that hate you
6:24 Ye cannot serve God and mammon
*7:2 It shall be measured to you again
8:8 but speak the word only
8:13 And Jesus said unto the centurion
8: 15 and ministered unto them
9: 17 and both are preserved
9:27 *Thou* son of David
10:25 If they have called the master of the house
10 :28 And fear not them
10:28 which kill the body
*10:28 which is able to destroy both soul (article)
*10:28 and body (article)
11:8 are in king's houses
11:16 It is like unto children
*12:6 in this place: is *one* greater than·the temple
12:21 And in his name
12 :28 But I f I cast out devils by the Spirit of God
12:32 And whosoever speaketh
12:35 bringeth forth good things
13:14 And in them is fulfilled

13:15 And I should heal them
13:27 from whence then hath it tares
13:28 Wilt thou then that we go and gather them
13:30 and in the time of harvest
3:33 and hid in three measures of meal
13:40 and burned in the fire
14:14 moved with compassion toward them
15:4 Honour thy father and mother
15:25 Then came she and worshipped him
15:32 they continue with me now three days
15:39 and took ship
16:28 There be some·standlng here
17:2 And his raiment was white
17:9 And as they came down from the mountain
17: 14 kneelin g down to him
17:27 the fish that first cometh up
18:4 whoevcr therefore shall humble himself
18:6 a millstone were hanged about his neck
18:28 Pay me that thou owest
18: 31 their lord
19:9 except *it be* for fornication
19:19 Honour thy father
19:26 all things are possible
20:2 And when he had agreed
20:3 about the third hour
20:4 And said unto them
*21:3 and straightway he will send them
21 :22 whatsoever ye shall ask
21:30 And he came to the second
21:41 and will let out *his* vineyard
22:37 Jesus said unto him
22:37 with all thy heart
22:37 with all thy soul
23:3 therefore whatsoever they bid you
*23:21 by him that dwelleth therein
23:36 All these things
23:37 *Thou* that killest the prophets
24 :2 that shall not be thrown down
24:20 neither on the sabbath
24:33 all these things
24:36 of that day and hour
25:3 took their lamps
25 :30 cast ye the unprofitable servant
26:4 take Jesus by subtility
26:11 For ye have the poor always

26:17 that we prepare
26:33 Though all *men* shall be offended
26:35 yet will I not deny thee
26:35 Likewise also
26:39 And he went a little further
26:59 to put him to death
26:71 and said unto them
26:74 Then began he to curse
27:33 that is to say
27:35 casting lots
27:44 cast the same in his teeth
27:46 Eli, Eli, lama sabachthani
28:9 Jesus met them
28:10 and there

Mark

1:6 And John was clothed
1:27 they questioned among themselves
1:37 All *men* seek for thee
1:38 that may preach there
21:1 again he entered into
2:8 they so reasoned
2:26 Abiathar the high priest
3:12 not make him,known
3:27 No man can enter
3:27 he will spoil
4:30 Whereunto shall we liken
4:31 *It is* like a grain
4:33 as they were able
4:37 the waves beat into the ship
5:3 among the tombs
5:3 no man could bind him
5:11 there was nigh unto the mountain a great herd of swine
5:16 And they that saw it
5:19 how great things the Lord hath done for thee
5:26 and had spent all that she had
5:40 When he had put them all out
.6:16 When He rod heard
6:17 bound him in prison
6:27 the king sent an executioner
6:31 and they had no leisure so much as to eat
6:37 two hundred pennyworth
6:52 their heart
7:24 entered into an house
7:26 a Syrophenician by nation

7:26 that he would cast forth the devil
7:32 and had an impediment in his speech
8:2 three days
8:3 for divers of them came from far
*8:13 and entereing into the ship again (article)
8:25 and saw every man clearly
8:31 and *of* the chief priests
*8:31 and-Scribes (article)
8:34 whosoever will come after me
8:35 shall lose his life
8:38 Whosoever therefore shall be ashamed
9:2 Peter, and James and John
9:3 And his raiment became shining
9:6 For he wist not what to say
9:22 hath cast him into the fire
9:38 And John answered him
9:41 in my name
9 :42 Whosoever shall offend
*10:2 And the Pharisees came (article)
10:16 and blessed them
10:21 and give to the poor
10:24 that trust in riches
10:27 but not with God
10:31 and the last first
10:43 shall be you minister
10 :44 And whosoever of you will be the chiefest
11:3 he will send
*11:4 and found the colt (article)
11:18 how they might destroy him
11:24 What things soever ye desire
11:29 1 will also ask
12:5 and killing some
12:26 how in the bush
12:28 the first conmandment of all
12:29 The first of all
12:33 and sacrifices'
12:36 said by the Holy Ghost
12:36 the Holy Ghost
12:36 the Lord said
12:43 hath cast more in
13:21 believe *him* not
13:31 shall pass away
14:6 on me
14:8 she hath done what she could
14:9 Wheresoever this gospel shall be preached

14:12 Where wilt thou that we go and prepare
14:25 of the fruit of the vine
14:31 I will not deny thee
14:33 Peter and James and John
14:35 he went forward
14:41 Sleep on now
14 :51 And there followed him
14:60 stood up in the midst
14:62 sitting on the right hand
14 :68 neither understand
14:71 began to curse and to swear
14:72 the word that Jesus said
15 :24 they parted his garments
15:31 Likewise also the chief priests
15:34 lama sabachthani
16: 1 and Mary the
16:1 the *mother* of James
16:18 it shall not hurt them

Luke
1:10 the people were praying
1:36 in her old age
1:44 the babe leaped in my womb for joy
2:12 lyng in a manger
2:20 And the shepherds returned
2:25 the Holy Ghost was upon him
2:39 to their own city
3:2 being the high priests
3:2 the son of Zacharias
3:10 What shall we do
3: 12 What shall we do
3:14 What shall we do
3:22 I am well pleased
4:4 That man shall not live
4 : 7 wilt worship me
4:7 all shall be thine
4:9 the son of God
4:11 And in *their* hands
4:18 because he hath anointed me
4:18 to preach the gospel
4 :29 unto the brow of the hill
4:35 had thrown him in the midst
4:38 Simons wife's mother
4:42 the people sought him
5:6 a great multitude of fishes

5:8 fell down at Jesus' knees
*5:19 could not find by what way
5:25 took up that whereon he lay
5:29 And Levi made
*5:30 eat and drink with publicans (article)
6 :23 Rejoice ye
6:34 for sinners also
6:35 the children of the highest
7:2 ready to die
*7:6 that thou shouldest enter under my roof
7:9 no, not In Israel
7:11 the day after
7: 16 fear on all
7:24 began to speak unto the people
7:34 a friend of publicans'
8:18 for whosoever hath
8:18 and whosoever hath not
8:33 entered into the swine
8:43 which had spent all her living upon physicians
8:51 And when he came into the house
9:5 And whosoever wi 11 not receive you
9:9 And Herod said
9:10 the city called Bethsaida
9:13 two fishes
9:27 standing here
9 :27 which 'shall not taste
9 :28 he took Peter
9:33 Peter said
9:33 one for Moses
9:34 For whsoever will save his life
*9:38 I beseech thee, look upon my son
9:40 to cast him out
9 41 Bring thy son hither
9:49 one casting out devils
9:62 And Jesus said unto him
10:2 that he would send forth labourers
10:6 And if the son
*10:6 the son of peace (article)
10:8 And into whosoever city ye enter
10:22 All things are delivered to me
10 :36 thinkest thou, was·neighbour unto him
10:40 hath left me to serve
11:8 and give him as many as he needeth
11:13 to give good gifts
*11:26 and they enter in, and dwell there

11:33 a secret place
11:44 the men that walk over *them*
11:54 Laying wait for him and seeking
12:4 that kill the body
1 2:15 a mans life
12:18 my fruits
12:53 The father shall be divided against the son
12:58 cast thee into prison
12 :59 the very last mite
13:6 he came and sought fruit
13:8 and dung *it*
13: 15 *Thou* hypocrite
13:34 which killed the prophets
l4:10 go and sit doWn in the lowest room
14:26 his father
14:27 cannot be my disciple
14 :28 intending to build
14:28 whether he have *sufficient* to finish *it*
14:32 while the other is yet a great way off
15:20 his father
15:26 one of the servants
16:9 when ye fail
16:15 is abomination in the sight of God
16:22 into Abrahams ,bosom
16:26 from hence to you
17:6 If ye had faith
17:7 Go and sit down to meat
17 :26 in the days of Noe
18:5 she weary me,
18:7 And shall not God avenge his own elect
18:9 And he spake this parable
18:14 *rather* than the other
18:28 Then Peter said
19:7 they all murmured
19:23 into the bank
20:5 Why then believed ye him not
20:35 nor are given in marriage
21:2 he saw also a certain poor beggar
21:12 before all these
21:22 may be fulfilled
21:34 your hearts be overcharged
22:3 Then entered Satan
22:4 the chief priests and captains
22:9 Where wilt thou that we prepare
22:18 of the fruit

22 :30 and sit upon thrones
22:32 that thy faith fail not
22:34 the cock shall not crow
22 :35 And they said, Nothing
22 :36 let him sell his garment
22:36 and buy one
22:45 was come to his disciples
22:47 went before them
22:47 and drew near unto Jesus to kiss him
*22:60 the cock crew (article)
22:66 and the chief priests and the scribes
22:66 their council
23:1 and let him unto Pilate
23:18 and release unto us Barabbas
23:26 one Simon, a Cyrenian coming
23:44 until the ninth hour
*23:54 the preparation, and the sabbath drew on (conjunction)
24:4 two men stood
24:18 a stranger in Jerusalem

John

1:39 for it was about the tenth hour
1:41 We have found the Messias
1:48 Jesus answered
2:17 hath eaten me up
2:19 Jesus answered
2:23 Now when he was In Jerusalem
3:5 Jesus answered
3:10 Jesus answered
3:36 shall not see life
4:13 Jesus answered
4:15 neither come hither
4:20 in this mountain
4:25 Messias
4:35 there are yet four months
4:46 So Jesus came again
4:47 for he was at the point of death
4:50 the word that Jesus
5:7 to put me into the pool
5:35 willing to rejoice
6:29 Jesus answered
6:39 at the last day
6:44 at the last day
6:45 taught of God
6:71 that should betray him

7:12 others said
7:27 Jesus answered
7:32 and the Pharisees and the chief priests sent officers
7:39 Jesus was not yet
7:41 Others said
7:53 went unto his own house
8:2 And early in the morning
8: 3 a woman taken in adultery
8: 3 in the midst
8:4 in adultery, in the very act
8:5 that such should be stoned
8:6 that they might have to accuse her
8:7 and said unto them
8:7 let him first cast a stone at her
8:12 Then spake Jesus again unto them
8:12 shall not walk in darkness
8:19 Jesus answered
*8:39 ye would do the works
8:44 Ye are of your father
8:52 he shall never taste of death
9:3 Jesus answered
9:15 He put clay upon mine eyes
9:21 he shall speak for himself
10:22 And it was at Jerusalem
10:23 In Solomon's porch
11:9 Jesus answered
11:20 heard that Jesus was coming
11:21 Then said Martha
11:32 fell down. at his feet
11:51 that Jesus should die
12:2 sat at the table with him
12:13 Blessed *is* the King
12:33 what death he should die
12:34 The Son of man must be lifted up
13: 37 Peter said unto him
13:38 The cock shall not crow
14:22 Lord, how is it that
14:23 Jesus answered
15:6 into the fire
15:16 he may give it you
16:7 for if I go not away
16:16 because I go to the Father
17:11 Keep through Thine own name those whom thou hast given me
18:8 Jesus answered
18:20 I ever taught in the synagogue

18:28 and it was early
18:36 Jesus answered
18:37 Jesus answered
19:7 because he made himself the Son of God
19:11 Jesus answered
19:12 Whosoever maketh himself a king
*19:16 And they took Jesus, and led *him* away
19:17 went forth Into a place
19:20 the place where Jesus was crucified was nigh to the city
19:23 the coat was without seam
19:26 behold thy son
19:27 that disciple took her
19:34 and forthwith came there out
19:35 and his record is true
19:39 arid aloes about an hundred pound *weight*
19:40 and wound it in linen clothes
20:14 that it was Jesus
20:15 tell me where thou hast laid him
20:28 And Thomas answered.
20:31 that Jesus is the Christ
21:3 entered in to a ship

Acts
1:18 with the reward
1 :24 show whether of these two thou hast chosen
2:37 what shall we do
3:3 asked an alms.
3:6 rise up and walk
3:13 Jesus; whom ye delivered
3:21 of all his holy prophets
3:23 every soul ,which will not hear
3:25 in thy seed.
*4:2 the resurrection from the dead
4:7 In the midst
4:15 conferred among themselves
4:16 What shall we do to these men
*4:21 how they might punish them
4:25 thy servant David
4:32 of the things which he possessed
4: 36 by the apostles
5:5 And Ananlas hearing
5:29 Then Peter...answered
5:36 joined themselves
6:3 Whom we may appoint
6:5 full of faith

164

7:5 that he would give it to him
7:11, and all his kindred
7:20 in his fathers house
*7:22 mighty in words and deeds
7:31 he wondered at the sight
7:36 signs in the land of Egypt
7:39 and in their hearts turned back
8:1 and they were all
8:7 crying with a loud voice
8:12 the name of Jesus Christ
8:32 before his shearer
9:7 stood speechless
9:8 and when his eyes were opened
9: 13 Then Ananias answered
9:21 and came hither for that intent
9:26 was come to Jerusalem
9:28 and going out at Jerusalem
10:3 about the ninth hour of the day
10:5 whose surname is Peter
10:19 While Peter thought on the vision
10:23 certain brethren from Joppa
10 :25 And as Peter was coming in
10:26 Peter took him up, saying
*11:26 When he had found him
11:26 assembled themselves with the church
11 :29 every man according to his ability
12:3 Then were the days
12:15 And they said unto her
12:22 *It is* the voice of a god
*12:23 he gave not God the glory (article)
13:2 Separate me Barnabas and Saul
13:4 and from thence they sailed
13:11 the hand of the Lord
13:19 divided their land to them by lot
13:27 they' that dwell at Jerusalem
13:29 had fulfilled all
13:41 Which ye shall in no wise believe
13:44 And the next sabbath day
13:48 they were glad
14:8 who never had walked
14:9 the same heard Paul speak
15:2 no small dissension
15:11 the grace of the Lord
15:22 with Paul .
15:32 And Judas and Silas

*16:12 we were in that city
16:34 and rejoiced
*16:37 and fetch us out
16:40 entered into the house
17:2 reasoned with them
17:7 these all do contrary
17:10 went into the synagogue of the Jews
17:25 and all things
17:26 the times before appointed
17:27 though he be not far
18:2 command all Jews to depart
18:17 Gallio cared for none of those things
18:19 and left them there
19:16 and overcame them,
25:20 I doubted of such manner
26:2 because I shall answer for myself this day before thee
26:7 I am accussed of the Jews
26:22 witnessing
26:22 for this thing was not done in a corner
27:10 not only of the lading
27:11 the centurian believed
27:23 this night
27:33 while the day was coming on
27:38 when they had eaten enough
27:39 if it were possible
27:42 and escape
28:3 came a viper out of the heat
28:16 to the captain of the guard
28:26 and say
28:27 and I should heal them

Romans
1:13 some fruit
4:4 but of debt
4:12 of that faith of our father Abraham, which *he had* being *yet*, uncircumcised
6:1 shall we continue in sin
7:6 that being dead – [Despite the conment of Hills arid others (KJVD p 208, JFB etc), the variation between the Beza and Stephanus text does not measurably affect the translation. The KJV does not here say that the law died, but rather we were dead when held under the Law. This reading is not cited by HF and therefore not added to the total.]
7:23 captivity to the law
8:10 because of sin
8:26 what we should pray for
8:36 For thy sake
11:7 that which he seeketh for

11:21 lest he aslo spare not thee·
13:1 there is no power but of God
13:2 I am nothing
13:9 as thyself
14:9 and revived
14:14 unclean of itself
14:22 have *it* to thyself
15:2 Let everyone of us
15:4 and comfort of the scriptures
15: 14 able also to admonish one another

1 Corinthians
3:1 could not speak unto you
3:11 which is Jesus Christ
3:14 work abide which he hath built
4:6 that no one of you be puffed up
6:7 a fault among you
7:24 abide with God
*7:39 but if her husband be dead
8:5 or in earth
10:7 as it is written
*11:18 when ye come together in the church
*11:27 of the body and blood (article)
12:21 the eye cannot say
12:25 should be no schism
13:2 I am nothing
13:9 For we know in part
14:5 except he interpret
14:26 Let all things be done
14:37 are the commandments of the Lord
15:23 they that are Christs
5:33 corrupt good manners
*15:49 we shall also bear the image

2 Corinthians
1:5 aboundeth by Christ
1: 15 I was minded to come unto you before
2:1 that I would not come again to you
3:3 tables of the heart
3:6 the letter killeth
3:10 which was made glorious had no glory
5 :21 that we might be made
9:5 and not as of covetousness
9:10 the frui ts of your righteousnesses
11:4 ye might well bear with him

11:16 that I may boast myself a little
12:21 my God will humble me

Galatians
1 :4 Who gave himsel for our sins
1:8 preach any other gospel
*4:24 these are the two covenants (article)
5:4 ye are fallen, from grace
5:7 who did hinder you
5:14 love thy neighbor as thyself
6:13 they themselves who are circumcised

Ephesians
1:10 are in heaven
1 :12 praise of his glory
1:20 from the dead
1 :23 that filleth all in all
2:21 all the building
3:5 which in other ages
3:8 least of all saints
4:27 Neither give place
5:14 Awake thou that sleepest
5 :23 For the husband
6:8 whatsoever good thing any man doeth
6:17 And taking the helmet of salvation
6:19 may be given unto me

Philippians
1:7 and in the defence
*1:23 For I am in a strait
1:30 which ye saw in me
2:1 if any bowels
2:11 should confess
2:21 not the thlngs which are Jesus Christ's
2:27 sorrow upon sorrow
3:1 but for you *it is* safe

Colossians
1:20 or things in heaven
*1:24 in my sufferings
1:27 what is the riches
*2:13 hath he quickened together with him
2:17 the body *is* of Christ
2:20 with Christ
3:12 bowels of mercies

3:20 pleasing unto the Lord
3:24 ye shall receive

1 Thessalonians
1:10 from the dead
2:6 nor *yet* of others
2:8 being affectionately desirous
2:11 and comforted and charged
2:14 have suffered like things
3:3 That no man should be moved
3:8 if ye stand fast
4 :1 Furthermore then

2 Thessalonians
*1:10, in all them that believe

1 Timothy
1:9 for murderers of fathers and murderers of mothers
5:21 doing nothing by partiality
5:25 cannot be hid
6:5 Perverse disputings
6:17 who giveth us richly all things to enjoy
6:20 that which is committed to thy trust

2 Timothy
1:14 That good thing which was committed unto thee
1:16 was not ashamed
3:6 lead captive silly women

Titus
2:2 aged men be sober
3:8 which have believed in God

Philemon
17 If thou count me

Hebrews
1:2 in these last days
3:13 lest any of you
*4:2 not being mixed with faith
5:4 as *was* Aaron
*6:3 And this will we do
6:9 better things
8:5 *that* thou make
8:6 a more excellent ministry

10:1 can never...make the comers
10:10 of Jesus Christ
10:34 knowing in yourselves
11:9 in the land
11:12 and as the sand
11:16 But now
12:2 and is set down
12:24 that speaketh better things
12:25 on earth
*12:28 whereby we may serve
13:5 nor forsake thee
*13:9 Be not carried about

James
1:13 tempted of God
1:27 before God
2:11 Do not commit adultery...do not kill
2:13 with out mercy
*2:13 and mercy rejolceth
2:13 mercy...judgment
3:3 behold...the horses
*4:7 Resist the deviil
*4:14 and then vanisheth away
5:7 hath long patience for it
5:7 until he receive
5:10 my brethren...of suffering affliction
5:12 lest ye fall into condemnation

1 Peter
*1:7 found unto praise and honour and glory
1:16 Be ye holy
2:12 Having your conversation honest among the nations
2:14 for the punishment of' evil doers
2:17 Love the brotherhood
3:1 may be won
3:5 who trusted inGod
3:7 that your prayers be not hindered
3:12 the eyes of the Lord
3:17 if the will of God be so
3:18 but quickened by the Spirit
3:21 whereunto
3:21 The like figure...doth also now save us
4:8 for charity shall cover
*4:11 as of the ability which God giveth
4:19 their souls

5:3 Neither as being
5:10 stabllsh, strengthen, settle *you*

2 Peter
1:12 to put you always in remembrance
*2:3 lingereth not
2:4 reserved unto judgment
2:12 and shall utterly perish
2:14 exercised with covetous practices
2:15 forsaken the right way
3:3 their own lusts

1 John
1:5 This then is
*3:15 abiding in him
3:18 neither in tongue
3:18 in deed
4:3 that Jesus Christ
5:6 Jesus Christ
*5:10 hath the witness in himself
5:15 whatsoever we ask

2 John
12 I would not

Jude
12 carried about of winds
13 darkness forever
14 ten thousands of his saints
15 to convince all
23 out of the fire

Revelation
*1:2 and of all things
1:4 Which are before
1:5 of the dead
1:5 unto him that loved us
1:8 I am Alpha and Omega
1:9 and companion
*1:9 in the kingdom and patience (article)
1:10 and heard behind me a great voice
*1:12 And I turned to see
1:12 the voicethat spake with me
1:13 like unto the son of Man
1:14 as white as snow

1:17 And he laid
1:17 His right hand upon me
1:18 and have the keys
1:20 and the seven golden lampstands
2:2 and thou hast tried them
2:2 which say they are apostles
2:4 Nevertheless I have
2:5 from whence thou art fallen
2: 8 of the church in Smyrna
2:9 but thou art rich
2:9 of them which say
2:10 whIch thou shalt suffer
2:10 tribulation ten days
2:13 those days wherein
2:13 where Satan dwells
2:14 But I have
2: 14 who taught
2:15 doctrine of the Nicolaitanes
2:17· which no man knoweth
2:20 Notwithstanding I have
2:20 because thou sufferest
2:20 Jezebel
2:20 which calleth herself
2:20 to seduce my servants
2:20 to eat things sacrificed unto idols
2 :22 I will cast her
2:23 he which searches
2:24 I will put
2:27 shall they be broken to shivers
3:1 thou hast a name
3:3 thou shalt not know
3:4 Thou hast a few names
3:5 I will confess his name
3:7 that hath the key
3:9 and to know that I have loved thee
3:12 which cometh down
*3:12 out of heaven from my God
3:15 I would that thou wert cold or hot
3:16 lukewarm, and neither
3:17 Because thou sayest, I am rich
3:17 wretched, and miserable
3:18 to buy of me gold
3:18 with eyesalve
3:19 be zealous
*4:1 a door was opened

4:1 talking with me
4:2 and *one* sat on the throne
4:3 in sight like unto an emerald
*4:4 four and twenty
*4:5 the seven Spirits of God (article)
4:7 a face as a man
4:7 was like a flying eagle
4:8 And the four beasts
4:8 had each of them
4:8 had each of them
4: 8 and they were full of eyes
4:8 saying, Holy
4:9 give glory
4:9 on the throne
*4:10 four and twenty elders
4:11 created all things
5:2 with a loud voice
5:2 who is worthy
5:3 was able '
5:3 nor...neither...neither
5:4 wept much
5:5 the lion of the tribe of Judah
5:5 to open the book
5:6 which are the seven
5:6 the seven Spirits of God
5 :6 sent forth
5:8 having everyone of them harps
*5:8 which are the prayers of the saints (article)
5: 11 round about the throne
5: 12 and riches
5:13 which is in heaven
5:13 and on earth
5:13 and such as are in the sea
5:13 an d all that are in them
5:13 upon the throne
5:14 beasts said, Amen
5:14 elders fell down
6:1 noise of thunder
6:2 he that sat on him
6:3 the second seal
6:4 horse *that was* red
6:4 that sat thereon
6:4 from the earth
6:4 that they should kill one another
6 :5 the third seal

6:5 that sat on him
6:7 beast say "
6:8 and Hell followed
6:8 wi th him
6:8 power...over the fourth part of the earth, to kill
6:10 And they cried
6:10 a loud voice saying
6:10 holy and true
6:10 on them tha t swell
*6:11 white robes were given
6:11 that they should rest
6:11 until their
6:11 an d their brethren
6:11 that should be killed
6:12 the sun became black
6: 13 stars of heaven fell
6:13 fig tree casteth
6:13 great wind
6:14 departed as a scroll
6:15 and the mighty men
*6:15 and every free man
6:16 on the throne
7:1 nor on any tree
*7:4 an hundred *and* forty *and* four thousand
7:4 were sealed
7:5 twelve thousand
7:5 were sealed
7:8 were sealed
7:9 which no man could number
7:9 no one could
7:9 stood before "
7:9 clothed with white robes
7:9 palms in their hands
7:10 And cried
7:10 which sitteth upon the throne
7:11 And all the anges stood
7:11 on their faces
7:14 And I said unto him
*7:14and made them white
7:15 on the throne
7:16 neither shall the sun light on them
7:17 For the Lamb...shall feed them
7:17 unto living fountains of waters
7:17 from their eyes
8:1 when he had opened

8:3 at the altar
8:3 that he should offer it
8:7 mingled with blood
8:9 creatures which were in the sea
8:11 called Wormwood
8:11 waters became wormwood
8:12 and the day shone not for a third part of it
8:13 flying through the midst
8:13 to the inhabiters
*9:4 but only those men
9:6 and shall not find It
9:6 death shall flee from them
*9:10 their power *was* to hurt men
9:11 but in the Greek tongue
9:14 saying
9:14 which had
9:16 of the army
9:18 by the fire
9:19 *were* like unto serpents
9 :20 repented not
*9:20 and idols of gold (article)
9:21 nor of their sorceries
*10:1 and a rainbow (article)
10:1 upon his head, and his face
10:2 he had
10:2 a little book
10:2 upon the sea...on the earth
10:4 and write them not
10:6 swore by him
*10:6 *that there should be time no longer
10:7 But in the days
*10:7 the mystery of God should, be finished
10:7 his servants the prophets
10:8 take the little book
10:8 which is open
10:8 the hand of the angel
10:9 the little book
10:10 And I took the little book
*10:11 before many peoples, and nations
11:1 Rise, and measure
*11:2 forty *and* two
11:4 standing before
11:5 if any man will hurt them
11:5 hurt
11:5 in this manner

11:6 These have power to shut heaven
11:6 that it rain not in the days of their prophecy
11:6 with all plagues, as often as they will
11:7 shall make war against them
11:8 their dead bodies
11:9 the people...shall see
11:9 their dead bodies
*11:9 three days and an half
11:10 they that dwell...shall rejoice over them
11:10 an d make merry.
*11:10 shall send gifts
11:11 entered into them
11:11 fear fell upon them
11:12 a great voice saying
11 :14 behold the third woe cometh quickly
11:15 saying
11:16 the four and twenty elders
11:16 which sat
11:16 fell upon their faces
11:19 was opened
12:2 cried, travailing
12:3 a great red dragon
12:3 seven crowns
*12:5 and *to* his throne
12:6 where she hath a place
12:6 prepared of God
12:6 should feed her there
12:7 Michael...fought
12:7 fought against the dragon
12:8 And prevailed not
12:8 neither
12: 8 their place found
12:9 the Devil, and Satan
12:10 saying in heaven
12:10 far...is cast down
12:12 rejoice, *ye* heavens
12:15 cast out of his mouth water as a flood
12:15 that he might cause her
13:2 *the feet* of a bear
13:3 one of his heads
13:3 as it were wounded
13:4 they worshipped the dragon
13:4 which gave power
13:4 power
13:4 they worshipped the beast

13:4 who is able
13:7 to make war
13:8 shall worship him
13:8 in the book
*13:12 causeth the earth
13:12 and them which dwell their in
13:13 so that he maketh fire come down from heaven
13:13 on the earth
13:14 And deceiveth them that dwell
13: 14 which had
*13:14 the wound (article)
13:14 by a sword and did live
13:15 to give life
13:15 as would not worship
13:15 worship the image
13:15 should be killed
13:16 to receive a mark
13:16 a mark
13:17 that no man might
*13:17 or the name
13:18 that hath understanding
*14:1 lo, a Lamb (article)
14:1 an hundred forty and four thousand
14:2 And I heard a voice
14:3 no man could learn
14:3 the hundred *and* forty *and* four thousand
14:4 whithersoever he goeth
14:5 And in their mouth was found no
14:6 fly in the midst of heaven
14:6 and to every nation
14:7 saying with aloud voice
14:7 and worship him that made heaven
14:8 she made all nations
14:9 If any man worship the beast
14:11 ascendeth up for ever and ever
14:12 the patience of the saints
14:13 Yea, saith the Spirit
14:14 *one* sat like unto
14:14.the Son of man
14:15 crying with a loud voice
14:18 and cried with a loud cry
14:19 the angel thrust in his sickle
14:19 the great winepress
14:20 without the city·
15:2 having the harps of God

15:4 for *thou* only *art* holy
15 :6 the Seven angels...having
15:6 pure and white linen
15 :8·the temple was filled with smoke
15:8 no man was able to enter
16:1 I heard a great voice
*16:2 upon the earth
16 :2 upon the men.
16:2 who worshipped his image
16:8 to scorch men with fire
16:10 they gnawed their tongues
16: 12 the great river Euphrates
16:12 kings of the east
16:13 three unclean spirits
16:13 like frogs
16:14 spirits of devils
16:17 poured out his vial into the air
16 :21 for the plague thereof was exceeding great
17:7 the Inhabitants of the earth have been...
*17:3 upon a scarlet coloured beast (article)
17:3 full of names
17:4 arrayed in purple
17:4 and scarlet colour
I7:4 with gold
17:4 a golden cup
17:6 drunken wi th the blood
*17:6 saints, and with the blood
17: 7 I will tell thee
17:8 they that dwell on the earth
17:8 in the book of life
17:8 when they behold
17:8 the beast that was (note especially the CR reading)
17:9 The seven heads are seven mountains
17:10 And there are seven kings
17:10 five are fallen
17:10 he must continue a short space
17:11 even he is the eighth
17:13 These have one mind
17:13 their power and strength
17:13 their strength
*17:16 and shall make her desolate and naked
17:17 and to agree
*17:17 until the words of God shall be fulfilled
17:18 over the kings of the earth
18:3 For all nations have drank

18:4 Come out of her
18:4 Come out of her, my people
18:5 and that ye receive not of her plagues
18:5 and God hath remembered her iniquities
*18:6 and double unto her double according to her works
18:7 hath glorified herself
*18:7 she saith in her heart, I sit a queen
18:8 death and mourning, and famine
18:8 Who Judgeth her
18:9 lament over her
18:10 in one hour
18:11 shall weep and mourn
18:12 and fine linen
18: 12 and purple
18:13 and chariots
18:14 thou shalt find them no more at all
18:16 fine linen
18:16 with gold
18:18 When they saw the smoke
18:19 that had ships
18:20 Rejoice over her
18:24· the blood of prophets
19:1 saying
19:2 which did corrupt the earth
19:2 at her hand
19:3 And again they said
*19:4 the four and twenty elders
19:4 that sat on the throne
*19:5 a voice came out of the throne
19:6 saying
19:8 is the righteousness of saints
19:9 unto the marriage supper
19:9 These are the true sayings of God
19: 10 I fell at his feet
19:10 the testimony of Jesus
19:11 I saw heaven opened
19:12 as a flame of fire
19:13 his name is called
19:14 upon white horses
*19:14 white and clean
19:15 he should smite the nations
19:17 I saw an angel
19: 17 cried wi th a loud voice
19:17 to all the flows that fly
19:17 unto the supper

19:18 both small and great
19:19 to make war
19:20 with him the false prophet
19:20 lake of fire burning
19:20 with brimstone
19:21 which *sword* proceeded out
20:1 having the key
20:2 and Satan'
20:3 that he should deceive
20:3 he must be loosed
20:4 worshipped the beast
20:4 neither
*20:4 upon their foreheads
20:4 reigned with Christ
*20:4 a thousand 'years (article)
*20:5 but the rest of the dead
20:6 the second death
20:8 Gog and Magog
20:8 gather them together to battle
20:9 compassed the camp
*20:9 from God out of heaven
20: 10 where the beast
20:11 a great white throne
20:11 that sat on it
20:12 an·d another book was opened
20:13 the dead which were in it
20:13 the dead which were in them
20:14 This is the second death
20:15 written in the book
21:1 were passed away
21:2 I...saw...coming down
*21:2 from God out of heaven
21:3 shall be his people
21:4 are passed away
21:5 that sat upon the throne
21:5 I make all things new
21:6 1 am Alpha and Omega
21:7 he shall be my son
21:8 But the fearful
21:8 and sorcerers
21:8 which is the second death
21:9 one of the seven angels
21:9 full of the seven last plagues
21:10 out of heaven from God
*21:12 and it had a wall great and high

21:12 *and* had twelve gates
21:12 twelve angels
21:12 tribes of the children of Israel
21:13 on the east
21:14 had twelve foundatlons
21 :16 and the length is as large as the breadth
21:16 twelve thousand furlongs
21:18 like unto
21:18 clear glass
21:20 the sixth, sardius
21:20 the ninth, a topaz
21:30 the twelfth an amethyst
21:21 as it were transparent glass
21 :21 transparent
21 :23 to shine in it: for the glory of God
21 :24 kings...do bring their glory and honour into It
21 :27 any thing that defileth
21:27 worketh abomination
22:2 and on either side of the river
22:2 yielded her fruit every month
22:3 no more curse
22: 3 shall serve him
22:5 giveth them light
22:6 he said unto me
22:8 And I John
*22:8 When I had heard and seen
22:8 I fell down to worship
22:8 which showed me these things
22:10 for the time is at hand
22:11 and he which is filthy
22:12 as his works shall be
22: 13 I am
22:13 Alpha and Omega
22:16 the offspring of David
22:17 Come...Come
22:17 the water of life
22:18 unto every man that heareth
22:18 shall add unto these things
22:18 God shall add
22:18 in this book
22:19 shall take away
22:19 in this book

Total   1179

He hath remembered his covenant for ever,
the word which he commanded to a thousand generations.

(Psalms 105:8)

APPENDIX 3

FURTHER WELL-SUPPORTED AV READINGS
REJECTED BY HODGES AND FARSTAD

The following KJV readings rejected by Hodges and Farstad are shown in their apparatus to either approach, equal, or exceed the *HF* reading. The variant proposed by them would affect the translation. Based on von Soden and his groupings, and Hoskier in Revelation these reading have at least "partial majority" support-M(pt). The early uncials *HF* lists are also given.

MATTHEW

9:5 thy sins be forgiven thee	M(pt)	
11:16 calling unto their fellows	M(pt)	
14:22 constrained his disciples	M(pt)	
24:27 so shall also the coming	M(pt)	
26:26 and blessed it	Mr	P45 Aleph B C

MARK

10:14 to come unto me and forbid	M(pt)	Aleph A C
10:29 for my sake, and the gospel's	M(pt)	A B2
10:33 and unto the scribes	M(pt)	CR A B
10:40 and on my left hand	Mr	
14:9 Verily I say unto you	M(pt)	A C
15:32 that we may see and believe	M(pt)	CR Aleph A B C

LUKE

2:21 The circumcising of the child	M(pt vid)	
6:10 he did so: and	Mr	
6 :26 all men	Mi	Cr P75(vid) A B
8:3 ministered unto him	Mpt	Aleph
16:25 but now he is comforted	Mr	

JOHN

1:29 John seeth Jesus	M(pt)	
1:42 And when Jesus beheld him	M(pt)	P75
1:43 and saith unto him	M(pt)	
3:2 The same came to Jesus	M(pt)	
4:30 Then they went out of the city	M(pt)	P66 Aleph
5:1 there was a feast	M(pt)	CR P66 75 A B
6:15 he departed again	M(pt)	CR P75 Aleph A B

6:70 Jesus answered them	M(pt)	[CR]	P75 B C
8:1 Jesus went unto	M1 2 3 5 7	CR	
8:2 he came again	M1 2 3 5 7	CR	
8:4 They say unto him	M1 2 5 7	CR	
8:5 What sayest thou	M1(pt) 5 6(pt) 7 CR		
8:7 he lifted up himself	M1(pt) 5 7		
18:2 Jesus of times resorted thither	M(pt)	CR Aleph A B C	
19:28 Jesus knowing	M(pt)	CR Aleph A B C	

ACTS

2:7 they were all amazed	M(pt)	A C
3:20 Jesus Christ	M(pt)	A C
3:22 the Lord your God	M(pt)	CR A
3:24 foretold of these days	Mr	
5:38 If this counsel	Mi	CR Aleph A B C
7:21 took him up	M(pt)	CR Aleph A B C
7:37 him ye shall hear	Mi	C
7:58 their clothes	M(pt)	CR Aleph A C
8:16 the Lord Jesus	M(pt)	CR Aleph A B C
9:18 he received sight forthwith	M(pt)	
9:28 coming in and going out	M(pt)	CR Aleph A B C
10:19 three men seek thee	M(pt)	CR Aleph A B C
12:25 returned from Jerusalem	M(pt)	A
13:17 this people of Israel	M(pt)	CR Aleph A B C
15:34, 35 Notwithstanding...to abide there still	M(pt)	
20:21 our Lord Jesus Christ	M(pt)	Aleph A C
22:12 all of the Jews which dwelt there	M(pt)	CR Aleph A B
22:20 and kept the raiment	M(pt)	CR Aleph A B
24:6-8 Whom we took...by examining	M(pt)	

ROMANS

13:9 Thou shalt not bear false witness	M(pt)	Aleph
15:7 Christ also received us	M(pt)	B

1 CORINTHIANS

5:7 Purge out therefore	M(pt)	C	
6:16 What? Know ye not	M(pt)	[CR]	P46 Aleph A B C
11:15 hair is given her	M(pt)	[CR]	Aleph A B
11:27 drink this cup of the Lord, unworthily	M(pt)	CR	P46 A B C

2 CORINTHIANS

5:14 that if one died for all	M(pt)	C*
7:13 in your comfort: yea...the more	M(pt)	
8:4 that we would receive	M	C

PHILIPPIANS

1:6 Jesus Christ	M(pt)	Aleph A
4:23 our Lord Jesus Christ	M(pt)	P46

COLOSSIANS

1:6 bringeth forth fruit	M(pt)
1:14 redemption through his blood	M(pt)
2:20 Wherefore If ye be dead	M(pt)

1 THESSALONIANS

2:19 our Lord Jesus Christ	M(pt)	
5:21 Prove all things	M(pt)	Aleph* A

2 THESSALONIANS

1:12 Our Lord Jesus Christ	M(pt)	A

1 TIMOTHY

5:4 good and acceptable	Mc(vid)

2 TIMOTHY

1:1 Jesus Christ	M(pt)	A

HEBREWS

2:7 and didst set him...hands	M(pt)	Aleph A C
11:26 the treasures in Egypt	M(pt)	
12:7 if he endure	M(pt)	

JAMES

4: 14 it is even a vapour	M(pt)

1 PETER

4:3 may suffice us	M(pt)	C

1 JOHN

4:16 and God in him	Mr	A
5:4 <u>even</u> our faith	M(pt)	CR Aleph A B

2 JOHN

3 Grace be with you	M(pt)

In Revelation, the following KJV readings have at least Me support (About 24 of Hoskier's MSS).

REVELATION

1:6 made us kings and priests	Mde		
1:8 the beginning and the ending	Mbe	Aleph*	
1:9 patience of Jesus Christ	Mde		
1:18 of hell and of death	Mde		
1:20 the seven candlesticks which thou sawest	Mcde		
2:3 has borne, and hast patience	Mcde(pt)		
2:7 in the midst of the paradise	Mbcde		
2:7 the paradise of God	Mde	CR	
2:10 behold	Mbde	CR	Aleph A C
2:14 to eat things	Mcde	CR	Aleph A C
2:16 Repent	Mcde	Aleph	
2:17 give to eat	Mcde		
3:1 that thou livest	Mcde	CR	Aleph A C
3:2 strengthen the things	Mbe	Aleph	
3:20 I will come	Mde	A	
4:2 And immediately	Mbcde		
4:4 And round about	Mbcde	CR	A
4:4 I saw four and twenty elders	Mc(pt)	(HF deficient)	
4:7 the fourth beast	Mcde	CR	Aleph A
4:8 Holy, holy, holy	Ma(pt) de	CR A	
4:11 they are and were created	Mbcde		
5:3 in heaven	Mcde(pt)		CR Aleph A
5:4 to open and to read	Mce(pt)		
6:1 I saw when	Mde	CR	Aleph A C
6:4 earth, and that	Mbe	CR	Aleph A C
6:7 I heard the voice	Mcde(pt)		CR Aleph A
6:11 a little season	Mde	CR	C
6:12 the moon	Mbce		
7:1 After these things	Mde		
7:11 throne	Mcde	CR	Aleph A C

7:17 and shall lead them	Mcde	CR	Aleph A
8:5 voices, and thunderlngs	Mcde		
8:7 The first angel	Mde		
8:8 burning with fire	Mbde	CR	Aleph A
8:13 and heard an angel	Mde		
9:2 a great furnace	Mde	CR	Aleph A
9:7 crowns like gold	Mbde	CR	Aleph A
9:16 of the horsmen	Mde	CR	P47 Aleph A
9:18 and by the brimstone	Mde	P47	
10:9 Give me	Mcde		
10:11 he said	Mcde		
11:4 Before the God	Mde		
11 :13 And the same	Mbcde	CR	P47 Aleph A C
11:16 before God	Mcde	CR	P47 Aleph A C
11:19 his testament	Mbde	CR	AC
12:14 where she is nourished	Mde	CR	A C
13:1 the name of blasphemy	Mde	P47	Aleph C
13:5 to continue	Mde	CR	P47 A C
13:6 and them that dwell	Mde		
13:7 over all kindreds	Mce(pt)	P47	
13:8 whose names	Mde		
13:10 he that killeth...must be killed with the sword	Mce		
13:16 in their foreheads	Mcde	P47	
14:1 and with him	Mcde	CR	Aleph A C
14:3 they sung	Mde	[CR]	A C
14:4 These were redeemed	Mbde	CR	P47 Aleph A C
14:7 Fear God	Mcde	CR	P47 Aleph A C
14:8 Babylon is fallen, is fallen	Mcde	CR	P47 A
14:12 here are they that keep	Mcde		
14:13 saying unto me	Mcde		
14:18 for grapes are fully ripe	Mcde	CR	Aleph (A) C
15:4 for all nations	Mcde	CR	P47 Aleph A C
15:6 came out of the temple...plagues	Mde	CR	P47 Aleph A C
16:1 pour out the vials	Mcde		
16:3 every living thing	Mcde	P47	Aleph
16:4 the third angel	Mbcde		
16:8 the fourth angel	Mbcde	Aleph	
16:10 the fifth angel	Mbcde		
16:12 the sixth angel	Mbcde(pt)		
16:17 the seventh angel	Mbcde		
16:18 there was a great earthquake	Mcde	CR	P47 (Aleph) (A)
17:1 talked with me saying unto me	Mde		
17:4 of her fornication	Mbcde	CR	A
17:8 whose names were not written	Mb(pt)cde		Aleph

18:1 And after these things	Mbcde				
18:6 as she rewarded you	Mcde				
18:6 in the cup	Mb(pt)cde	CR	A C		
18:13 and beasts and sheep	Mcde	CR	Aleph A C		
18:15 weeping	Mbcde	CR	Aleph A C		
18:19 and waiting, saying	Mb(pt)de(pt)	CR	Aleph C		
18:23 for thy merchants were	Mcde	CR	Aleph A C		
19:1 And after these things	Mcde				
19:12 written, that no man knew	Ma(pt)de(pt)	CR	A		
19:15 the fierceness and wrath	Mde				
20:2 Satan	Mde		CR Aleph A		
20:3 and after that	Mb(pt)cde				
20:7 and when the thousand years	Ma(pt)cde	CR	Aleph A		
20:8 the number	Mb(pt)cde				
20:13 according to their works	Ma(pt)cde	CR	Aleph A		
21:5 he said unto me	Ma(pt)b(pt)cde	Aleph			
21:5 these words are true	Mcde(pt)				
21:6 the beginning	Mbd	CR	Aleph A		
21:6 I will give	Mcbd	CR	Aleph A		
21:9 the bride, the Lamb's wife	Mde				
21:12 which are the names	Mcde				
21:15 had a golden reed	Mde				
21:16 twelve thousand	Mb(pt)e		CR	Aleph	A
21:17 he measured the wall	Mcde		CR	Aleph	A
21:19 And the foundations	Mb(pt)cde		Aleph*		
21:26 into it	Mbcde(pt)		CR	Aleph	A
22:5 there shall be no night there	Mb(pt)cde				
22:5 and they...neither light of the sun	Mb(pt)cde				
22:6 the holy prophets	Mde				
22:7 Behold	Mb(pt)ce				
22:13 the beginning...last	Mcde(pt)				

Total Matthew to Jude   79
Total for Revelation   105

Total for Matthew to Revelation   184

The preliminary. evidence given above indicates substantial MS support for these KJV readings rejected by Hodges and Farstad. They also have the combined support of the two standard Received Text editions—the 1550 Stephanus and the 1624 Elzevir. The two exceptions being: 3 John 3 Elz. supports KJV with *Grace be with you*, while Steph. reads with HF *Grace be with us*. In Rev. 13:5 Steph. supports KJV *power was given unto him to continue*, while Elz. sides with HF *power was given unto him to make war*.

SELECT BIBLIOGRAPHY

WORKS CONSULTED FOR MANUSCRIPT DIGEST

Aland, Kurt. *Synopsis Quattuor Evangeliorum*, Stuttgart: Wurttembergeshe Bibelanstal,1964.

Aland, Kurt; Black, Matthew; Martini, Carlo; Metzger, Bruce; Witgren, Allen (eds.). *The Greek New Testament*, 3rd Edition Corrected, New York: American Bible Society, 1983.

Alford, Henry. *The Greek Testament*, Chicago: Moody Press, 1968.

Charles, Robert H. *A Critical and Exegetical Commentary on The Revelation of St. John*, Edinburg: T&T Clark, 1920.

Hodges, Zane C. and Arthrur L. Farstad (eds.). *The Greek New Testament According to the Majority Text*, Nashville: Thomas Nelson, 1982.

Hoskier, Herman C. *Concerning the Text of the Apocalypse*, London: Bernard Quartich, 1914.

Legg, S. C. E (ed.). *Novum Testamentum Graece Secundum Textum Westcotto-Hortianum. Evangelium Secundum Marcum.* Oxonii: E. Typographero Clarendoniano, 1935.
    — *Novum Testamentum Graece Secundum Textum Westcotto-Hortianum.* Evangelium Secundum Mattaeum. Oxonii: E. Typographero Clarendoniano, 1935.

Metzger, Bruce M. *A Textual Commentary of the Greek New Testament*, Stuttgart: United Bible Society, 1975.

Nestle, Irwin and Kurt Aland. *Novum Testamentum Graece*, 26th Edition, Stuttgart: Wurttembergeshe Bibelanstal,1979.

Soden, Hermann F. von. *Die Schriften des Neuen Testaments,* Gottingen: Vandenhoeck und Ruprecht, 1911.

The American and British Committees of the International Greek New Testament Project. *The New Testament in Greek,* The Gospel According to Luke, (Part One, Chs. 1-12), Oxford: Clarendon Press, 1984.

Tischendorf, Constantine von. *Novum Testamentum Graece.* Editio octava critica maior. Lipsae: Giesecke and Devrient, 1869.

OTHER WORKS CONSULTED

Aland, Kurt, and Barbara Aland. *The Text of the New Testament*, Grand Rapids: Eerdmans, 1987.
— "The Text of the Church," *Trinity Journal*, 8NS, 1987.

Birdsall, J. Neville. "The Text of the Revelation of Saint John," *The Evangelical Quarterly*, 33-1961.

Brown, Andrew. –Concerning von Soden's Accuracy-, *Trinitarian Bible Society Quarterly Record*, January 1983.

Burgon, John W. and Edward Miller. *The Traditional Text of the Holy Gospels,* Collingswood NJ: The Bible for Today Press, 1998.

Dabney, Robert. "Dabneys Discussions Evangelical and Theological," reprinted by the Trinitarian Bible Society n.d.

Ehrman, Bart D. "Methodological Developments in the Analysis and Classification of New Testament Documentary Evidence," *Novum Testamentum*, 29 –1987.

Elliott, J. K. "The International Project to Establish A Critical Apparatus to Luke's Gospel," *New Testament Studies,* No. 29, 1983.
— "An Eclectic Textual Commentary on the Greek Text of Mark's Gospel," *New Testament Textual Criticism, Its Significance for Exegesis, Essays in Honour of Bruce M. Metzger*, Oxford: Clarendon Press.

Cloud, David W. *The Bible Version Question/Answer Database*, Port Huron MI: Way of Life Literature, 2005.

Gaussen, Louis. *Theopneustia: The Plenary Inspiration of the Holy Scriptures.* Edinburgh & London: Johnstone & Hunter, 1850.

Greenlee, J. Harold. *Introduction to New Testament Textual Criticism*, Grand Rapids: Eerdmans, 1964.

Henry, Matthew. *Matthew Henry's Commentary.*

Hodges, Zane C. "Modern Textual Criticism and the Majority Text: A Surrejoinder," *Journal of Evangelical Theological Studies*, June 1978.
— "The Ecclesiastical Text of Revelation," *Bibllotheca Sacra*, April 1961.

Hoskier, Herman C. *Genesis of the Versions*, London: Quaritch, 1911.
— -Review of von Soden Apparatus-, *Journal of Theological Studies*, 15-1914.
— *Codex B And its Allies*, London: Quartch, 1914.

— - Concerning Erasmus' Manuscript of Revelation-, *The John Rylands Bulletin*, 19 -1922/23.

Hills, Edward. *The King James Version Defended*, Des Moines: The Christian Research Press, 1984.

Khoo, Jeffrey. "Errors in the King James Version? A Response to William W. Combs of Detroit Baptist Seminary", *Dean Burgon Society eNews*, 89- Sept. 2009.

Maynard, Michael. *A History Of The Debate Over 1 John 5:7-8*, Tempe Az: Comma Publications, 1995.

Metzger, Bruce H. *The Text of the New Testament*, 2nd edition, Oxford: Clarendon Press, 1968.

Miller, H. S. *General Biblical Introduction*, Houghton: The Word-Bearer Press, 1960.

Milne, H.J.M. and T.C. Skeat. *Scribes and Correctors of Codex Sinaiticus*, London: British Museum, 1938.

Pickering, Wilbur. *The Identity of the New Testament Text*, Nashville: Thomas Nelson, 1980.
— "Queen Anne...And All That: A Response," *Journal of the Evangelical Theological Society*. June 1978.

Plummer, A. *The Epistles of St. John, The Cambridge Bible for Schools and Colleges.* Cambridge: University Press, 1896.

Robinson, Maurice A. and William G. Pierpont (eds.). *The New Testament in the Original Greek: Byzantine Textform*, Southborough MA: Chilton Book Publishing,2005.
— 1991 Edition, internet.

Robinson, Maurice A. *How Many Manuscripts are Necessary to Establish the Majority Text*, unpublished paper, 1978.
— 2010 Interview, sermonindex, internet.

Royse, James R. "Von Soden's Accuracy," *Journal of Theological Studies*, 30-1979.

Schmid, Josef. *Studien Zur Geschichte Des Griechischen Apokalypse-Textes*, Munchen: Karl Zink, 1956.

Scrivener, F. H. A. *A Plain Introduction to the Criticism of the New Testament*, Cambridge: Deighton, Bell, 1883.

Sturz, Harry A. *The Byzantine Text-Type and New Testament Textual Criticism*, Nashville: Thomas Nelson, 1984.

Voobus, Arthur. *Early Versions of the New Testament,* Stockholm: Estonian Theological Society in Exile, 1954.

Wisse, Frederik. *The Profile Method for the Classification and Evaluation of Manuscript Evidence,* Grand Rapids: Eerdmans, 1982.

INDEX OF WORDS AND PHRASES

1/3 directly affect the KJV translation, 9, 44

"046," 5, 26, 32, 33, 34, 35, 36, 37, 38, 40, 41, 43, 45, 46, 108, 111, 112, 113, 122, 128, 130, 131, 132, 138, 150

12 groups, 38

120 MSS, 24, 26

1200 changes into the text, 43

150 Byzantine readings, 14

1500 differences, 12

165 Kx MSS, 28

170 Byzantine readings, 14

1800 places, 9, 12

2,343 lectionaries, 17

2,808 cursives, 17

200 plus MSS, 31

256 (just above 300 now) MSS, 33

3,000 clear differences, 19

30% of the New Testament, 14

375 passages, 11

39 MSS remain as valuable, 40

40 directly cited MSS, 28

414 MSS, 23, 26, 28

4th century, 32

5000 separate items, 19

55 directly K MSS, 24

5555 MSS, 17, 28

57 of the MSS, 36

559 directly affect the KJV translation, 44

8000 places, 12

83 MSS, 38, 40, 41

839 readings, 14

900 MSS, 28

99 of the 120 MSS, 24

A, 2, 5, 6, 7, 9, 11, 12, 14, 17, 19, 21, 24, 25, 27, 33, 35, 36, 40, 44, 46, 49, 52, 53, 54, 55, 56, 57, 58, 59, 60, 61, 62, 65, 66, 69, 70, 72, 73, 76, 77, 78, 79, 80, 81, 82, 83, 84, 85, 86, 87, 89, 91, 93, 94, 95, 96, 97, 98, 99, 100, 101, 103, 105, 106, 107, 108, 109, 110, 111, 112, 113, 114, 115, 116, 117, 118, 119, 120, 121, 122, 123, 124, 125, 126, 127, 128, 130, 132, 133, 134, 136, 137, 141, 142, 144, 145, 146, 147, 148, 149, 151, 153, 183, 184, 185, 186, 187, 188, 189, 190, 191

a few old uncials, 43

Acts of the Latern Council, 141

Africa, 49, 64, 81, 89, 93, 104, 110, 114, 117, 133, 134, 137, 149, 201

Aland (Kurt), 14, 17, 189

Aland (Barbara), 8, 18, 24, 189, 190

Alands Synopsis, 47

Alcuin, 141

Aleph, 5, 8, 14, 17, 18, 19, 33, 35, 36, 45, 46, 49, 50, 51, 52, 53, 54, 55, 56, 57, 58, 59, 60, 61, 62, 63, 64, 65, 66, 67, 68, 69, 70, 71, 72, 73, 75, 76, 77, 78, 79, 80, 81, 82, 83, 84, 85, 86, 87, 88, 89, 91, 92, 93, 94, 95, 97, 98, 99, 100, 101, 104, 108, 109, 111, 112, 113, 114, 117, 119, 120, 121, 122, 125, 126, 127, 130, 133, 134, 136, 146, 183, 184, 185, 186, 187, 188

Aleph and B, 5, 17, 19, 92, 146

Aleph-B, 8, 17, 18

Alexandria, 8, 49, 50, 51, 52, 53, 54, 56, 59, 63, 64, 66, 70, 71, 72, 73, 75, 76, 77, 78, 79, 82, 84, 85, 87, 88, 89, 91, 92, 93, 94, 96, 98, 99, 101, 106, 109, 111, 117, 119, 120, 121, 130, 133

Alexandrian (H), 24

Alexandrian tendency, 37

Alford (Henry), 24, 32, 46, 51, 60, 85, 143, 189

Alfred Martin, 12

Ambrose, 49, 63, 68, 81, 85, 88, 89, 92, 93, 94, 121, 122, 123, 124, 130, 132, 135, 137, 138, 139

Amiatinus, 147

Andrean MSS, 33, 35, 38, 41

Andreas, 5, 32, 33, 34, 35, 36, 37, 38, 40, 41, 80, 82, 83, 84, 86, 98, 99, 100, 101, 102, 103, 104, 105, 106, 107, 108, 109, 110, 111, 112, 113, 114, 115, 116, 117, 118,

ABOUT THE AUTHOR

Dr. Moorman & His Wife Dot

Dr. J. A. Moorman studied for a while at the Indianapolis campus of Purdue University, attended briefly Indiana Bible College, and graduated from Tennessee Temple Bible School. Since his graduation, he has been involved in church planting, Bible Institute teaching, and extensive distribution of Scriptures and gospel tracts in Johannesburg, South Africa from 1968—1988, and in England and London since 1988. More recently he has been seeking to get Scripture portions into Latin Europe. He married his wife, Dot, on November 22, 1963.

Dr. Moorman has written the following scholarly books defending the King James Bible and the Hebrew, Aramaic and Greek Words that underlie it:

1. *When the King James Bible Departs from the So-Called "Majority Text"* (the current volume).
2. *Early Manuscripts, Church Fathers, and the Authorized Version.*
3. *Forever Settled.*
4. *Missing in Modern Bibles—The Old Heresy Revived*
5. *The Doctrinal Heart of the Bible—Removed from Modern Versions.*
6. *Samuel P. Tregelles—The Man Who Made the Critical Text Acceptable to Bible Believers.*
7. *8,000 Difference Between the Textus Receptus and the Critical Text.*

All of these scholarly and well-documented works by Dr. Moorman are replete with manuscript and other evidence which he has gleaned from his own vast resources as well as references found in the British Museum and other libraries in the London area.

Pray for this humble friend of this vital cause as he continues his evangelistic, research, and preaching ministries.

Dr. Moorman is currently pastor of Bethel Baptist Church in London, England and is serving as a missionary to England and Europe. He is known for standing on street-corners many hours handing out gospel tracts throughout England and Europe. May God bless his unfailing service to the Lord Jesus Christ.